Sustainable Building (

Theory and Practice of Responsive Design in the Heritage Environment

Oriel Prizeman

RIBA Publishing

Sustainable Building Conservation

© RIBA Enterprises Ltd, 2015

Published by RIBA Publishing, The Old Post Office, St Nicholas Street,
Newcastle upon Tyne, NE1 1RH

ISBN 978 1 85946 542 4

Stock code 82398

The rights of RIBA Enterprises Ltd to be identified as the Authors of this Work have been
asserted in accordance with the Copyright, Designs and Patents Act 1988 sections 77 and 78.

British Library Cataloguing-in-Publication Data
A catalogue record for this book is available from the British Library.

Publisher: Steven Cross
Commissioning Editor: Sharla Plant
Production: Richard Blackburn
Cover Design: Ashley Western
Page Design: Tom Cabot/Ketchup
Typeset by Academic + Technical, Bristol
Printed and bound by W&G Baird Ltd in Great Britain
Cover image: The Ford Piquette Avenue Plant Museum Detroit USA © Oriel Prizeman

www.ribaenterprises.com

In memory of my father, John Prizeman AAdip FRIBA FRSA 1930–1992,
who sought to persuade every bright young person he met to become
an architect and to do so at the Architectural Association.

Contents

Preface and acknowledgements   iv

Contributors   v

Introduction Oriel Prizeman   ix

Part 1: Evaluations – Theories   1

Chapter One   3
The English climate and enduring principles of environmental design Dean Hawkes

Chapter Two   39
The energy context of domestic traditional buildings for the UK Simon Lannon,
Heledd Iorwerth, Xiaojun Li and Diana Waldron

Chapter Three   65
Retrofitting heritage buildings Peter Cox

Chapter Four   87
Containing the questions Douglas D Kent

Part 2: Responses – Practices   113

Chapter Five   115
*An integrated approach to heritage and sustainability: four academic building projects
in the US* Tom Hotaling

Chapter Six   159
New Court, Trinity College, Cambridge: continuing a legacy of inhabitation Oliver Smith

Chapter Seven   193
*Four case studies demonstrating the impacts of energy conservation in traditional
domestic buildings* Oriel Prizeman

Chapter Eight   219
*Sustaining heating in places of worship: Physical, social, organisational and
commercial factors as determinants of strategic decision-making and practical
outcomes* Bruce Induni

Part 3: Conclusions   247

Glossary   253

Bibliography   257

Image credits   265

Index   267

Preface and acknowledgements

••

This book was commissioned by Sharla Plant in 2013 to help build up a body of work on the subject of conservation for RIBA publications. The number of CPD courses and the proliferation of accreditation schemes is now expanding the number of building professionals who consider conservation a key skill. It is very evident that the majority of architects have been encouraged to shun the label of 'conservationist' despite often developing a deep affection for and understanding of architectural history. Conservation has been pitted against development as a regressive, inarticulate and unimaginative mode of control whereas arguably it is quite the reverse. The marriage of concerns associated with sustainability and conservation are becoming more apparent in every sector of stewardship governance. This book is a call to architects to apply their significant domain knowledge and take pride and care in the future treatment of historic buildings. The complexity of arguments regarding energy use and adaptation often confound swift negotiation. They require skills that a lengthy and hard-earned education can and should address.

Many thanks to each of the contributors for their patience, efficiency and goodwill. Thanks to Maney Publishing for permission to reproduce in substantial form Oliver Smith's chapter from *The Historic Environment: Policy and Practice* special issue *Energy Efficiency and Heritage Values in Historic Buildings* (Maney Publishing, 5:2 (2014)). Keith Jones of the National Trust is owed specific thanks, as are my colleagues Andy Faulkner, Tim Forman and Chris Whitman together with all Sustainable Building Conservation MSc students at the Welsh School of Architecture, Cardiff University. Thanks to my patient clients who have allowed me to write about their homes and to my commissioning editor and her team at RIBA publications as a whole. Thanks, most of all to Nic, Matilda and Stella Rhode, and my mother Willow Prizeman.

Contributors

PETER COX

Peter Cox is president of the ICOMOS (International Council on Monuments and Sites) International Scientific Committee for Energy and Sustainability. He is the founding member of Carrig and brings over 30 years of stone conservation experience in historical buildings and all types of porous building materials. Peter is responsible for the company development and has brought many exciting projects to be worked on by the team. Peter remains involved in all projects which are handled by the Carrig team.

From 1985 to 1994, he operated as European Marketing Director for ProSoCo Inc and its subsidiary MNSC, which specialised in laboratory analysis of prescribed cleaning and treatment systems for all porous building materials. While in the United States, he was involved in projects such as Grand Central Station, New York, and the US Capitol Building in Washington, DC, and in the UK he worked with prestigious buildings such as Lloyd's Register of Shipping, London, Tate Gallery of Modern Art, Bankside Power Station and Fort Dunlop.

Peter is currently vice-president of ICOMOS Ireland, having been President from 2004 to 2006. Peter has played a big role in the Stone Federation of Great Britain, chairing the technical committee, and served as vice chair of the approved contractors' scheme. While working in the USA, he was an active member of the Association of Preservation Technology (APT). He has served on the committee researching chemical consolidation methods for decay and is an associate of the International Institute of Conservation.

TOM HOTALING

Tom Hotaling is a principal and designer with Ann Beha Architects (ABA), a Boston-based design firm whose work is marked by its strong historic and cultural content. ABA's work ranges from renovations and adaptive reuse combining preservation with contemporary design, to new buildings in historic settings. The firm is currently designing renovations to the campus of the United States Embassy in Athens, whose landmarked Chancery building was designed by Walter Gropius in 1961.

In the greater Boston area his cultural and academic clients include Old North Church, the Museum of Fine Arts, the Massachusetts Institute of Technology, the New England Conservatory of Music, and Louis Kahn's Library at Phillips Exeter Academy. Nationally, his clients have included the University of Pennsylvania, Washington University in St Louis, the Arizona State Museum, and the Portland Art Museum in Oregon.

He has served as a grants reviewer for the Pew Charitable Trust and teaches a course in preservation and adaptive reuse at Harvard University. He is a Commissioner for the Boston Landmarks Commission and a trustee for the Instituto Internacional, an educational and cultural centre in Madrid whose building is a Spanish national landmark.

DEAN HAWKES

Dean Hawkes is emeritus professor of architectural design at the Welsh School of Architecture, Cardiff University, and an emeritus fellow of Darwin College, University of Cambridge. He taught and researched at Cambridge from 1965 to 1995, when he was appointed professor of architectural design at Cardiff. Following his retirement in 2002 he returned to Cambridge as a fellow of Darwin College.

Dean has held visiting professorships at schools of architecture in Hong Kong, Singapore, Glasgow, Huddersfield and Leicester. His research is in the field of environmental design in architecture. His books include *The Environmental Tradition* (1996), *The Environmental Imagination* (2008) and *Architecture and Climate* (2012). His buildings, in partnership with Stephen Greenberg, have received four RIBA Architecture Awards. In 2010 he received the RIBA Annie Spink Award in recognition of his contribution to architectural education.

BRUCE INDUNI

Dr Bruce Induni, born of a line of Italian marble carvers, trained in stone conservation at Wells Cathedral. After accumulating 13 years' experience as a conservation contractor, Bruce moved into academia as a senior lecturer in building conservation. His doctorate examined the survival of medieval plaster in Dorset churches. This built on and extended a particular interest in how the heat and humidity inside ancient buildings impacts on mortar, masonry and decoration.

He is currently teaching at Kingston and Plymouth Universities and the Building Crafts College, and has just written the course material for a major educational initiative jointly sponsored by the North of England Civic Trust and English Heritage.

Future plans include the completion of a handbook of applied conservation and an independent review of the methods of ruin conservation adopted by the Ministry of Works.

DOUGLAS KENT

Douglas Kent is a chartered building surveyor specialising in building conservation and is currently the Technical and Research Director at the Society for the Protection of Ancient Buildings (SPAB). He oversees the SPAB's technical activities, which embrace advice, publications and courses of a technical nature, as well as its supporting research. Douglas has also worked in the public and private sectors, offering advice on historic buildings to a range of organisations, such as the Ministry of Defence and English Heritage.

Douglas's technical knowledge is underpinned by his formal qualifications, including an MSc in the Conservation of Buildings, coupled with extensive practical experience. This has been gained from leading volunteer working parties to repair old buildings, along with a project to renovate his own Grade I-listed medieval timber-framed house in Essex. The conservation of his 17th-century pargeting (decorative external render) was joint winner of a prestigious Museum + Heritage Award for Restoration or Conservation.

Douglas publishes and lectures regularly on building conservation and has contributed to various radio and television programmes. He also serves on many committees for organisations devoted to safeguarding the historic built environment and is chairman of the Hundred Parishes Society.

SIMON LANNON, HELEDD IORWERTH, XIAOJUN LI AND DIANA WALDRON

Simon Lannon

Simon Lannon is a research fellow at the Welsh School of Architecture, Cardiff University, where he has developed models and tools based on building physics principles to be used at all scales of the built environment, from individual buildings to regional energy and emissions models. The main focus of his research has been the development of software to model the energy use and emissions for large urban areas using geographic information systems (GIS) and simulation software.

Heledd Iorwerth

Heledd Iorwerth is a researcher at the Welsh School of Architecture, Cardiff University, with a background in mathematics and building physics. Her interest lies in the use of GIS and statistical data to aid in modelling energy use at an urban and regional scale.

Xiaojun Li

Xiaojun Li is a researcher at the Welsh School of Architecture, Cardiff University. She has an architectural background, and has been involved in a series of projects on low carbon built environment. Her research interest lies in integrative design, and environmental performance prediction through simulation tools at a building or community scale.

Diana Waldron

Diana Waldron is a researcher at the Welsh School of Architecture and the environmental sustainability officer for the Sustainable Building Envelope Demonstration Project (SBED) at Cardiff University. Her research projects and interests have been mainly focused on finding strategies to improve the sustainable development of the built environment. She has been assisting with the development of dynamic simulation models and software tools for energy use in buildings.

The four co-authors have been researching the built environment as part of the Smart Operation for a Low Carbon Energy Region project, and the Low Carbon Environment project supported by the European Regional Development Fund through the Welsh Government.

OLIVER SMITH

Before founding 5th Studio, Oliver had worked with Sir James Stirling and then Sir Richard MacCormac on a number of international and national gallery, museum and higher education projects.

For a period of over 12 years Oliver combined practice with studio teaching at the University of Cambridge School of Architecture, focusing on attitudes to materiality and construction. This research has been extended through the practice's work to develop a critical approach to sustainable construction and in particular to the adaptation of existing fabric.

Recent project work at 5th Studio includes the award-winning low-carbon projects at St Catharine's College, Russell Street, and the Wolfson Flats, Churchill College in Cambridge, which have established the practice's reputation for innovative new build and retrofit housing.

Current projects in Oxford, London and Cambridge are developing this approach over a wide range of projects, at scales from minor works to campus master-planning and urban infrastructure. Oliver is also leading the highly sustainable refurbishment of the Grade I-listed buildings at New Court in Trinity College Cambridge.

Introduction

∙∙∙

Oriel Prizeman

The engagement of concerns regarding sustainability and building conservation has had a long incubation. Government initiatives such as the Green Deal bring urgency for the issue to be addressed and understood by architects not simply in technical but also in philosophical terms. Internationally, focus is drawn to the challenges of developing conservation strategies against the tide of new development. Unlike the period of development that took place during the Industrial Revolution in the UK, the climate change agenda focuses on issues of conservation in its broadest terms and lends the debate serious responsibility in the context of contemporary global development.

CONTEXT

The 2013 UNESCO Hangzhou Declaration '*Placing Culture at the Heart of Sustainable Development Policies*' made a call to 'Build on Culture to promote environmental sustainability'.[1] It stated:

> The safeguarding of historic urban and rural areas and of their associated traditional knowledge and practices reduces the environmental footprints of societies, promoting more ecologically sustainable patterns of production and consumption and sustainable urban and architectural design solutions. Access to essential environmental goods and services for the livelihood of communities should be secured through the stronger protection and more sustainable use of biological and cultural diversity, as well as by the safeguarding of relevant traditional knowledge and skills, paying particular attention to those of indigenous peoples, in synergy with other forms of scientific knowledge.

The mention of both traditional and scientific knowledge is rightly identified as critical to the context of historic environments, but the notion of a 'synergy' between them is lacklustre. As Elefante pointed out a decade ago,[2] desires for sustainability and building conservation share significant areas of common ground, yet they marry philosophies that were born in very different philosophical camps. There is opportunity for both conflict and creativity in this context, and the aim of this book is broadly to encourage architects and anyone engaged in development within the built environment to step into the foreground of the debate and to participate in the creation of the emerging tools of practice relevant to this sphere.

The natural environment is perceived as one that requires the highest level of protection and itself constitutes the victim of climate change, whereas the built environment is presumed less valuable because, being manmade, it can in theory be rebuilt. As everyone involved in building work will acknowledge, the shifting technological, economic and skills transformation of the workforce over time prevents this from being a reality with all but the humblest or most lavish of exceptions. Economic viability is a huge factor that works in sometimes unexpected but always powerful ways. The capacity to think strategically about long-term, potentially generation-skipping gains will both elude the poor and be dismissed by the profit-seeking.

The contributors who have been selected here are chosen specifically to represent a diverse range of insights. Their approaches are at times in direct contrast to one another, yet their goals may be shared on some level. As practitioners from both Europe and the US, academics, representatives of advisory bodies and even representatives of international scientific committees, they collectively speak on the same subject but not in unison. They speak in their own voices, they do not address their neighbours' arguments, but state their own. The aims in broad terms may be similar, but the methods and practices explored either for enhancing arguments or resolving technical issues in very specific contexts are often contradictory. This conflict deliberately challenges readers to address such concerns themselves. The book sets out the conflicts and potential overlaps in the interests of energy conservation and building conservation. The relevance and necessary adjustments of qualitative and quantitative frames of reference are made evident through the various expertise of the contributors.

QUESTIONS

While almost all designers adopt the ethical tenets of sustainability, relatively few acknowledge conservation skills, which are often seen as a force against progress. Both concerns are heavily regulated in the UK, yet the balance between them often leaves the architect to take a preferential stance in favour of one or the other. The forefront of research in terms of both conservation and sustainability is held in the realms of the physical sciences – where quantifiable evidence can provide demonstrable results. However, for practitioners, the ethical and practical lead needs further bolstering beyond what are ultimately economic drivers. Arguments in favour of preserving the historic environment are, in ICOMOS terms,[3] 'values-based' – values of heritage assets are established through rarity. Architects need to develop better fluency in the archaeologist's language of 'valorisation', as they have already done to address the heat loss and carbon emission metrics of physicists.

The potential of design in the context of historic buildings requires greater credit. A huge proportion of the work that architects do relates to existing buildings. At a wider level, environmental design that responds best to climate is widely regarded to be derived from vernacular traditions. A large proportion of our built environment is historic, creating a climate and context in itself. It is recognised by global policymakers that the next critical task in policymaking is to address the task of making this environment more responsive to needs for reduction in energy use in buildings. That said, the very assertion of any universal policy often leads to significant debate. While metrics are used to determine prescribed performance parameters for new and proposed buildings, these are applied meaninglessly to existing buildings. Very little has been achieved to assist in the accurate day-to-day assimilation of the performance of historic building fabric. Calculations have baseline data in terms of life cycle costing, which is wildly at variance with other methods, yet the results are used as benchmarks. The eco-bling aspect of sustainable features or renewable additions to a building or site is not necessarily one that is meaningful but it can be marketable – is this the right stance to take in the context of an irreplaceable environment?

ICOMOS was set up after the Second World War to vehemently challenge the perceived risk posed by rebuilding programmes, principally across Europe. A deeper question emerges here: should the role of standardisation be limited? In 20th-century architecture, bolstered by the necessity of two waves of postwar rebuilding, universal construction standards have been developed and championed to meet both the demands of a drastically depleted skills base and demands for greater efficiency against huge budget constraints. Since then it has sought to rewrite its hugely Euro-centric sphere of influence with greater emphasis placed upon the identification of quieter voices and subtler forms of heritage, such as intangible heritage. In many ways local technical knowledge needs to be atomised and then made accessible, as opposed to being generalised. Today we translate everything into a commodity and then seek to trade our debts, for example in a global forum for the exchange of carbon offsets: will we eventually exchange equal credits with international heritage values?

Here, we are concerned firmly with built architecture, yet in several of the accounts presented it is the modification of human behaviour, allowing design to act as a complex imaginative tool, that promises to deliver the greatest gains. This is not quite the same as introducing a culture of recycling; it is the promotion of a willingness to submit to the operational rules of the existing built environment. At this point we need to recognise that if we choose to sustain the historic environments we have, we may need to make adjustments ourselves, as opposed to making adjustments to those buildings. In this respect, the role of the designer here reverses the entire thrust of the environmental movement. Environmental design principles are based on the notion that people are victims of their environments. Environments therefore should be designed to support and maintain the wellbeing of their inhabitants. On the other hand, historic buildings are broadly perceived to be at the mercy of their inhabitants. Applying the same criterion of demand to them as to new buildings is ridiculous; in the same way that budgets do not necessarily ensure the most effective distribution of funds, the prediction of human demand does not necessarily ensure the most effective calculation of performance.

At the National Trust,[4] trials are under way to equip staff with battery-powered heated vests in order to overcome legislative requirements for the maintenance of comfortable working conditions. Will such practices become commonplace in the future? Many of our most venerated institutions are housed in historic buildings; their age lends status to our government, our seats of learning and our national collections. Will the cluster of power in buildings around St James's and Trafalgar Square see Members of Parliament, civil servants in Whitehall, and visitors to the National Gallery adjusting their own attire in order to maintain that of their architecture?

AIMS

The key aim here is to adjust the frame of reference. The book aims to provide a theoretical context which is both global and local, as opposed to a technical manual or textbook. The patently inadequate means to benchmark the performance of historic buildings call for an urgent overhaul. One of the key concerns for architects emerging through the increasingly polarised nature of research in the built environment is that they are regarded as insufficiently equipped to evaluate responses in terms of physical science and historical merit, yet are constantly required to discount one at the expense of the other. The vast majority of refurbishment work to historic buildings is carried out and overseen by small practices and sole practitioners who do not yet have access to sufficiently powerful calculation tools. While practitioners are likely to develop a close understanding of local building technology through experience, they are unlikely to have time to programme the full nuances of its performance within a dropdown menu of construction materials in a modelling programme.

Despite the associated connotations of autonomy in the title 'architect', many practising will admit that their conscience is dominated by charges of responsibility. The duty of care to the client is extended to that of the planet and to future generations. To this end, the demands of political and liberal philosophy extend across a wide spectrum. The year after the publication of the 1987 United Nations' Brundtland Report, Our Common Future,[5] introduced the term 'sustainable development', Edith Brown Weiss traced the concept of intergenerational relationship through political philosophy.[6] Citing Edmund Burke in the 18th and John Rawls in the 20th century, she demonstrated the breadth of the political spectrum behind the delivery of what we recognise as a conservationist or sustainable agenda. Burke's interpretation of the Social Contract (in contrast to that of Marx, Hobbes, Locke and Rousseau) was cited as a root within conservative liberal political philosophy for highlighting the importance of the generational transaction of responsibility. Burke's statement 'Each generation should provide its members with equitable rights of access to the planetary legacy of past generations and should conserve this access for future generations'[7] is presented together with Rawls's comments on inheritance and responsibility from his *Theory of Justice* (1971). Weiss drew together the articulation of apparently diverse concerns. Economic Liberalism that underpins Conservative political philosophy is conventionally seen as a threat to ecological systems. Conversely, from a Conservative perspective, freedom of the individual is presumed to sustain instincts to protect family, natural environment and tradition; the shift in thinking is from ecology to economy. Magazines with titles such as *Shooting and Conservation* seek to make this apparent anomaly a misreading.

Another root of the conservation movement, the mobilisation of the middle-class connoisseurship that founded the great amenity societies, initially threatens a disastrous debate against the empiricists. Their authority was founded on qualified reasoning, prior knowledge and an assumption of hierarchy. There is an absolute demand today to reason in both quantified and qualified terms. As a result a skills gap has emerged. The highly technical tends to outwit the impassioned, and the notion of intergenerational justice is at risk of miscalculation. Strung between legislative goals and charged to deliver the environments of the past for the appetites of the present, architects are under significant pressure to present flawless solutions to possibly unanswerable demands. At current rates of pay and costs of tuition, the profession is at risk of collapse, as was recognised in the 2014 Farrell Review. Is it now essential for architects to take a greater and more innovative role in the meting out of these concerns and if so, to consider how best they might they be supported.

METHODS

This book is simply divided into two sections: theory and practice. It is not necessarily intended to be read through in sequence, but rather to provide a set of voices in discussion over a contested ground. The structure of the book deliberately avoids the pretence of providing a set of recipes; as all involved in conservation are aware, the potential risk of ubiquitous rules causing harm to historic fabric when applied unthinkingly is colossal. There are case studies, but these are not intended as models: they are intended to provide moments for reflection. The contributors to the book come from a wide range of backgrounds – practitioners, academics, amenity societies. They are divided between those who reason in a predominantly numerical way and those who reason by citation and the collation of historical evidence. They are perhaps unified in their recognition of a conundrum.

The practice section here specifically introduces the concerns of three types of interested owner or developer. There are obviously others, and notably, for example, it excludes the commercial client. On the basis that academic institutions have perhaps the most secure tenancies and predictive usage patterns, examples are presented here from both the US and the UK demonstrating contrasting contexts for similar problems. Architects working in this arena have the privilege of arguing for the longest-term payback, for the economic recovery by the client of the work implemented now. By contrast, in the domestic home-owner context, as evidenced in my own chapter, the strategic domain and perspective are severely limited by immediate interest.

NOTES

1   UNESCO, *Hangzhou Declaration: Placing Culture at the Heart of Sustainable Development Policies* (Hangzhou, China, 2013).

2   Carl Elefante, 'Historic preservation and sustainable development: lots to learn, lots to teach', *APT Bulletin* 36:4 (2005).

3   International Council on Monuments and Sites.

4   Tredegar House cf Keith Jones.

5   World Commission on Environment and Development, *Our Common Future* (Oxford: Oxford University Press, 1987).

6   Edith Brown Weiss, *In Fairness to Future Generations: International Law, Common Patrimony, and Intergenerational Equity* (Tokyo, Japan, and Dobbs Ferry, NY: United Nations University Transnational Publishers, 1988).

7   Ibid cites pp139–40 Edmund Burke, James Dodsley and Isabella Metford, *Reflections on the revolution in France: and on the proceedings in certain ocieties in London relative to that event. In a letter intended to have been sent to a gentleman in Paris*, The fourth edition (London: Printed for J. Dodsley, in Pall-Mall, 1790).

PART 1

Evaluations – Theories

The evaluation of concerns regarding climate change can be seen to emanate from, and add weight to, a wide range of political and theoretical agendas. The aim of the first part of this book is to present a diverse range of interests and perspectives that are generated through historical, theoretical and practical research and experience. Certain conclusions overlap and others diverge: the reader is invited to join in with the debate. The chapters set out the conflicts and potential overlaps in the interests of energy conservation and building conservation. The relevance and necessary adjustment of qualitative and quantitative frames of reference are introduced alongside the various expertise of the contributors.

ONE

The English climate and enduring principles of environmental design

···

Dean Hawkes

INTRODUCTION

The western and northern parts of the United Kingdom lie close to the normal path of the Atlantic depressions and are mostly cool and windy. The lowlands of England have a climate similar to that of the Continent: drier, with a wider range of temperatures than in the north and west. However, the winters are not as severe as those on the Continent. Overall, the south of the United Kingdom is usually warmer than the north, and the west is wetter than the east. The more extreme weather tends to occur in the mountainous regions, where it is often cloudy.[1]

In the broadest of terms, the inhabitants of these islands would have recognised this modern description of the climate of the British Isles at any moment in the last four centuries. They would also have been accustomed to the vagaries and unpredictability of the weather, with the changes from hour to hour and day to day that we continue to endure. This is the background against which the following narrative is set, in which we trace the way in which British architecture has been shaped by the climate and, reciprocally, how it provides us with a vivid, alternative climate history.

HARDWICK HALL AND THE CLIMATE OF SHAKESPEARE'S ENGLAND

Hardwick Hall (Fig 1.01), with its tall, glassy facades and clusters of chimneys seen high above its monogrammed parapets, stands on a hilltop in the middle of England. Completed in 1597,

Fig 1.01 Robert Smythson, Hardwick Hall, Derbyshire, West Front

the house is the masterwork of Robert Smythson (1535–1614), the greatest architect of the Elizabethan age. It is also a remarkable demonstration of how a building may aspire to architectural greatness and also exhibit a deep understanding of, and response to, the physical climate in which it is set.

At the end of the 16th century Britain, and the whole of northern Europe, was in the midst of the so-called Little Ice Age.[2] It has been calculated that the average annual temperature at the end of the 16th century was between 1° and 1.5°C colder than in the present day.[3] There is, however, evidence that, even in this chilly period, respite would occur in pleasant, mild summers. This was the context in which Hardwick was conceived and first inhabited. We should imagine a climate setting not unlike that we experience in the 21st century, but with generally much colder winters. We should also consider that the weather would be as unpredictable as ours.

Hardwick's hilltop site, 181 metres above sea level, exposes the house to the elements from all directions. This appears directly to contradict the general perceptions of the time on the placement of houses, which were declaimed by William Harrison in *The Description of England*, published in 1587:[4]

> In this island … the winds are commonly more strong and fierce than in any other places of the main …. That grievous inconvenience also enforceth our nobility, gentry and commonality to build their houses in the valleys, leaving the high grounds unto their corn and cattle, lest the cold and stormy blasts of winter should breed them greater annoyance.

Hardwick's owner was Elizabeth, Countess of Shrewsbury, usually known as Bess of Hardwick, one of the most important figures of the age and, among women, second only to Queen Elizabeth.[5] For her, the modesty and shelter of the valley floor would have been inconceivable. The house is clearly an object of display. Its tall silhouette, with the initials 'ES', for Elizabeth Shrewsbury, carved into the parapets, declares her dominant presence across the Derbyshire landscape. Robert Smythson's task was, therefore, to meet his patron's seemingly complex expectations for grandeur and display, while shaping a building that provided protection from the testing context of this Derbyshire hilltop.

Two important facts should be stated here. First, the Elizabethan climate was unmeasured. The instruments for giving numbers to meteorological phenomena were yet to come.[6] But both chill and warmth were keenly felt and, perhaps, given most eloquent expression by Shakespeare (1564–1616), who lived at precisely the date of Hardwick:

> When all aloud the wind doth blow,
> And coughing drowns the parson's saw,
> And birds sit brooding in the snow,
> And Marion's nose looks red and raw,
> When roasted crabs hiss in the bowl ...
> *Love's Labour's Lost*, Act V, Scene ii

> Shall I compare thee to a summer's day?
> Thou art more lovely and more temperate:
> Rough winds do shake the darling buds of May,
> And summer's lease hath all too short a date:
> Sometimes too hot, the eye of heaven shines,
> And often is his gold complexion dimm'd ...
> *The Sonnets*, 18

These descriptions are certainly as potent as a modern weather forecast.

In environmental design in architecture, climate is, of necessity, connected to the idea of *comfort*. At the end of the 16th century comfort was quite unlike that of our modern perceptions and expectations.[7] The numerical codification of modern *comfort theory* began in the 20th century in the work of, for example, Bedford and Dufton in the thermal environment, Luckeish and Walsh in lighting and vision, and Knudsen and Hope Bagenal in acoustics.[8] Before then, just as with the perception of climate, comfort was subjective and, equally important, it was a *relative* concept. Before the development of modern mechanical services for managing the environments within buildings, which permit the maintenance of constant conditions at all seasons of the year and times of the day, the inhabitants would expect the internal conditions to be directly connected to the state of the natural climate. These would, therefore, vary widely, and both

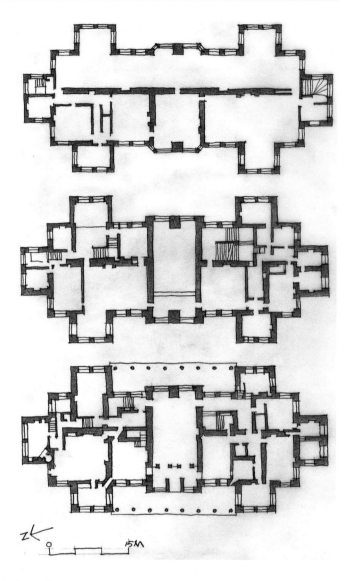

Fig 1.02 Hardwick Hall, floor plans

temporally and spatially. Such conditions were the expectation and experience of the occupants of Hardwick Hall.

The plans of Hardwick (Fig 1.02) are the key to its environmental logic. Peter Smithson, Robert's 20th-century architect namesake, offered the following analysis of the house:

> In Hardwick New Hall there is a gallery which runs along the whole extent of the house. What's nice about [the plan] is that it indicates the thick spine wall, where the fireplaces are ... and the perimeter windows that let in the light. ... in the winter you have screens around the gallery against the fireplaces and in the summer you moved into the bay windows.[9]

This captures the environmental essence of the house. The spine wall and the corresponding internal walls on the more compartmented lower floors contain a total of 28 fireplaces. In winter it is likely that fires would burn continuously and would heat the thermal mass of the masonry at the heart of the plan. These would create localised warm places throughout the house, which would be enhanced by the use of enclosing screens to form smaller enclosures by the fireplaces.[10] More generally, the heat in the spine walls would offset the heat loss through the glass of the bay windows.

Peter Smithson's account proposes that, in the summer, the house became a completely different place, with the occupants moving to the perimeter to enjoy the sun's warmth. The long axis of the house is oriented almost exactly north–south, and this clearly influenced the disposition of rooms. This is most strikingly seen in the location and arrangement of Bess's own apartments at the southern end of the first floor, where they enjoy the best of the sun. They also receive protection from the floors above and below. The great staterooms of the second floor, the Long Gallery (Fig 1.03) and the High Great Chamber (Fig 1.04), are equally carefully oriented. The Long Gallery, as mentioned by Peter Smithson, occupies the entire east side of the house. These rooms were used for indoor exercise, which was taken in the morning,

Fig 1.03 Hardwick Hall, Long Gallery

Fig 1.04 Hardwick Hall,
High Great Chamber

warmed by the early sun. The High Great Chamber was where the grandest events in the life
of the household took place. At the south–west corner it is filled with south and west light,
bringing with it the sun's warmth.

The symbolic purpose of this great house was to proclaim the status of its remarkable owner.
This was the genesis of its striking appearance on its exposed hilltop; but beyond appearances
lay a rich and sophisticated response to the English climate, at a time of extremes. Four
centuries ago Robert Smythson demonstrated that significant architecture could reconcile the
symbolic with the functional and the environmental.

CHRISTOPHER WREN: ENVIRONMENTALIST

Within less than a century after the construction of Hardwick Hall, architecture in England
had undergone a profound transformation as classicism had become the dominant style. At
the same time, although unremarked in the standard architectural histories, the understanding
of the environmental context of architecture had taken an equally significant step. It was now

possible to give number to the temperature of the air and to the pressure of the atmosphere, and the science of meteorology was born. It was almost certainly in England that a direct link was first established between architecture and meteorology, in the works of Christopher Wren (1632–1723), who was both scientist and architect.

Before examining the connection between Wren's science and his architecture, we should renew our description of the climate of England as it was seen from a 17th-century viewpoint. The river Thames had frozen in London in most years since the reign of Henry VIII, but in the extreme winters of the 17th century the frosts lasted for months, permitting the establishment of 'Frost Fairs' on the ice. The winter of 1683–84 was the most severe in memory, and John Evelyn (1620-1706) recorded in his diary entry for 24 January 1684:

> Frost ... more & more severe, the Thames before London was planted with bothes [booths] in formal streets, as in a Citty ...[11]

This event is illustrated in a contemporary engraving (Fig 1.05), which is captioned:

> A Exact and Lively Mapp or representation of Boothes and all the varieties of Showes and Humours upon the ICE on the River of THAMES by London During the memorable frost ... MDCLXXXIII

Fig 1.05 Thames Frost Fair of 1683

Evelyn provides a further significant insight into the climate of London in *Fumifugium*.[12] Here, the subject is the pollution of the atmosphere caused by the burning of coal:

> that Hellish and dismall Cloud of SEA COAL ... so universally mixed with the otherwise wholesome and excellent Are, that her Inhabitants breathe nothing but an impure and thick Mist ...

This condition is contrasted with the virtues of the natural qualities of London's situation:

> the City of London is built upon a sweet and most agreeable Eminency of Ground, at the North-side of a goodly and well-condition'd River, towards which it hath an Aspect by a gentle and easie declivity, apt to be improv'd to all that may render her Palaces, Buildings and Avenues usefully graceful and most magnificent.

This implies that the climate of London in Wren's day was inherently agreeable, and even the rigours of the severe winters were turned to advantage by the citizens. On the other hand, *Fumifugium* is a reminder that man's impact on climate is not a new phenomenon.

This is the context in which Christopher Wren made his most direct contribution to the science of meteorology, with his project for a *History of the Seasons*:[13]

> His proposal ... was to comprehend a *Diary* of wind, weather and other Conditions of the Air, as to Heat, Cold and Weight; and also a *general Description* of the Year .... And because of the difficulty of a constant *Observation of the Air*, by Night and Day, seem'd invincible he therefore devised a *Clock* to be annexed by a Weather-Cock which mov'd a Rundle cover'd with Paper, upon which the Clock mov'd a black Lead Pencil, so that

Fig 1.06 Christopher Wren, Weather Clock

the Observer by the Traces of the Pencil on the Paper, might certainly conclude what Winds had blown in his Absence for twelve Hours space: After like manner he contrived a Thermometer with its own Register ...

Although the project was never realised, Wren did make a number of designs for weather clocks (Fig 1.06), one of which he demonstrated at a meeting of the Royal Society in 1662. It is against this background that Wren's architecture may be interpreted as the first to be explicitly *environmental*. The following analysis aims to show this in the case of the churches that Wren built in London following the Great Fire of 1666.

WREN'S CHURCHES AND THE CLIMATE OF 17TH-CENTURY LONDON

St James's, Piccadilly (1676–84) (Fig 1.07), is perhaps the example that most clearly demonstrates the principles that Wren applied to all of these remarkable designs. The situation of the church is clearly seen from the map in Strype's *Survey of London*, 1720 edition (Fig 1.08), where it stands between Piccadilly to the north and German (now Jermyn) Street

Fig 1.07 Christopher Wren, St James's Piccadilly Exterior

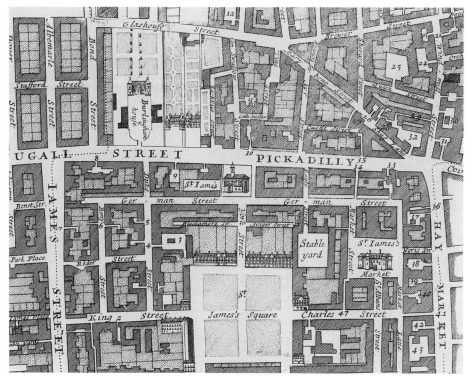

Fig 1.08 St James's, Piccadilly, site plan, Strype's *Survey of London*

to the south. Looking at the map, we should recall that in the 17th-century winter even this elegant quarter of the city would suffer from the bitter cold of the Little Ice Age. Similarly, the atmosphere would often be dank and polluted from the effects of coal smoke. Nonetheless, there would be times when the atmosphere was clear and the air warm and pleasant in sun-filled streets.

These churches were the first to be purposely built for the reformed (Anglican) religion. In 1708, after his work in building the new churches was completed, Wren wrote a major commentary on the basis of church design.[14] There he stated that the aim should be to ensure that 'all who are present can both see and hear'. St James's has a simple rectangular plan, with aisles and side galleries (Fig 1.09). The orientation, dictated by the alignment of the streets, is rotated to the north of east–west. The present-day surroundings are denser than those of the 17th century, but the interior is filled with daylight. This is, I suggest, a product of Wren's deep understanding of natural light and the sun's geometry that came from his astronomy and from his interest in climate. The arrangement of the windows, with five tall openings to each side of the nave above the galleries and smaller openings below to light the aisles (Fig 1.10), ensures that the sky is seen above the adjoining buildings. These windows were originally, as today, clear glazed, offering little obstruction to this light. The walls were originally painted a bright, pale stone colour to reflect the direct light. The entire arrangement complies with the

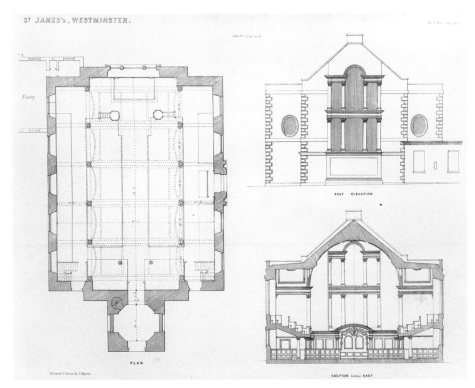

Fig 1.09 St James's, Piccadilly, plan and section

principles of daylight design later explained by modern building science.[15] In the 17th century, Sunday services were held in the morning and afternoon to take advantage of the natural light. Artificial lighting, by candles mounted on free-standing metal candelabra, was a poor substitute, with a church of this size probably having only four or six of these.[16]

When first built, these churches had no heating. We must imagine what it would have been like to attend Evensong in the winter of the Little Ice Age; but these worshippers would have had no other expectation. Initially the churches were sparsely furnished, with each parish responsible for fittings in the unadorned shell. Wren had strong ideas on this subject and declared: 'A Church should not be so fill'd with pews, but that the Poor may have room enough to stand and sit in the Alleys ...'[17] Very soon after their construction, however, the city churches were furnished with box pews. These often spacious enclosures were owned by individual families and were a source of income for the parishes. They also provided a small degree of thermal comfort by sheltering against draughts and capturing the bodily warmth of their well-wrapped occupants.

In most respects the environmental capacity of 17th-century buildings had advanced little from that of the previous century. Although the classical language was now in full command, construction methods and materials had not changed, and the environments within were still

Fig 1.10 St James's,
Piccadilly, interior

at the mercy of the weather outside. But in the work of Wren, scientist become architect, the
conception of environments had moved on from the subjectivity and intuition of Smythson to
embrace a new objectivity and method. In the next century, this movement gathered pace.

THE ENVIRONMENT OF ENGLISH PALLADIANISM

In 1715 the first English translation of Andrea Palladio's *I Quattro Libri dell'architettura* was
published.[18] An important theme of this work is its extensive discussion of the relationship
between buildings and climate – the *Italian* climate, of course. The year 1715 also saw
the publication of the first volume of Colen Campbell's *Vitruvius Britannicus.*[19] This work,
eventually in three volumes, presented a collection of designs for English country houses, all
in the classical manner.[20] It is essentially a visual presentation and lacks the practical themes
that are present in Palladio's text; but important treatises on the model of Palladio were also
published, first by Robert Morris (1734), and later by William Chambers (1759).[21] In these, the
question of design in relation to the climate was directly addressed by explaining how the
Italian prescriptions of Palladio should be adapted to English conditions.

In the 18th century, observing the climate became a popular pastime. Both city and country dwellers kept weather diaries. Some recorded subjective observations in written – often extensive – notes. Others benefited from the ready availability of meteorological instruments and kept both quantitative and qualitative records. A particularly important record is that kept between 1698 and 1731 by William Derham. This recorded events first at Upminster in Essex and later at Windsor, and extracts were published in the *Philosophical Transactions of the Royal Society*.[22] Towards the end of the century, Gilbert White's *The Natural History of Selborne* presents a remarkable description of English rural life.[23] White possessed both thermometers and barometers, and while these were not used to keep the detailed records of Derham and others, he did use them to give emphasis to his accounts of extremes of winter cold and summer heat.[24]

From these records it is possible to construct a synoptic picture of the climate of Palladian England.[25] Over the 18th century there were wide variations of temperature. The first two decades were relatively quiet, except for the 'Great Storm' of the night of 26–27 November 1703, which produced much damage across the south of the country, and the winters of 1708–09 and 1715–16, when frost fairs were once again held on the Thames. The 1730s was a surprisingly mild decade, but with an extreme frost in January 1731. Another very cold winter came in 1740, and this marked the beginning of lower winter temperatures that continued through the second half of the century. In contrast, the mean summer temperatures were generally high, at or above 15°C throughout the century. The summer of 1719 was one of the hottest for many years, and excellent grape harvests were gathered at Richmond upon Thames in both 1718 and 1719, but – this being England – the summer of 1725 was so cold that the Richmond grape harvest failed completely.

It is against this background of a more extensive and quantitative understanding of the climate that we may return to the writings of Morris and Chambers. In the second of his Lectures, Morris – almost certainly influenced by Isaac Newton's *Opticks*, which had been published in 1704 – wrote about the orientation lighting of rooms:

> OPTICKS will be requisite to understand, as far as they relate to the Proportions of Light in large or small Rooms, or as the Situation is as to the four Cardinal Points ...

In Lecture VI, Morris is more specific on these matters:

> The South Aspect is most preferable for the principal Front, if it can be conveniently had, in which should be the Rooms of State and Grandeur. The East is most proper for a Library because in the Morning Sun gives an enlivening Warmth to Nature, and then the Spirits are more active and free in the Choice of beautiful ideas ...

> In Hunting Seats ... as the Seasons for Hunting are in that Part of the Year which is generally cold, and require a temperate Warmth ... preserve the Lodgings as warm as can

be, by making as few Doors and Windows into these Rooms as Conveniency will permit …. All Winter Houses should be so contriv'd, whilst those for Summer should be more open, to cool and make the Dwellings comfortable and agreeable.

This Lecture also discusses the design of 'Chiminies' and the basis upon which the dimensions of windows should be determined in relation to the size of the rooms that they serve:

Let the Magnitude of the Room be given, and one of those Proportions I have propos'd to be made use of, or any other; multiply the Length and the Breadth of the Room together, and the Product multiply by the Height, and the Square Root of that Sum will be the Area or superficial Content in Feet, etc. of Light requir'd.

Palladio's treatise is a clear influence on both the content and the structure of the Lectures, but it is equally clear that Morris was alert to the different conditions of the Italian and English climates. It is also striking how closely calibrated his prescriptions are to the exact experience of climate in the 18th century, with its seasonal extremes, as is suggested by his emphasis on the very different needs of 'Summer and Winter Houses'.

The translation of Palladio's Italian formulae lies at the centre of William Chambers' recommendations:

I have generally added the depth and the height of the rooms on the principal floor together, and taken one eighth part thereof, for the width of the windows; a rule to which there are but few objections; admitting somewhat more light than Palladio's, it is I apprehend, fitter for our climate than his rule would be.

A further difference lay in the question of placing chimneys:

The Italians frequently put their chiminies in the front walls, between the windows, for the benefit of looking out while sitting by the fire; but this must be avoided; for by so doing that side of the room becomes crowded with ornaments and the other sides are left too bare … and the chimney shafts at the top of the building, which must necessarily be carried higher that the ridges of the roofs, have from their great length, a very disagreeable effect.

PALLADIO IN ENGLAND: HOUGHTON HALL AND CHISWICK HOUSE

Houghton Hall in Norfolk (Fig 1.11), the home of Sir Robert Walpole, who was to become Prime Minster, was built between 1722 and 1735. The design was the work of a number of architects. John Harris lists 'a real compote of architects', including Ripley, Gibbs, Kent, Campbell and Ware.[26] If we consider the plan of the principal floor (Fig 1.12), we see a

Fig 1.11 Houghton Hall, exterior

compact rectangle with a north–south long axis, and with Palladian principles of formal symmetry observed about the east–west axis. The formal entrance was originally from the east by a grand staircase, now demolished. This led into the Stone Hall, a grand reception room from which you enter the west-facing Saloon. To the south, grouped around the rooflit great staircase, are the private apartments of the Walpole family. The north side of the plan is occupied by the state apartments.

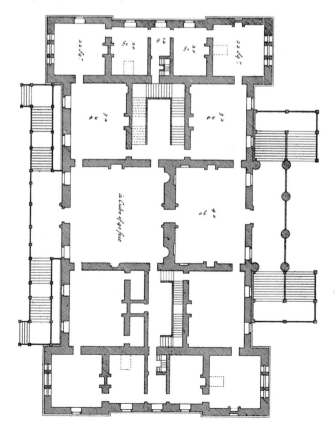

Fig 1.12 Houghton Hall, principal floor plan

An environmental analysis shows some surprising similarities with Hardwick Hall. All the fireplaces are placed in the core of the plan, just like at Hardwick and anticipating Chambers' later prescription, and the placement of the family rooms to the favoured south is similar to that of Bess's apartments at Hardwick. The principal rooms here are the east-facing Common Parlour, where family meals were taken, receiving morning sun, and, at the west, the Yellow Drawing Room, which would be agreeable in late afternoon and evening. The corresponding state rooms to the north of the Stone Hall are the Marble Parlour, or Great Dining Room, facing east, and the Velvet Drawing Room (now White Drawing Room), which balances the Yellow Parlour on the west front. In contrast to the almost medieval rigours of Hardwick, these interiors provide an entirely different idea of comfort. The adoption of classical proportions for determining the relationship of windows to rooms, adapted by both practice and theory to the English climate, establishes a greater harmony between inside and out at all seasons. Rooms would be cool in summer and more readily warmed in winter. Further benefits followed from the materials and decorations of these rooms. The fashion for wall linings such as velvet and luxurious carpets laid on timber or stone floors brought, in the language of building science, readier 'thermal response' to the warmth of open fires. The softer forms and enveloping designs of furniture also helped this warmth to be localised and retained.

Lord Burlington's Chiswick House (1725–29) more closely resembles the Palladian model than does Houghton (Fig 1.13). The centralised plan, with its domed octagon (Fig 1.14), is reminiscent of Palladio's Villa Rotonda, the Villa Capra near Vicenza (c1550). Chiswick also shares its orientation with the Rotonda. At both houses, north lies across the diagonal of the square plan. The result at Chiswick is to give preferential orientation to significant rooms in the manner that we saw at both Hardwick and Houghton. The room that enjoys the greatest

Fig 1.13 Lord Burlington, Chiswick House, entrance front

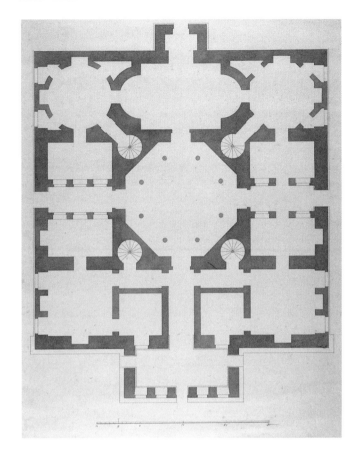

Fig 1.14 Chiswick House, plan

benefit is the Blue Velvet Room at the southern corner. This was Burlington's own study and has windows, one to the south-east and two to the south-west, that fill this quite small room with sunlight both morning and afternoon. In an inventory of the contents of the house taken in 1770 it is noted that the windows of this room, and the others for Burlington's personal use that lie adjacent, were fitted with 'Spring Window Blinds'.[27] It is unclear whether these were original fittings or were added after the completion of the house. In this context they suggest that a design on English Palladian principles could require some degree of sunlight control.

Chiswick is closest to the Italian model in placing the fireplaces on the outside walls, precisely in contradiction of William Chambers' later advice. Here they offer the advantages of simultaneous enjoyment of both view and warmth. Chambers was exercised about the practical disadvantage of this arrangement, which should, he argued, be taken above the ridge-line of the roof to ensure good combustion. The other disadvantage is that external flues take longer to become warm, and therefore burn less well than those within the fabric of the building and retain less warmth. Burlington's chimneys were in the form of obelisks, four to each side, and their height was well below the ridge.[28]

It may be suggested that 18th-century architecture in England, in both its theory and its practice, was influenced to some degree by the emerging natural sciences. The quantitative prescriptions of Morris and Chambers for dimensioning and positioning window openings and fireplaces, although clearly influenced by Palladio's earlier Italian formulations, represent a major step in bringing architecture into a new and more precise relationship with the nature of the English climate.

CITY AND COUNTRY: TWO PERSPECTIVES ON THE 19TH-CENTURY CLIMATE

At the end of the 18th century the relationship between buildings and climate changed fundamentally when, as a direct outcome of the events of the Industrial Revolution, mechanical devices for the warming, ventilating and lighting of buildings were first manufactured and brought into use. Until relatively recently these events were omitted from the standard histories of architecture, but following the publication of Reyner Banham's *The Architecture of the Well-tempered Environment* (1969),[29] the field has become a fruitful area of study.

The significance of these new technologies was that, for the first time in the history of building, the prospect opened up of fashioning buildings that could be comfortably inhabited at all seasons of the year and at all times of day and night. This became one of the great themes of the architecture of the 19th century as cities grew and new building types were conceived to meet the expectations of the new urban populations. But in the latter half of the century English architecture developed a further and influential theme. This was the fashion among the newly wealthy industrial and commercial classes to build houses for their families in the newly accessible countryside around the urban centres. These houses, many of which were designed by architects devoted to William Morris's ideas of Arts and Crafts, were rooted in an understanding of the English climate. So in considering the relationship between architecture and climate in the 19th century, we will see two quite distinct conditions and responses. First, we have the new 'technological' buildings of the industrial city, with new degrees and sources of atmospheric pollution, and set in relation to this we have houses of great sophistication and beauty located in settings that are climatically seen to be refuges from that city.

THE CLIMATE OF LONDON

Nineteenth-century England saw the growth of the great industrial cities of the Midlands and the north. Common to these and to the capital was the effect on the climate of the new, densely inhabited urban expansion in which industry, commerce and housing consumed quantities of coal for heating buildings and in fuelling industrial processes. In London this condition was nothing new, but the problem now reached unprecedented dimensions.[30]

The science of meteorology made further advances at this time. A major contribution was that of Luke Howard (1772–1864), who made extensive observations in London from 1801 to 1831. These were published as *The Climate of London*.[31] Howard's daily readings were taken in what where then suburbs at Plaistow and later at Tottenham. He collated them into monthly summaries, which gave daily values of wind direction, maximum and minimum barometric pressure, maximum and minimum temperature, evaporation, humidity and rainfall. In scope and detail this data exceeded anything that had previously been recorded. In addition to the scientific evidence, the climate of London in the 19th century was vividly described in literature and art. Charles Dickens's novels are full of references to the dire state of the atmosphere in the winter months:

> Implacable November weather …. Smoke lowering down from chimney-pots, making a soft black drizzle with flakes of soot in it as big as snowflakes – gone into mourning, one might imagine, for the death of the sun …. Fog everywhere …. Chance people on the bridges peeping over the parapets into a nether sky of fog, with fog all around them, as if they were up in a balloon and hanging into the misty clouds.
> Charles Dickens, *Bleak House*

Painters, from JMW Turner at the beginning of the century to Claude Monet at its end, depicted the foggy city. Monet, who made his atmospheric London paintings between 1899 and 1904, carefully chose to visit the city only in the winter months:

> I so love London! But I love it only in the winter. It's nice in the summer with the parks, but nothing like it is in the winter with the fog, for without the fog London wouldn't be a beautiful city.[32]

With the advent of new technologies for environmental management in buildings it became possible, for the first time, to design *against* the effects of climate rather than to shape form and material in conjunction *with* climate to fashion improved environments within. This was a significant moment in the history of architecture and, in England, architects of the highest standing were quick to explore these new possibilities in buildings for many purposes. The list included John Soane, who was one of the earliest, followed by, among others, Charles Barry, Robert Smirke and Alfred Waterhouse. It is important to note that, alongside the architects, there grew new professions of engineers and 'experts', who provided the equipment and expertise for the design and installation of systems for warming, ventilating and illuminating buildings.

This new emphasis was expressed by Soane in the eighth of the lectures that he delivered between1810 and 1820 when he was Professor of Architecture at the Royal Academy of Arts:

> The due and equably warming of rooms in cold climates, it must be admitted, is of great importance to the health and comfort of the inhabitants of every dwelling, from the

cottage of the servant to the palace of the sovereign. So necessary is warmth to existence that we cannot be surprised at the various inventions that have been produced for the better and more economical warming of our houses.[33]

In his own practice, Soane's engagement with *warming* applied to all building types, not just the houses he referred to in the lecture. His own house at 12–14 Lincoln's Inn Fields in London, where he lived from 1792 until 1837, was the test bed for his experiments.[34] One of Soane's assistants in his office at Lincoln's Inn was Charles James Richardson, who in 1837 published *A Popular Treatise on the Warming and Ventilation of Buildings*.[35] This was devoted entirely to descriptions of installations of the Perkins system. These included a system installed in 1837 at Robert Adam's Edinburgh Register Office, first built in 1774. Richardson also noted that Smirke, who had been articled to Soane, made widespread use of Perkins systems in his buildings, including in his own home, Stanmore House in Middlesex. Soane himself put Perkins systems into many of his projects, including designs for the Bank of England and the Law Courts at Westminster. Richardson's book contains drawings that show the system at Lincoln's Inn Fields in plan and cross section (Fig 1.15).[36]

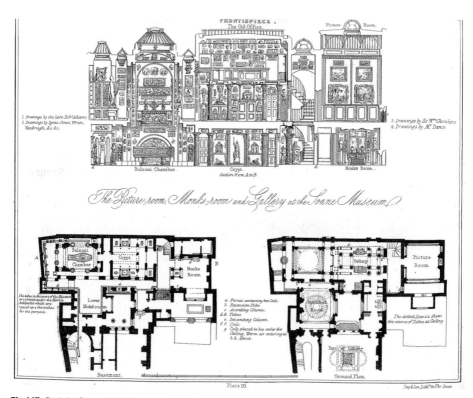

Fig 1.15 Sir John Soane, 12–14 Lincoln's Inn Fields, plan and section

The story of the warming and ventilating of the new Palace of Westminster, built to Sir Charles Barry's design following the destruction of the earlier building by fire, shows that these early systems frequently failed to meet expectations. The chambers of the House of Lords and the House of Commons in the old building had long suffered from inadequate ventilation, so a select committee of Members, appointed in 1835 shortly after the fire, concluded that 'special provision should be made for the due ventilation of all the rooms in the new House'. In August of the same year, an expert committee was commissioned to investigate 'The Ventilating and Warming of the New House'.[37] One of the members of the committee was Dr David Boswell Reid. He was an acknowledged expert on the subject and was responsible for the ventilation system in the temporary chamber for the House of Commons that was constructed within the shell of the former House of Lords. This incorporated a 25-horsepower steam engine to drive the extract ventilation. Following Barry's appointment as architect for the new building in 1836, Reid became his adviser. This ensured that physical provision was made for warming and ventilating, in the form of plant areas and distribution ducts. Both intake and extract air were at high level, clear of the polluted air at ground and river level. These, together with the magnificent lantern above the central lobby, were seized upon as opportunities in developing the building's picturesque silhouette (Fig 1.16). Extensive voids were provided beneath and above the principal spaces, and networks of ducts were threaded throughout the fabric (Fig 1.17). The relationship between Barry and Reid quickly deteriorated, and the performance of the systems was judged unsatisfactory for many decades after the building was opened. Nonetheless, the project serves to show how architectural ambition and technological expertise were brought together in pursuit of new standards of comfort in the first decades of the 19th century.

In the year after he was appointed architect for the Palace of Westminster, Barry was successful in the competition for the design of the Reform Club in Pall Mall. The building, which was constructed between 1838 and 1840, is possibly the most assured example of the extent to which architects and engineers created controlled environments in the Victorian metropolis. Barry adopted the model of the Renaissance Italian palazzo, specifically Sangallo's

Fig 1.16 Sir Charles Barry, Palace of Westminster, exterior

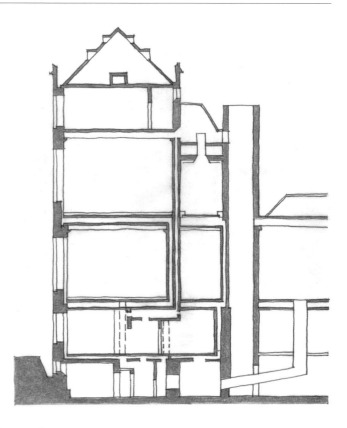

Fig 1.17 Palace of
Westminster, section showing
ducts

Palazzo Farnese in Rome (1515–41). Here is a further instance of an Italian exemplar serving
to inform the design of a building in England, but the transformation from 16th-century
Rome to 19th-century London is more radical than the subtle adjustments made by the
English Palladians a century earlier. Barry's competition design followed the original closely by
proposing that the central *cortile* should be open to the sky, as in Rome, albeit surrounded by
a glazed rather than an open colonnade. Following his appointment, however, Barry decided,
in discussion with his client, that the best solution in the atmosphere of London would be
to cover the courtyard with a glazed roof.[38] This allows the courtyard, the Saloon, to be
inhabited at all times of year, whatever the state of the outdoor climate. The principal rooms
are disposed around the central space, with the most important, great rooms overlooking the
gardens to the south (Fig 1.18). As we have seen in so many of these buildings, orientation
is a major consideration in designing in the English climate. Here, in the heart of the city,
the perhaps fortuitous orientation of the site, with Pall Mall to the north–west and Carlton
Gardens to the south–east, is used to advantage.

The relationship between the Reform Club and the Palace of Westminster in the matter of
the warming and ventilating systems is uncertain, but it is clear that the later building was
seen from the outset as a being fully serviced. Here, however, Dr Reid played no part and the
club's building committee authorised Barry 'to confer with Mr. Oldham in conjunction with

Fig 1.18 Sir Charles Barry, The Reform Club, view from Pall Mall

Messrs. Manby and Price'.[39] John Oldham, born in Dublin, was both an artist and an inventor, and had installed systems of warming and ventilation at the Bank of Ireland and in part of Soane's Bank of England.[40] The system used a 5-horsepower steam engine, located in vaults beneath the pavement of Pall Mall, to drive air, warmed by a heat exchanger, through a system of ducts to all the principal rooms, where it was introduced at ceiling level through openings concealed in the decorated cornices.

The building had an extensive gas lighting installation. This served its evening requirements, but it was likely that it was also used to provide light when the frequent fogs made day into night. A connection was made to the mains gas supply that had been laid along Pall Mall in 1820, and gasoliers were installed in the principal rooms. The combustion of gas requires that the waste products should be conducted away, and this was achieved through another system of ducts concealed in the detailing of the ceilings. The flues of the splendid fireplaces in the great rooms also assisted the ventilation process. A 'sun burner'[41] at the centre of the glass and iron rooflight lighted the Saloon. This was directly ventilated to the atmosphere and provided propulsion for the ventilation of the Saloon itself.

In contrast to the difficult experience at the Palace of Westminster, the Reform Club achieved a successful synthesis of architecture and environmental technologies. It was followed by many other successful collaborations in important buildings in London and other British cities in the 19th century as buildings accommodated new public uses in serving the needs of the increasing urban populations.[42]

LIVING IN THE COUNTRY

The English climate in the later part of the 19th century had recovered from the last vestiges of the Little Ice Age that were still experienced at the century's beginning. The Met Office Central England Temperature records show that these decades were relatively quiet, neither unusually hot or cold nor very wet. In the country beyond the cities, this was an ideal setting in which to build houses. It is the period when English domestic architecture reached a high point, as a group of architects associated with the Arts and Crafts ideas of William Morris were commissioned by the new middle classes to build houses for their families in the countryside outside the cities. This was now accessible by the expanded railway networks, so the family could remain in the clear air while the breadwinner commuted to and from the still-polluted city.

The Arts and Crafts house was a sophisticated translation of the principles of English vernacular building to meet the needs of this new clientele. MH Baillie Scott, one of the leading architects of the movement, finely summarised the essence of such a house:

> The house which, for want of a better word, we must continue to differentiate from the ordinary house as 'artistic', bases its claims not on its frillings and on its adornments, but on the very essence of its structure. The claims of commonsense are paramount in its plan, and its apartments are arranged to secure comfortable habitation for its inmates.[43]

At this date the idea of 'comfortable inhabitation' would be very different from that experienced by Bess of Hardwick or by a Palladian. These 'inmates' would expect to be warm in the winter and not suffer from the heat of a summer's day. Such expectations became a vital aspect of the designs and were achieved through a new analysis and interpretation of the climate and how to build in response to it.

The most perceptive contemporary commentary on the Arts and Crafts house was made by Hermann Muthesius in his book *Das Englische Haus*, published in Germany in 1904–05.[44] Here Muthesius, an architect who served for three years as cultural attaché at the German embassy in London, identified the climate as a strong influence on the design of these houses:

> The English climate is fundamentally different from that of the continent; in particular, it is milder, the air is extremely damp and it is generally inhospitable …. It is extremely rare for snow and ice to persist in England, and the day-time temperature in winter seldom falls below freezing point. There are short periods of great heat during the summer, but in general summers are rather cool …

Charles Francis Annesley Voysey was one of the greatest of the Arts and Crafts architects. Like many of his contemporaries, he took pains to articulate the principles by which he designed. Here we find explicit reference to climate:

Will it not be better for soul and body to capture the early morning sun, which is never too hot in England, and is a great purifying influence .... You will tell me, small windows, when rightly placed, in conjunction with white ceilings and friezes, may produce very light rooms, and have the advantage of preserving equable temperatures throughout the year ... It is pleasant to feel well protected when the weather is disturbed and angry; so you will not give me great sheets of plate glass.[45]

The interpretation of these principles may be seen in Voysey's 'Moorcrag' (1898), built above Lake Windermere for a Manchester industrialist. The long, rectangular plan is set on a platform excavated from the hillside, with its long axis orientated east–west (Fig 1.19). Orientation, or aspect in the terminology of the time, was a consistent concern of Arts and Crafts architects, with clear distinction being made between the hostile north and the benign south. 'Moorcrag' is entered from the north via a sheltered porch, and the principal rooms all face to the south, where they enjoy the warmth of the sun and views along the lake below. The south face of the house is a complex composition of gables, dormer windows and bay windows, with a sheltered veranda beneath the sweeping roof. Rising above are three tall chimney stacks. This is all as

Fig 1.19 CFA Voysey, 'Moorcrag', Windermere

purposeful as it is picturesque. The bay windows capture sun throughout the day at all seasons and allow the inhabitants of the house to sit on window seats in solar warmth. The veranda, where there is a comfortable seat, provides a sheltered microclimate against the breezes of the northern weather. The enclosing roof and tall chimneys are both functional and symbolic of the house's place in relation to the climate. Voysey wrote:

> a careful study of our climate makes us emphasise our roofs to suggest protection from weather. Large, massive chimneys imply stability and repose.[46]

The elements of the Arts and Crafts house were consistently conceived to bring comfort in the English climate. This is shown most eloquently in the houses of MH Baillie Scott, who, like Voysey and many others, put these principles into both word and form. In 1906 Baillie Scott published *Houses and Gardens*.[47] The benefits of a southerly orientation are expressed where, in talking about the design of a dining room, Baillie Scott tells us: 'Modern science has shown that sunlight is the great health-giver and germ destroyer and few rooms should be deprived of it.'[48] For Baillie Scott, as the title of his book declares, house and garden were seen as interdependent parts of a whole in creating rich environments in the English climate:

> Human life, like plant life, flourishes in sun and air and grows pale and anaemic when it is deprived of these.
> And so the garden is conceived as an outdoor extension of the house, with its sheltered apartments for the sunshine or for the shade.
> But in our inconsistent climate it is not always possible to use the garden entirely. It is desirable, for instance, that meals should be taken in summer weather out of doors ... and so the need for a wide verandah or garden-room is increasingly felt ...[49]

On the question of winter warmth, Baillie Scott, like many of his associates, rejected the potential of central heating in favour of the open fire:

> I suppose it must be conceded that the open fire is an extremely unscientific and unsatisfactory arrangement. But the modern scientist satisfies himself with putting the matter to the test of the thermometer, and the value of the system is judged by its effects on mercury, rather than on the complex human ...
> In the house the fire is practically a substitute for the sun, and it bears the same relationship to the household as the sun does to the landscape.

These principles are translated into form in the house at 48 Storey's Way in Cambridge, completed in 1912. The plan (Fig 1.20) has much in common with 'Moorcrag', with entry from the north and all the principal rooms to the south. Here in the gentler climate of the outskirts of the university city, the continuity of house and garden is more fully realised than it is on the Cumbrian uplands. The living room is a perfect example of Arts and Crafts domestic space,

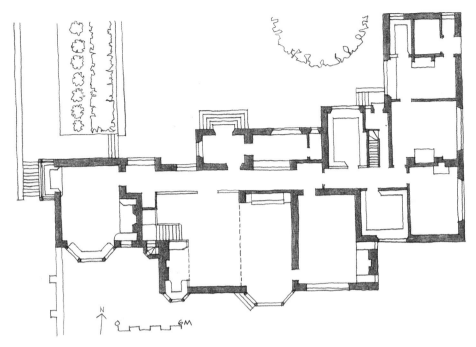

Fig 1.20 MH Baillie Scott, 48 Storey's Way, Cambridge, plan

with bay window and inglenook providing quite distinct microclimates in response to the different needs of day and night and the seasons. The inhabitants would sit in the bay in warm sun on clear winter's days and retreat to the open fire – the sun's substitute – in the evenings. Functionally and compositionally the arrangement is compelling (Fig 1.21).

Fig 1.21 48 Storey's Way, living room

THE 20TH CENTURY: NEW TECHNOLOGIES AND NEW FORMS

At the beginning of the 20th century all of the technological elements of modern environmental management were in place. The systems of warming and ventilation that were applied by master architects of the 19th century were becoming more refined and the possibility of mechanically cooling buildings was just around the corner. General availability of mains electricity supplies and the invention of the incandescent light bulb, almost simultaneously in 1879 by Edison in America and Swan in Britain, promised to release architecture from its historic relationship with climate. The prospect appeared of buildings that could be occupied for all purposes at all times of year and all times of day and night.

Architects were eager to explore this new world. In 1920 Le Corbusier wrote in *L'Esprit Nouveau*:

> There is a new spirit of construction and synthesis guided by a clear conception. Whatever may be thought of it, it animates today the greater part of human activity.[50]

Most of the early explorations of the influence of new technologies in architecture were concerned with structural and constructional methods. But Le Corbusier was quick to move on to the environmental. In his Buenos Aires lectures of 1929, he proclaimed the new environmental principle:

> Every country builds its houses in response to its climate. At this moment of general diffusion, of international scientific techniques, I propose only one house for all climates.[51]

The lecture was illustrated with diagrams showing the principles of *batiments hermetiques*: Corbusian towers served by umbilical *usine à air exact*, which is an air conditioning plant in broad principle. Theory was translated into practice in the design of the Cité de Rèfuge in Paris in 1932, where Le Corbusier collaborated in the design of a sealed double glass skin, a 'neutralising wall'.[52] In many ways this was a prototype for the sealed glass boxes, wrapped around air-conditioned interiors, that were to become the overwhelming stereotype of late 20th-century commercial architecture.

Modernism proceeded more slowly in England, and few, if any, large public buildings were experimental environmentally. The 'Modern House', however, was a success and many good designs were built. What is interesting here, however, is that most of these embraced environmental principles little different from those of the Arts and Crafts. Houses by Berthold Lubetkin, Wells Coates, Maxwell Fry and others carefully observed principles of orientation and planning that would have been recognised by Voysey and Baillie Scott, whatever they may have thought of the language and detail of this new 'white' architecture.[53] A particularly

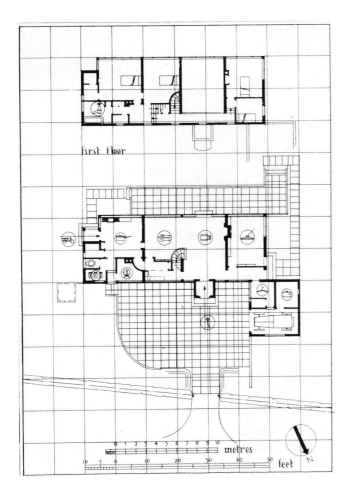

first floor

metres

feet

N

Fig 1.22 George Checkley, Thurso House, plan

good example is the Thurso House at Cambridge, built in 1932 by George Checkley, a New Zealander, who taught in the school of architecture at Cambridge. The plan (Fig 1.22) exhibits all the concern for orientation that was ubiquitous in Arts and Crafts planning, and this is continued in the design of the elevations, although reinterpreted here in the language of white Modernism (Fig 1.23).

At the same date the Royal Institute of British Architects (RIBA) commissioned a study, *The Orientation of Buildings*.[54] This was a clear indication of the significance attached to the question by the architectural establishment at the time. An important contribution to the study was made by the building scientists at the Building Research Station, which had been established in 1921 to undertake research in connection with building materials.[55] Particular attention was paid in the report to the value of sunlight in the design of school buildings, and principles of proper orientation were applied in designs for schools by the younger, more experimental architects. A fine example is the kindergarten built in 1937 as part of a housing

Fig 1.23 Thurso House, south front

project at Kensal Rise in west London by Maxwell Fry, who was one of the leading English Modernist architects. The footprint of a demolished gasholder that formerly occupied the site determined the circular form of the plan, but the classrooms and outdoor play areas of the school are scrupulously orientated towards the sun (Fig 1.24).

Fig 1.24 Maxwell Fry, Kindergarten, Kensal Rise, exterior

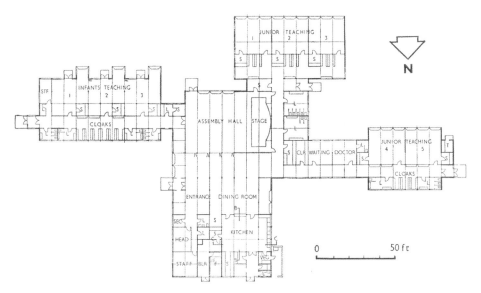

Fig 1.25 Morgan Road School, Hertford, plan

In the years following the Second World War, principles of environmental design were formally incorporated into the official guidelines for the design of schools.[56] The work of the architects at Hertfordshire County Council was notable, and they enlisted the expertise of the Building Research Station, located within the county at Garston, to provide support for design. Particular emphasis was given to the achievement of quantitatively defined standards of daylight, and the orientation principles of the prewar designs continued to be applied, as may be seen in the plan of Morgan's Road School at Hertford, where all the classrooms face due south (Fig 1.25).

Late in the 1950s a seemingly unlikely source made a significant contribution to the history of school building in Britain and to the continuing evolution of architecture's relationship with climate. St George's School at Wallasey on the Wirral peninsula, just across the river Mersey from Liverpool, was designed by Emslie Morgan, the assistant borough architect. Morgan educated himself in the principles of solar heating and applied this knowledge to the design of a building that would obtain much of its heating needs from the sun. With its 9-metre-high, south-facing 'solar wall' (Fig 1.26), the building achieved this goal to a remarkable degree. The conventional heating system that was installed as a precaution was rarely, if ever, used in the first 25 years of the building's life.[57] Despite this success, the building had little influence on wider design practice for many years until, following the so-called energy crisis of the 1970s, the possibility of low energy design – the precursor of sustainability – led to the understanding of new relationships between architecture and climate. In the years that have followed, these ideas of passive solar architecture and energy-conscious design – of *sustainability* – have informed the work of an increasing number of architects in Britain who place environmental concerns at the heart of their practice.

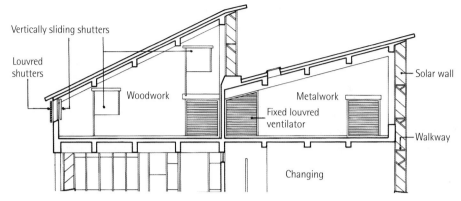

Fig 1.26 Emslie Morgan, St George's School, Wallasey, cross section

CONCLUSION

In this chapter I have traced a history of English architecture that begins in the reign of Elizabeth I, when England was in the grip of the Little Ice Age, and ends at the beginning of the 21st century, when the climate is once again a prominent factor in architecture. In the first two centuries of the narrative, from 1600 to 1800, buildings mediated between the extremes of the natural climate, winter cold and summer heat, through the organisation of form and material. Life within buildings of all purposes was conditioned by the seasonal and diurnal variations of climate. In winter, meagre artificial lighting and the limited warmth of open fireplaces governed life, spatially and temporally. In summer, life expanded, within and around buildings, as daylight filled rooms that were thermally comfortable. These buildings, by architects as different as Smythson, Wren and Burlington, nonetheless provided settings for lives that were often socially and culturally sophisticated and, in a sense different from our modern definition, comfortable.

At the beginning of the 19th century, however, it became possible to redefine the relationship between buildings and climate. The Industrial Revolution produced the means by which the interiors of buildings could be made warm even on the coldest winter days and, as the century progressed, could be brightly illuminated after dark. The unpredictability and variability of climate had, seemingly, been conquered. For the first time in history, the form and material of buildings entered a partnership with mechanical devices, and architects collaborated in their design with the new profession of engineering. From the earliest cases, in the works of Soane, the new elements were effectively incorporated into the building fabric and, in the middle years of the century, Barry, Waterhouse and their contemporaries achieved a comprehensive synthesis of form, material and machine. It should also be noted that it was at this moment that buildings began to consume large quantities of energy in the form of coal for boilers, and gas – and later electricity – for lighting.

In the 20th century, the potential of this marriage of architecture with engineering was eagerly realised – first in America, then in Europe, and then in the remainder of the planet – as economic development took place. The glass skyscraper is the ubiquitous symbol of this success.[58] A major contribution made by Banham to the theory of environmental architecture is his definition of three distinct 'modes' of environmental control: the *conservative*, the *selective* and the *regenerative*. In later work, the present author proposed a simpler, two-part distinction between the *selective* and the *exclusive* modes.[59] In this, the *selective* embraces the environmental method of all historic buildings up to the introduction of mechanical services and those of a later date that continue to give priority to natural light, ventilation and energy. The *exclusive* defines buildings that prioritise mechanical, energy-consuming methods of environmental provision and, in their later manifestations, have sealed envelopes. This is the present state of environmental design practice. Do we design *with* or *against* climate? That is our choice.

NOTES

1 National Meteorological Library and Archive, *Climate of the British Isles Fact Sheet 4* (Exeter: Met Office, 2013).

2 See Bryan Fagan, *The Little Ice Age: How Climate Made History 1300–1830* (New York: Basic Books, 2000).

3 Mike Hulme, 'Climate', in Bruce Smith (ed), *The Cambridge Shakespeare Encyclopedia: Volume I, Mapping Shakespeare's World* (Cambridge: Cambridge University Press, 2015).

4 William Harrison, *The Description of England* (1587; repr ed New York: Dover, 1994).

5 See Mary S Lowell, *Bess of Hardwick: First Lady of Chatsworth* (London: Abacus Books, 2007) and David N. Durrant, *Bess of Hardwick: Portrait of an Elizabethan Dynast* (London: Peter Owen, 1999).

6 See WE Knowles Middleton, *The Invention of the Meteorological Instruments* (Baltimore: Johns Hopkins University Press, 1972).

7 Before 1200, the definition of *comfort* (n) was 'a feeling of consolation'; by *c*1340 *comfortable* (adj) had the meaning 'pleasant, enjoyable'. *Chambers Dictionary of Etymology* (Edinburgh & New York: Chambers, 1988).

8 This is discussed in more detail in Dean Hawkes, *The Environmental Tradition: Studies in the Architecture of Environment* (London & New York: E & FN Spon, 1996).

9 See Catherine Spellman and Carl Unglaub (eds), *Peter Smithson, Conversations with Students: A Space for Our Generation* (New York: Princeton Architectural Press, 2005).

10 An inventory of the contents of the house in 1601 describes each fireplace in detail and refers to the number of 'skreynes' (screens) in each room. See Lindsay Boynton, *The Hardwick Inventory of 1601* (London: The Furniture History Society, 1971).

11 John Evelyn, *Diaries*, cited in Fagan, *The Little Ice Age*.

12 John Evelyn, *Fumifugium, or The Inconveniencie of the Aer and Smoak of London Dissipated Together With Some Remedies Humbly Proposed* (London, 1661).

13 The proposal is described in Christopher Wren, *Parentalia: Or, Memoirs of the Family of Wren …* (London: T. Osborn and R. Dodsley, 1750).

14 'Letter to a Friend on the Commission for Building Fifty New City Churches', ibid.

15 A comprehensive source of the fundamentals of daylight design is, RG Hopkinson, *Architectural Physics: Lighting* (HMSO, 1964).

16 See Paul Jeffrey, *The City Churches of Sir Christopher Wren* (London: Hambledon Continuum 1996).

17 Wren, 'Letter to a Friend'.

18 This version, with the illustrations redrawn by Giacomo Leoni and text translated by Nicholas Dubois, appeared in instalments over several years. Other editions were by Edward Hoppus (1736) and Isaac Ware (1737). This information from John Summerson, *Architecture in Britain: 1530-1830*, 9th rev ed (New Haven: Yale University Press, 1993).

19 Colen Campbell, *Vitruvius Britannicus, or The British Architect* (1715, 1717 and 1725; unabridged facsimilie ed, New York: Dover, 2006).

20 In the first volume the architects included Wren, Thomas Archer, Inigo Jones, Thomas Talman and Campbell himself.

21 Robert Morris, *Lectures on Architecture: Consisting of Rules Founded upon Harmonic Architectural Proportions in Building* (London, 1734). William Chambers, *A Treatise on the Decorative Part of Civil Architecture* (London, 1759).

22 William Derham, 'The history of the great frost in the last winter 1703 and 1708/9', *Philosophical Transactions of the Royal Society*, 26 (1708-09), 454-78; and William Derham, 'Concerning frost in January 1730/1', *Philosophical Transactions of the Royal Society*, 37 (1731-32), 16-18.

23 Gilbert White, *The Natural History of Selborne 1788-1789* (Harmondsworth: Penguin Classics, 1987); Gilbert White, *The Journals of Gilbert White* (London: Futura, 1982).

24 See Vladimir Jankovic, *Reading the Skies: A Cultural History of English Weather, 1650-1820* (Chicago: University of Chicago Press, 2000).

25 This overview is constructed from the data collated in G Manley, 'Central England temperatures record: monthly means 1659 to 1973', *Quarterly Journal of the Royal Meteorological Society*, 100 (1974), 389-405.

26 John Harris, 'The architecture of the house', in Andrew Morris (ed), *Houghton Hall: The Prime Minister, the Empress and the Heritage* (London: Philip Wilson, 1996).

27 TS Rosoman, 'The Chiswick House inventory of 1770', *Furniture History*, 22 (1986), 81-105.

28 The present obelisk chimneys were reconstructed during restoration works in 1956-57. Nineteenth-century images show more conventional chimneys that were probably built to overcome practical difficulties with the originals.

29 Reyner Banham, *The Architecture of the Well-tempered Environment*, 2nd rev ed (London: The Architectural Press, 1969).

30 An excellent review is Peter Brimblecombe, *The Big Smoke: A History of Air Pollution in London since Mediaeval Times* (London: Methuen, 1987).

31 Luke Howard, *The Climate of London*, 2 vols (1818; 2nd ed, 3 vols, London, 1833).

32 Claude Monet, cited in Brimblecombe, *The Big Smoke*.

33 Sir John Soane, Lecture VIII, Royal Academy Lectures. The lectures are reproduced in full, with an extensive commentary, in David Watkin, *Sir John Soane: Enlightenment Thought and the Royal Academy Lectures* (Cambridge: Cambridge University Press, 1996).

34 See Todd Wilmert, 'Heating methods and their impact on Soane's work: Lincoln's Inn Fields and Dulwich Picture Gallery', *Journal of the Society of Architectural Historians*, 1:2 (1993), 26-58.

35 Charles James Richardson, *A Popular Treatise on the Warming and Ventilation of Buildings Showing the Advantage of the Improved System of Heated Water Circulation* (London: John Weale Architectural Library, 1837).

36 See Dean Hawkes, *The Environmental Imagination* (London & New York: Routledge, 2008), and Dean Hawkes, *Architecture and Climate* (London & New York: Routledge, 2012) for further discussion of Soane's environmental achievements.

37 See Denis Smith, 'The building services', in MH Port (ed), *The Houses of Parliament* (New Haven: Paul Mellon Center for British Art/Yale University Press, 1976).

38 See John Olley, 'The Reform Club', in Dan Cruickshank (ed), *Timeless Architecture* (London: The Architectural Press, 1985).

39 Ibid.

40 See *Oxford Dictionary of National Biography* (Oxford: Oxford University Press, 2004–09). A description of Oldham's system is in CW Williams, 'Mr Oldham's system of warming and ventilating', *Civil Engineer and Architects' Journal*, 2 (1839), 96–7.

41 A 'sun burner' was a gas light fitting which incorporated built-in flues that carried away the noxious fumes from the gas burner. Sun burners were installed in the Upper Library and the saloon at the Reform Club.

42 In addition to Reyner Banham's pioneering *The Architecture of the Well-tempered Environment*, there is a growing literature that describes these developments. See, for example, Robert Bruegmann, 'Central heating and forced ventilation: origins and effects on architectural design', *Journal of the Society of Architectural Historians*, 37 (1978), 141–60; Robert Bruegmann and Donald Prowler, 'Nineteenth century mechanical system design', *Journal of Architectural Education (JAE)*, 30:3 (1977), 11–15. The essays collected in Cruickshank (ed), *Timeless Architecture*, describe a range of buildings by Soane, Barry, Waterhouse, Prior and, in Brussels, Victor Horta. Oriel Prizeman, *Philanthropy and Light: Carnegie Libraries and the Advent of Transatlantic Standards for Public Space* (Farnham: Ashgate, 2012), presents a detailed study of the environmental intentions of the Carnegie libraries that were built in British and American industrial cities.

43 MH Baillie Scott, *Houses and Gardens* (London: George Newnes, 1906).

44 Hermann Muthesius, *Das Englische Haus* (Berlin: Wasmuth, Vols 1 and 2 1904, Vol 3, 1905), ed Denis Sharp, trans Janet Seligman (London: Crosby Lockwood Staples, 2007).

45 CFA Voysey, 'Ideas in Things II', in T Raffles Davidson (ed), *The Arts Connected with Building* (London: Batsford, 1909).

46 Ibid.

47 Baillie Scott, *Houses and Gardens*.

48 Ibid.

49 Ibid.

50 Le Corbusier, 'Programme', *L'Esprit Nouveau*, 1 (1920).

51 Le Corbusier, *Precision on the Present State of Architecture and City Planning* (Cambridge, MA: MIT Press, 1991).

52 The idea of the *neutralising wall* or *mur neutralisant* is discussed at some length by Reyner Banham in *The Architecture of the Well-tempered Environment*, 157–60.

53 These designs are discussed in detail in Hawkes, *Architecture and Climate*.

54 RIBA Joint Committee on the Orientation of Buildings, *The Orientation of Buildings* (London: RIBA, 1933).

55 See FM Lea, *Science and Building: A History of the Building Research Station* (London: HMSO, 1971).

56 See Andrew Saint, *Towards a Social Architecture: The Role of School Building in Post-War Britain* (New Haven & London: Yale University Press, 1987).

57 The building was first brought to wide attention in Banham, *The Architecture of the Well-tempered Environment*. Further, more technical discussion is in Hawkes, *The Environmental Tradition*. This draws upon a substantial body of research into the performance of the building published by MG Davies, *International Journal of Energy Research*, 11:1 (January/March 1987).

58 See Banham, *The Architecture of the Well-tempered Environment*, for an account of this history up to the mid 20th century.

59 Hawkes, *The Environmental Tradition*.

TWO

The energy context of domestic traditional buildings for the UK

···

Simon Lannon, Heledd Iorwerth, Xiaojun Li and Diana Waldron

INTRODUCTION

The majority of traditional stock will be still in use in 2050, when the UK government has set a target of 80% reduction in carbon emissions.[1] To achieve these ambitious targets there is a push to improve the energy efficiency of all buildings in the UK. This chapter will explore traditional residential buildings, which currently represent approximately 22% of the building stock, to establish the impact of these policy pressures. The types of buildings considered in this chapter range from the exemplar one-off or individual building to the mass-built solid-wall stock constructed as part of the industrialisation of the UK, often referred to as pre-1919 dwellings. The terraces of the industrial towns have considerable heritage value but are often in locations where house prices and incomes are low and, as such, are prone to fuel poverty issues. Both 'retrofitting the fabric first' and 'retrofitting the systems first' methods of retrofit will be tested through energy demand modelling, providing possible routes to low energy and low carbon emissions for traditional dwellings.

Having set out the context for carbon reductions and energy efficiency, the process of retrofit and the opportunity to change the performance of the buildings will be explored through simulation. These changes can be 'whole house' as a managed project, or 'stepwise' in a more ad hoc manner, where the refurbishment is ongoing and continues through the life of the buildings. Traditional buildings in the UK are not as they were originally built, but more a mix of refurbishments and retrofits. As such, they are complex one-off properties in need of careful consideration regarding retrofit routes.

Fig 2.01 Typical terraces of the industrial town

The UK policy on energy efficiency considers national energy infrastructures and buildings
as a whole. The overall targets allow for variance in the performance need for each building
but require action from all building owners. In essence, the UK needs these buildings to
be retrofitted, but in a manner that is both practical and of a high standard. The following
sections will address domestic energy consumption, starting with UK policy, then will analyse
the stock profile for the UK. Simulation techniques used to understand the impact of retrofit
processes from simple to complex tools will be described. The process of retrofitting the
buildings will be explained in terms of both the overall process chosen and the order in which
it is undertaken. Finally, the chapter will explore through a series of case studies the benefits
of careful evaluation of the retrofit design process through computer simulation methods at
different scales: regional, community and building.

POLICY CONTEXT

Carbon emissions

The UK government has set an ambitious target of 80% reduction in carbon emissions by
the year 2050. As part of this target, it is predicted that the emissions related to buildings in
2050 will need to be close to zero. While the design of new zero carbon buildings has been
well researched, the potential for zero emission retrofit is less explored. As the vast majority
of buildings that will exist in 2050 have already been built, the interactions of the carbon
emission reduction methods, such as fabric improvements, occupant behaviour and renewable
technologies in the retrofit design process, need to be researched further.

Future electricity generation

The supply of electrical energy in the UK is usually through the national grid, which uses a
mix of fuel sources to generate electricity. This mix, which includes fossil fuels, has an overall

Table 2.1 UK electricity fuel for 2014

Energy source	%	kg/kWh
Coal	46.8	0.91
Natural gas	27.1	0.40
Nuclear	8.4	0.00
Renewables	11.9	0.00
Other fuels	5.8	0.77
Overall average		0.42

Source: Carbon Trust, *Building the Future Today*

emission rate for each unit of energy delivered to houses. The figures for 2014 show that currently the UK is heavily reliant on coal and natural gas (Table 2.1) covering over 73% of the generation.[2] The government plans to reduce this emission rate by decarbonising the grid through new nuclear power stations and investment in large-scale renewable technology. In addition, the move from coal, which has a high emission rate of carbon per kWh, to gas power stations will drive the emissions rate down.

Many pathways and scenarios have been created to show how emission reduction targets can be achieved, such as the Carbon Trust's report *Building the Future Today*,[3] but they are generally based on a top-down approach. They therefore tend to give broad guidance on the impact of the work on the ground. The *grid decarbonisation pathways* chosen for the modelling process have taken data and waypoints from the UK Energy Research Centre (UKERC) 2050 Carbon Pathway.[4] Concepts regarding affordability of energy efficiency measures have been taken from the Carbon Trust *Building the Future Today* research.[5] The outcome of the review of scenarios available presents three possible future pathways:

Scenario 1 – Faint hearted
Generally business as usual, with some minor attempts to decarbonise the grid and continued slow energy efficiency update.

Scenario 2 – Low carbon reference
The government invests in partial decarbonisation of the grid through reduced dependence on fossil fuels. Large investment in energy efficiency, small-scale renewable installations, and some change in occupant behaviour.

Scenario 3 – Super ambitious
The government invests in full decarbonisation of the grid through large-scale renewable energy (wind and solar farms), nuclear power stations, and huge investment in energy efficiency and small-scale renewables. There is also widespread change in occupant behaviour, reducing the personal demands for heat and energy.

Each of these scenarios can be broken down into four components that have an impact on the emissions of buildings: electric national grid, small-scale renewable technologies, energy efficiency and occupant behaviours. Choices for these components are introduced in the model as variables, covering the range of change corresponding to the scenarios described above.

The outcome of the scenarios mentioned is a range of electricity grid carbon emissions, from 'faint hearted' with 0.42kg CO_2 per kWh, which represents little change from current levels, to 'super ambitious' with 0.08kg CO_2 per kWh, which represents a reduction of 80%.[6]

Fuel poverty

The accepted definition of a household as being fuel poor has been until recently that more than 10% of the household income is spent on fuel to maintain comfortable conditions within the dwelling. Since 2013 the official definition of fuel poverty is based on the concept of 'Low Income High Costs',[7] where a household is fuel poor if:

- they have required fuel costs that are above average (the national median level)
- were they to spend that amount, they would be left with a residual income below the official poverty line.

The fuel use considered within this definition includes heating, hot water, lighting, appliances and cooking, rather than just the fuel for heating.

The number of fuel poor households in England has been estimated at 2.28 million in 2012, which is a drop from 2.39 million in 2011.[8] When the age of dwellings is considered, it is clear that traditional buildings are more likely to have fuel poor households. In 2012, 18% of households living in properties built before 1919 were considered fuel poor compared with 13% of households living in properties built between 1919 and 1964, and 6% of households living in properties built after 1964.

Another aspect of the fuel poverty problem is the source of finance for the retrofitting of energy efficiency measures. Large-scale retrofit has predominately been undertaken in the UK's public stock. In 2011, 94% of pre-1919 dwellings were privately owned or rented and therefore unlikely to have access to the finance required.[9]

Finally, the value of the house limits the ability to access finance as the cost of retrofit approaches the value of the house. If council tax banding is used as an indicator of dwelling value, the percentage of pre-1919 houses in council tax band A for England and Wales is 32%, whereas for post-1919 only 22% is in band A. This suggests that low-value dwellings are more likely to be traditional properties. In 2013, research also suggested a link between energy efficiency and house prices,[10] where increased SAP rating band[11] through retrofitting was correlated to an increase of value compared to un-retrofitted houses. The issues of fuel poverty, private ownership and the low value of some of the UK's traditional stock suggest that there is a need for retrofitting if the stock is to be of a decent standard and achieve carbon reduction targets by 2050.

STOCK PROFILE FOR UK

The distribution of traditional buildings varies greatly between administrative areas, resulting in a range of challenges with distinct problems and solutions (Fig 2.02). For example, 67% of Kensington and Chelsea dwellings were built pre-1919, while areas of newer settlements such as Basildon, at the other extreme, have less than 1% of these older buildings. When delving into smaller geographical areas, these extremes become even more pronounced; when combined with other energy usage issues such as rurality, lack of mains gas, and economic and social issues, energy efficiency improvement to the housing stock becomes incredibly complex.

The age of a dwelling is a key indicator of the building's characteristics and ultimately the efficiency of its fabric. Although identifying a building's age is challenging, major changes in building techniques make it possible to roughly estimate the period in which they were built. Pre-1919 buildings of traditional construction are mostly buildings with solid masonry walls that both absorb and readily allow the evaporation of moisture. These buildings generally pre-date those constructed with walls incorporating cavities and damp-proof membranes, which became widespread from the 1920s.[12]

The pre-1919 housing category ranges from exemplar individual buildings to the mass-built solid-wall stock constructed as part of the industrialisation of the UK. In analysing the energy efficiency and potential improvements to buildings, a range of variables is usually used to further categorise properties within age groups. A property's typology and dimensions are key, as is the type of fuel used and its system efficiencies.

Another crucial issue to consider when analysing the potential of any building stock is the extent to which these older buildings can accommodate change without harming their special interest. Some traditional buildings such as the mass-built solid-wall terraces that are widespread in a considerable number of the UK's towns and cities may be able to accommodate significant change. Others, including those that are listed (1%) or are in conservation areas (5%), are sensitive to even slight internal or external alteration. New regulations came into force in January 2013,[13] stating that listed buildings no longer require Energy Performance Certificates (EPC) unless they are being considered for the 'Green Deal'.[14] It is evident that this new update aims to protect the character of listed buildings,[15] as compliance with minimum energy efficiency requirements could unacceptably alter their character or appearance.[16] It is also to be noted that within current building regulations special considerations can be applied to non-exempt buildings, such as those of traditional construction.[17] Works are required to comply with the energy efficiency requirements as far as is reasonably practicable – that is, not to unacceptably alter the character of the building or increase the risk of long-term

Age of Dwellings (VOA)
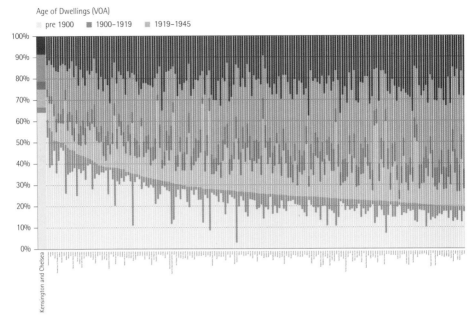

Fig 2.02 Distribution of property build period by administrative area, March 2014 (Valuation Office Agency)

deterioration. However, particular buildings that might be exempt from having an EPC can be thermally upgraded if appropriate measures can be applied. These must be carefully considered and submitted for planning approval, since they must avoid controversies of street-scene blight through some commonly applied measures that can cause irreversible damage. External solid-wall insulation, for example, which in many cases has proved not to perform up to standards, has ruined original features of building facades.

These regulations can provide the flexibility needed to improve the energy efficiency of pre-1919 houses responsibly. Blanket solutions are usually inappropriate and can inadvertently cause irreversible damage to the building fabric. If energy efficiency measures are to be applied to such traditional buildings, it is essential that their significance is thoroughly understood and that the physics of air and moisture movement through older buildings is taken into account. With great care and understanding, building conservation and energy conservation do not have to remain mutually exclusive. Both have a significant role to play in protecting the rich heritage of the UK's building stock.

EXPLORING THE POTENTIAL FOR ENERGY REDUCTION THROUGH ENERGY MODELLING TECHNIQUES

The modelling of domestic energy consumption is an important tool to establish the benefits of energy efficient refurbishment. The methods employed are similar to those of design: an initial

Age of Dwellings (VOA)
■ 1945–1964   ■ 1964–1982   ■ post 1982

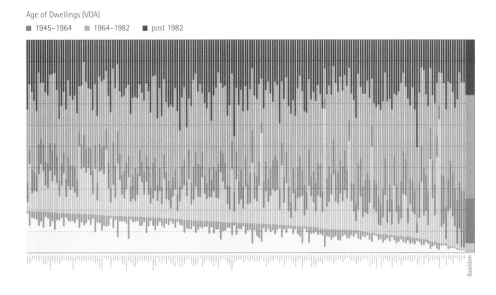

case will be tested using a simple model to provide confidence in the effectiveness in terms of energy and cost/payback. Typically the model used in the UK is the Standard Assessment Procedure (SAP), which forms part of the UK government's flagship energy efficiency policy instrument the 'Green Deal', which was announced as part of the Energy Act 2011.[18]

If the results of this initial work show potential then more detailed work can be undertaken to explore the implications in terms of thermal comfort, or humidity and moisture problems. The tools used in this instance are generally known as dynamic simulation tools, for example EnergyPlus,[19] Therm,[20] and HTB2.[21]

STANDARD ASSESSMENT PROCEDURE (SAP)

Work at neighbourhood and regional scale allows a deep understanding of potential energy efficiency to be gained, enabling limited financial resources to be targeted. The general concept is to use archetypes or typical buildings as a base to establish the current and potential energy efficiency state of properties. A lack of confidence in the outcomes of these techniques recognised as the difference between the predicted and actual energy use of an individual building, commonly known as the performance gap.

SAP is a simplified building performance prediction tool, and is the most commonly used tool for assessing the performance of domestic buildings in the UK and producing the

Energy Performance Certificate. SAP is based on a worksheet that considers the heat transfers in the building including fabric heat losses, ventilation, domestic hot water demand, solar gains, appliance loads and the type of heating system. When considering the fabric of the building, it deals with the design in a non-geometric way: for example, the external walls are not considered individually, but rather similar constructions are summed to form a single area for the calculation of heat loss. The method also takes into consideration the thermal mass of the building through the heating utilisation factor, which adjusts the assumed internal temperature for the heating calculation. Other simplifications are undertaken regarding solar gains, occupancy, and incidental gains from appliances and occupants.

SAP is often criticised because of the discrepancies found between modelled consumption and reality. Research has been carried out to investigate the limitations of SAP[22] and how to further improve it.[23] While anecdotal evidence from professional and academic circles suggests that SAP is inadequate, Scott Kelly states that there is a serious lack of recent experimental analysis testing its validity and robustness in regard to calculating building performance.[24] This can be said to be especially true for pre-1919 building stock.

A study by English Heritage in 2007 compared records of energy use in a number of traditional dwellings with their EPC assessments.[25] Typically, the actual energy use was some 40% less than the EPC estimate. Recent developments to the reduced SAP that is often used to generate EPCs for existing buildings allows assessors to enter actual U-values for elements of a structure rather than notional estimates taken from a database. Such developments are anticipated to have increased SAP's ability to represent the performance of traditional properties, due to the imposition of a standard U-value measured in ideal conditions.

Reduced SAP for existing buildings calculates the energy efficiency of properties based on assumptions related to the type and age of the building. This means that reduced SAP gives an indication of energy consumption across large populations of buildings with similar general characteristics, rather than the energy consumption of individual buildings. This may lead to inaccurate estimates of energy consumption and overall energy performance for single properties but theoretically should mean that SAP is capable of representing consumption on a larger scale where the result of individual occupancy patterns are averaged out.

The SAP calculation procedure is central to government policy for estimating building performance in the UK. According to Kelly,[26] it is the primary method for assessing the efficiency of the building stock and for meeting EU policy directives regarding improvements to building efficiency. Consequently SAP and EPCs play a significant role in assessing the reduction of energy consumption in the building stock, but it is crucial that the underlying data and calculation procedures used by SAP are understood and validated when used to predict the impact of strategies to improve performance.

SAP MODELLING OF BUILDING STOCK

A new method of using SAP to predict domestic energy use on an urban scale was developed,[27] based on a method of applying sets of results from a sensitivity tool to a local authority, using and extracting data from a geographical information system (GIS).[28] The model's results were validated by comparison with the Department of Energy and Climate Change's (DECC) data on actual residential gas and electricity consumption per UK census area. Results of this validation created a case for modifying variables and assumptions in SAP to better reflect consumption patterns in UK households.[29]

The main finding was that using an internal temperature of between 18 and 19°C (rather than the default 21°C used in SAP calculations) improves the accuracy of consumption prediction on an aggregated level. Fig 2.03 shows the comparison with DECC meter readings when the model was run under five different mean internal temperatures, from

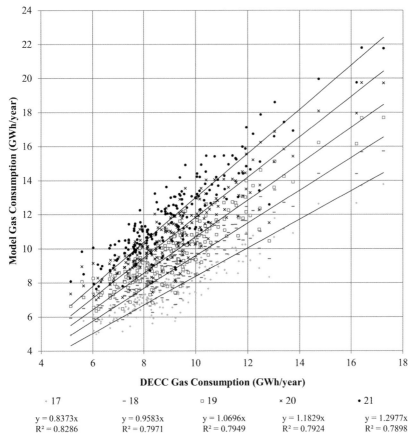

· 17	- 18	□ 19	× 20	• 21
y = 0.8373x	y = 0.9583x	y = 1.0696x	y = 1.1829x	y = 1.2977x
$R^2 = 0.8286$	$R^2 = 0.7971$	$R^2 = 0.7949$	$R^2 = 0.7924$	$R^2 = 0.7898$

Fig 2.03 Refined model's calculated domestic gas consumption with five internal temperatures compared to DECC gas meter readings per LSOA

17°C to 21°C. It is understood that internal temperatures are highly dependent on occupants, but currently these models do not attempt to represent the diversity and complexity of occupants' heating regimes. This alteration to the model does not imply that all dwellings are heated to 18.5°C but that a default value of 18.5°C is a better representation of reality than a default value of 21°C.

This work has allowed more confidence to be attached to the cluster-based results, but still leaves room for more detailed modelling to provide the information for a specific building.

DYNAMIC SIMULATION MODELS

As advocated in local, regional and national policies and regulations, analysing a new build or an existing building to predict how energy efficient it will be and how comfortable it is to occupy has been an important part of the design process. Architects are required to consider a new building's energy performance, impacts to the environment and possible overheating risks when locating it in a neighbourhood, designing its shape and orientation, and arranging its functional layout. Therefore, an effective and user-friendly tool is in great demand.

Dynamic building simulation allows the creation of a detailed thermal model of a proposed building to provide accurate assessment of any possible cooling, heating and ventilation issues it may have once built. However, most dynamic simulation tools are not user-friendly and require the mastering of detailed knowledge. They are therefore much more often used by system engineers at the detailed design stage to compare different system options, rather than by architects to explore energy optimisation from the early design stage. Simulation is an important part of low energy or low carbon design,[30] but at present computer programs are arguably too expensive for architects to afford and too cumbersome for use at the early design stage. When using an integrative design process the team can involve stakeholders from the very early stage, enabling architects to work on design optimisation in relation to building energy and environment performance. In these circumstances, dynamic simulation modelling can be carried out by engineers or relevant professionals in the group, and options for different design aspects tested as soon as possible, such as:

- site (impacts from microclimate, overshadowing from the neighbourhood)
- building shape and orientation
- glazing ratio, natural lighting and solar shading
- fabric insulation (solid wall insulation or cavity wall insulation, roof or loft insulation)
- ventilation (natural or mechanical ventilation)
- materials (with thermal mass or not)
- heating and cooling systems (convection or surface radiation system, mechanical ventilation heat exchange systems)
- renewable technologies (photovoltaic, solar thermal, wind).

Through modelling, the energy performance and environmental impact of different cases can be assessed and compared, including heating and cooling loads, electricity and gas demand, carbon dioxide emission, and indoor air temperature and humidity in extreme weather condition. The most energy-efficient and environmental friendly cases can then be identified. When this information is combined with cost data, the relevant cost-effectiveness can be analysed as well. Cases could also be modelled with future weather data to predict overheating risks in summer due to climate change. During the simulation process, all the components of the building are measured to generate an inventory of the fabric and systems. This inventory can be used to assess the life cycle costs or the embodied energy of the retrofit by comparing the impacts of different materials, allowing the estimation of the carbon costs of local rather than imported materials or manmade versus natural building elements.

With the help of simple interfaces, it is possible for architects to work on their own. SketchUp, an early stage design tool, has been used to provide easy access to dynamic simulation.[31] Through a bridge between design software SketchUp and dynamic simulation tool HTB2, people without environmental engineering expertise are able to carry out environmental studies when required. Architects can easily adjust their models in SketchUp, and test their performances in HTB2 for environmental design optimisation.

RETROFIT MEASURES

The potential options for retrofit measures are predominately based on what is readily available in the market. One source of information commonly used is Appendix T of the official SAP2009 document.[32] This not only gives a list of potential retrofits but also includes the circumstances in which recommendations for improvements are made in EPCs for the properties and the extent to which features should be improved. A short list of frequently recommended improvements is provided in the order in which they would appear in EPCs. Table 2.2 highlights the recommendations considered, and the values used in the official SAP2009 document and in our modelling. The order of recommendations in the document might imply an increase in technical difficulty. However, the cost implications, the potential for funding to be accessed to retrofit the dwelling, the potential lock-out of other retrofit measures and the lack of reversibility of the measures also need to be taken into account.

WHOLE HOUSE OR STEPWISE RETROFIT

The retrofit process can be considered as a managed or unmanaged undertaking, but it is also important to look at the timescale over which it happens and whether it is a one-off or over-time retrofit.[33] Examples of managed and one-off can be found in the TSB Retrofit for the Future project, which targeted an 80% reduction of carbon emissions for domestic properties in a one-off process. Most of the projects were managed by single organisations

Table 2.2 Circumstances for improvements, values used in the modelling from Appendix T of SAP 2012 document

Measure		Condition for improvement	Recommended improvement
Loft/roof insulation		≤150mm insulation or U-value entered by assessor ≥0.35 (U-value ≥0.35)	250mm insulation (U-value 0.2)
Wall	Cavity wall insulation	Wall U-value >0.6 (U-value >0.6)	Cavity filled wall (U-value dependent on age of wall) (U-value 0.3)
	Solid	Wall U-value >0.6 (U-value >0.6)	Internal or external wall insulation with U-value of 0.3 (U-value 0.3)
Floor insulation		Floor is as built (if built <2006) Or U-value >0.5 (U value >0.45)	150mm of floor insulation (U-value 0.25)
Draught-proofing		Less than 100% draught proofing of windows and doors (poor or normal infiltration rate: approx. $10m^3/m^2$ air changes per hr or more)	100% draught proofing (good practice infiltration rate: maximum of $5m^3/m^2$ air changes per hr)
Low energy lighting		Low energy lighting <100% of fixed outlets (Low energy lighting <100% of fixed outlets)	Low energy lighting in all fixed outlets (Low energy lighting in all fixed outlets)
Upgrade heating system		Any component of system is below A rating (Age of system unknown)	System that is A rated (Age of system 2006 to present)
Solar water heating		No solar thermal panel (No solar panel)	$3m^2$ solar thermal panel ($3m^2$ solar)
Double glazing		Less than 80% of windows with multiple glazing (U value <3)	All single glazed windows replaced by double glazing with U-1.5 and G = 0.63 (U value 1.4)
Photovoltaics		No photovoltaics (No PV panels)	Photovoltaics, 2.5kWp (2.5kWp PV panels)

or architectural practices that considered the whole house when choosing the measures undertaken. As these projects were considered to be whole house, many of them added space or changed internal layouts, using software to predict the impact of the design decisions.[34] This managed approach delivered 86 projects throughout the UK, which included more than 100 properties both pre-1919 and post-1919.

Managed projects that have not been whole house have been undertaken throughout the UK as part of the Energy Company Obligation, where energy efficiency measures are applied to buildings in an area to reduce carbon emissions. These dwellings may require further work at a later date to achieve the 80% targets. When work is undertaken in an over-time manner, there is potential for lock-out,[35] where measures may conflict with or obstruct each other: for example, if single glazing is replaced with low-standard double glazing rather than triple, the full potential for carbon reduction has been locked out.

CASE STUDIES

The case studies described in the next section are based upon work carried out to target and implement retrofit in domestic properties. They will provide the vehicle to describe the different scales of modelling undertaken on traditional buildings in Wales. The energy modelling starts at the urban scale, considering the impact of changes on the stock as a whole. This will provide information on the potential for changing the energy performance of archetypes, rather than of specific buildings. This type of technique is helpful for local authorities or landlords to target funding and get the best value for money when refurbishing their stock. Once the areas have been identified it is possible to create the next level of detail, as described in the Gwynedd and Castleland case studies. This allows the exploration of the impact at a building scale of different energy retrofit processes, including system first and fabric first, to achieve low carbon buildings.

Modelling pathways to 2050

A bottom-up engineering modelling approach has been used to investigate the pathways to a 2050 low carbon residential building stock. The impact of housing retrofit, renewable technologies, occupants' behaviour and grid decarbonisation is measured at a local authority scale. The results of this exercise were visualised using a web application, or 'demonstrator', which was developed to allow stakeholders to engage with the modelling process.

The web application or demonstrator aims to provide a clearer understanding of how urban transitions can be undertaken to achieve UK and international targets to reduce carbon emissions. It enables researchers and stakeholders, including policymakers, to look at how the spatial and temporal distribution of energy efficiency measures may impact upon likely regional outcomes for a given future state. This takes the form of a *spatio-temporal* exploration and visualisation tool for building-level energy efficiency modelling outputs such as the energy rating of the building, the likely energy demand of the building and the related CO_2 emissions. A finite series of modelled scenario permutations have been 'pre-built', providing a controlled number of parameters to be interactively altered to explore the spatio-temporal consequences of various policy measures.

A cluster analysis technique was used to identify dwellings with similar energy consumption and carbon dioxide emissions. The cluster analysis procedure 'forces' dwellings into a specified number of groups, or 'clusters', based on selected built form characteristics and the age of the dwelling. The five characteristics used to describe an individual dwelling in order to create clusters are:

- heated ground floor area (m²)
- facade (m²)
- window to wall ratio
- exposed end area (m²)
- property age.

These features are considered to have the greatest influence on domestic energy performance.

A SAP result was calculated for each of the 100 'house types' found in the case study data. Further SAP analysis was undertaken to allow for the effect of the different combinations of the three interventions considered: small-scale renewable technologies, energy efficiency and occupant behaviour. An example of one of the clusters, in this case cluster 2, is a 90m² two-storey solid wall construction mid-terrace house built before 1919. Results for this further analysis on a sample cluster show that the reductions in carbon emissions can vary greatly (Fig 2.04). In this instance only 10 of the 625 pathways achieved the 80% overall reduction target; the remaining pathways were mostly hampered by limited grid decarbonisation and the lack of change in occupant behaviour.

Energy efficiency of dwellings at a local authority scale

There is a growing recognition that action by local authorities will play a significant role in reducing emissions from existing dwellings, which is crucial to the success of the UK government's 2050 target to cut greenhouse gas emissions by 80%. According to DECC, local authorities are uniquely placed to assess the needs of their local areas and residents. This, however, is an enormous challenge for local authorities due to the lack of consistent publicly available tools and methods for calculating the potential carbon savings.[36]

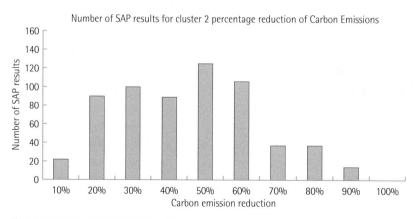

Fig 2.04 SAP analysis for cluster 2 for all the scenarios

The model presented in this section aims to provide local authorities with the foundation needed to develop robust strategies and therefore tackle the inefficiency of dwellings. The model can estimate the energy consumption of small geographical areas, allowing users to explore refurbishment options. As a result, it is hoped that well-informed decisions can be made, enabling local authorities to succeed in their challenging role as catalysts for change.

The objective of the modelling technique was to utilise information available to local authorities to approximate the impact of refurbishment options. Available energy performance certificates were analysed to approximate the current state of all dwellings within the local authority, providing a valuable knowledge base for future housing energy efficiency plans whatever the upcoming national and international strategies might be. To enable decision-makers to explore the potential options for refurbishment, pathways for improvements were created in line with current energy efficiency targets. These were applied to suitable dwellings and areas so that the effect of potential improvements and associated costs could be explored. Areas or dwelling types could be compared and detailed approximations calculated for the selected properties. The model's results revealed a great deal about the complexities involved in area-based retrofit. Results exposed and clarified aspects of the relationship between the current state of properties and possible pathways to improvement:

- **Effectiveness of types of measures** – Results clearly identified that the consumption reduction / cost ratio of measures is greatly reduced if refurbishment measures have already been carried out to reduce consumption: eg improving the fabric of properties after installing efficient heating systems would result in less consumption reduction for the same cost than if the fabric were improved as the primary step.
- **Combination of measures** – Applying systems, fabric or renewables alone would improve efficiency only up to a certain point. Going beyond this requires a mixture of improvement types applied in combination or succession over a period of time.
- **Targeting subsets of areas** – It is evident that if subsets of properties are targeted rather than whole areas, concentrating on the least efficient properties would most definitely have the greatest impact on overall consumption reduction.

The significance of retrofitting decisions could be better understood and appreciated by combining these modelled results with wider related issues. For example, analysing the relationship between the energy consumed and its cost could provide a case for investing larger amounts of money to drastically reduce consumption and therefore minimise the effect of possible rises in future energy prices. Moreover, combining this model's result with work on reducing fuel poverty would mean that decisions could be made combining both economic and social arguments.

Refurbishment of renewal areas

To provide area-based guidance on reducing carbon emissions of a housing stock, it was essential to identify the properties' physical characteristics and current state of energy efficiency. The construction date and typology of dwellings are primary indicators of their fabric characteristics; therefore each dwelling within the area was classified in terms of its age and typology. A sample of EPCs was used to further identify the range in energy efficiency performance within these classifications (ie improvements to the original fabric, and the current heating system type and efficiency). By developing a detailed database for the sample area (ie about half of the properties) and using GIS, the data of all properties was mapped and regions of particular interest pinpointed. Moreover, alternative routes and associated costs of achieving lower carbon emissions have been laid out for the area using the database and SAP2009 recommendations of improvement.

To find possible routes to improve the energy efficiency of the existing housing stock, data was collected from all the available EPCs (568 EPCs) in the case study area: Castleland renewal area of Barry, Wales, UK. Each EPC was identified by its typology and was further grouped in terms of its SAP rating. The data collected from the EPCs was recorded and analysed, identifying the main building characteristics affecting the energy performance of each group (cluster analysis). This made it possible to identify the recommended measures required for each cluster to achieve an acceptable level of performance as outlined in the UK Government Housing Health and Safety Rating System (HHSRS),[37] which is an evaluation tool to help local authorities measure risks and hazards to health and safety in a dwelling, and the more ambitious 2050 targets.

It can be observed in Table 2.2 that the retrofitting interventions proposed are focused on the 'fabric first' approach. For Castleland renewal area, however, the initial funding stage was focused on 'systems first'; therefore the analysis considered two different orders of interventions, which can be seen in Table 2.3.

A baseline for each group was created depending on the average current SAP rating and dwelling floor area of the sample. If conditions for improvement shown in Table 2.2 were

Table 2.3 Order of interventions: Fabric First and Systems First

Fabric first	Systems first
Roof	Heating
Wall	Lighting
Floor	Draught
Draught	Roof
Lighting	Wall
Heating	Floor
Solar	Windows
Windows	Solar
PV	PV

Table 2.4 Cost of retrofit measures

	Mid-terrace	End-terrace / semi-detached	Flats
Roof insulation	£250	£250	–
Wall insulation	£7,602	£14,415	£3,801
Floor insulation	£530	£530	–
Draughtproofing	£100	£100	£100
Low energy lighting	£50	£50	£50
Heating	£2,300	£2,300	£2,300
Solar	£4,800	£4,800	£4,800
Windows	£4,900	£4,900	£4,900
Photovoltaics	£8,750	£8,750	£8,750

met, recommendations were applied in order of relevance using the SAP sensitivity tool.[38] The improvement with each recommendation was recorded at each step. This made it possible to identify which measures were needed to achieve the HHSRS target and the 2050 target for each of the groups. Both sets of recommendations were 'applied' to all pre-1919 dwellings within the renewal area. As the sample represented the renewal area well in terms of typologies, the recommendations for groups were applied to the dwellings in the area per typology in line with the representation of the groups within that typology in the sample.

An average cost deduced from the sample EPCs was used to estimate the cost of separate measures. However, Warm Wales (project partners) provided actual costs of wall insulation and upgrading of heating systems in the area; therefore those figures were used instead of the EPC estimated averages. Table 2.4 outlines the costs used for each measure. The cost of achieving the two standards was calculated for the most common properties in each group before extrapolating the results and calculating the total for all properties in the area.

Fig 2.05 shows the effect of individual measures on each of the representative dwellings and assumes that all measures are needed in all cases. It shows the impact of individual measures as the difference in SAP score before and after a measure is applied. The element under analysis is assumed to be improved from an inefficient state to an efficient one (see the table above Fig 2.05 for assumptions used).

Figs 2.06 and 2.07 show the relative costs of measures for single dwellings compared to the improvement gained in terms of SAP rating score for both approaches, fabric first (Fig 2.06) and system first (Fig 2.07). The dotted lines represent measures that are not needed for that certain group and therefore the cost would not need to be applied. This is highlighted in the bars above the graph, which indicate the recommendations and costs applied to rating groups as well as the total costs of all measures. Note that the costs provided in the bars above the graph are the overall costs of the properties of different bands to achieve the 2050 target;

Moderately efficient gas boiler 1996–2006	→	Efficient gas boiler 2006 to present
0% efficient lighting	→	100% efficient lighting
Poor draught proofing	→	Good draught proofing
No roof, wall or floor insulation	→	200mm roof insulation, solid wall insulation, floor insulation
Single glazing	→	2012 standard double glazing
No solar thermal	→	3m² solar thermal
No PVs	→	2.5kWp PVs

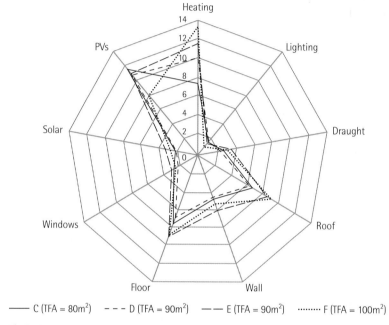

——— C (TFA = 80m²)   – – – D (TFA = 90m²)   —— E (TFA = 90m²)   ········ F (TFA = 100m²)

Fig 2.05 SAP improvement of individual measures for typical pre-1919 mid-terraced houses of stated band and floor area

that is, a C-rated pre-1919 mid-terrace house would cost approximately £14,130 to achieve the 2050 target. This same typology graded as F or G in the SAP rating might cost twice as much, approximately £29,282.

DYNAMIC SIMULATION OF PRE-1919 END-TERRACE HOUSE

This section describes dynamic simulation for a retrofit case study of a pre-1919 end-terrace house. It aimed to examine the current performance, assess the effectiveness of different retrofit strategies, and assess the best group of options available, aiding decision-making in advance of retrofitting. Simulations were carried out in two stages through building energy model HTB2, which has been applied in many research and design projects. The house to be modelled is a

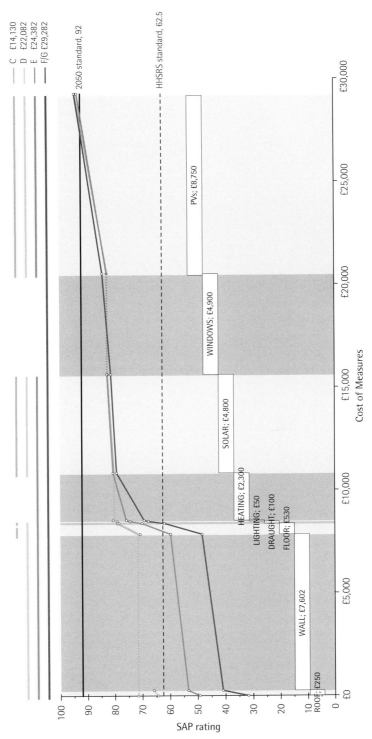

Fig 2.06 Fabric First: Cumulative cost and SAP improvement of measures per band for pre-1919 mid-terraced houses

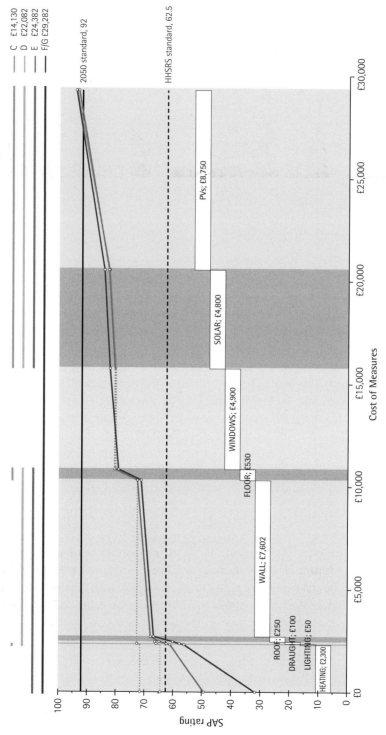

Fig 2.07 Systems First: Cumulative cost and SAP improvement of measures per band for pre-1919 mid-terraced houses

Fig 2.08 Case study house before retrofit, after retrofit, and thermal image after retrofit

typical Welsh valleys pre-1919 end-terrace house with two bedrooms (Fig 2.08), located outside any conservation area. This study modelled the occupancy of two adults with a child.

The strategies tested at the early stage include external wall insulation (without insulation, rear wall insulation, rear and side walls insulation, all external walls insulation), external window insulation (single glazing, double glazing, low-E double glazing), improvements of airtightness (related to window performance), and different design temperatures for heating (heating control: 22°C vs 20°C). Simulation results are summarised in Fig 2.09. It can be seen that around 66% of heating demand could be reduced if maintaining the current design temperature for heating, while a higher decrease rate of 77% could be achieved if reducing the design temperature by 2°C. External wall insulation showed a more positive impact on building energy optimisation than window improvement as replacing double glazing with low-E double glazing shows only a small reduction in energy consumption.

Based on findings at early stage, more strategies were discussed and analysed, including roof insulation, LED lighting, mechanical ventilation heat recovery (MVHR) system, photovoltaic roof and battery storage, system boiler, and immersion heater by the excess electricity from the photovoltaic array. These strategies were grouped (Table 2.5) and modelled step by step to show how building performance was optimised in an assumed retrofit process. According to the simulation results (Fig 2.10), heating and hot water demand could be reduced by 75%, while for electricity demand only 9.8% reduction could be achieved, with 1794kWh surplus power exported to the grid if all proposed strategies were applied (case ABCDE). Overall, fabric insulation showed the most effective impact on building energy optimisation. Most of the power generated by photovoltaic panels was exported to the grid, except a small portion used to provide electricity for LED lighting. If an immersion heater powered by the photovoltaic panels was installed, around a third of this photovoltaic power could be used to provide domestic hot water.

Above all, the case study showed how dynamic simulation could aid decision-making for building retrofit. For the next step, a more comprehensive study will be carried out to take

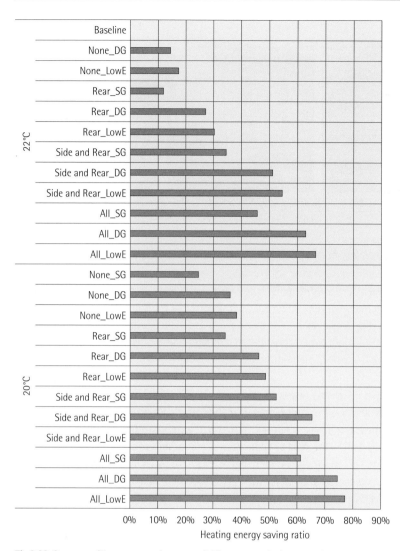

Fig 2.09 Summary of the energy performance of different cases (at later stage)

Table 2.5 Strategy groups

No.	Strategies details
A	Fabric insulation: solid wall insulation, loft insulation, flat roof insulation (rear extension), double glazing
B	LED lighting
C	Mechanical ventilation heat recovery (MVHR) system
D	Photovoltaic roof and battery storage
E	System boiler, hot water cylinder + photovoltaic immersion heater

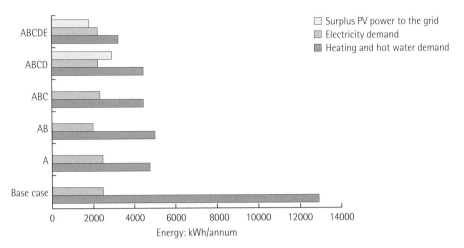

Fig 2.10 Final summary of the energy performance of different cases (at later stage)

more factors into consideration, including future weather data and retrofit cost. These findings could be a good reference for retrofit work in practice.

CONCLUSION

When considering the retrofit of unlisted traditional buildings outside conservation areas, the policy drivers are carbon emission targets and fuel poverty. Traditional buildings are particularly problematic for both of these as they have low energy efficiency and are generally privately owned, with a high likelihood of fuel poverty. The stock is also variable in its nature, some areas of the UK having significant numbers of traditional buildings. The need to retrofit is clear, but the route is less so and unmanaged projects run the danger of locking out measures unless careful design assessment is undertaken.

Software tools can help designers and managers of retrofit projects to produce evidence for the choices made, but such tools need to be more widely available. Simulation can provide information to target the potential for energy efficiency retrofitting in traditional buildings. The pathway chosen should be guided by the cost benefits, financial incentives that are available, energy efficiency and, as it is unlikely that the building owner will be able to undertake a whole house approach, the potential for stepwise improvements. Removing the potential lock-out of future measures is critical if the stepwise approach is to be successfully undertaken.

ACKNOWLEDGEMENTS

This work comes in part from research undertaken as part of the Smart Operation for a Low Carbon Energy Region project, and the Low Carbon Environment project supported by the

European Regional Development Fund through the Welsh Government. The scenario modelling (http://steevsrv.edina.ac.uk/) was undertaken as part of the Information Environment Programme, Geospatial strand.

NOTES

1 The UK 2008 Climate Change Act sets a legally binding climate change target which aims to reduce the UK's greenhouse gas emissions by at least 80% (from the 1990 baseline) by 2050.

2 Department of Energy and Climate Change (DECC), *Fuel Mix Disclosure Data Tables* (London: DECC, 2014).

3 Carbon Trust, *Building the Future Today*, http://www.carbontrust.com/resources/reports/technology/building-the-future [accessed 30 June 2015].

4 Department of Energy and Climate Change (DECC), *DECC 2050 Pathways Calculator*, (London: DECC 2011).

5 Carbon Trust, *Building the Future Today*.

6 DECC, *DECC 2050 Pathways Calculator*.

7 Department of Energy and Climate Change (DECC), *Fuel Poverty Methodology Handbook* (London: DECC, 2013).

8 Department of Energy and Climate Change (DECC), *Annual Fuel Poverty Statistics Report* (London: DECC, 2014).

9 Department of Energy and Climate Change (DECC), *United Kingdom Housing Energy Fact File: 2013* (London: DECC, 2013).

10 Department of Energy and Climate Change (DECC), *An Investigation of the Effect of EPC Ratings on House Prices* (London: DECC, 2013).

11 SAP (Standard Assessment Procedure) National Calculation Method for the UK used to predict the energy consumption and associated carbon emissions for domestic properties.

12 English Heritage, *Research into the Thermal Performance of Traditional Brick Walls* (English Heritage, 2013).

13 The Energy Performance of Buildings (England and Wales) Regulations 2012.

14 UK government's flagship energy efficiency policy instrument.

15 Department for Communities and Local Government (DCLG), *Energy Performance Certificates for the Marketing, Sale and Let of Dwellings* (London: DCLG, 2012).

16 Department for Communities and Local Government (DCLG), *Improving the Energy Efficiency of Our Buildings* (London: DCLG, 2012).

17 The Buildings Regulations 2010, Conservation of fuel and power, Approved Document L1B, Existing dwellings.

18 DECC, *DECC 2050 Pathways Calculator*.

19 Energyplus, *Energyplus Energy Simulation Software*, http://apps1.eere.energy.gov/buildings/energyplus/ [accessed 30 June 2015].

20 Lawrence Berkeley National Laboratory (LBNL), *Therm Two-Dimensional Building Heat-Transfer Modeling*, http://windows.lbl.gov/software/therm/therm.html [accessed 30 June 2015].

21 PT Lewis and DK Alexander, 'HTB2: A Flexible Model for Dynamic Building Simulation', *Build Environment*, 25:1 (1990), 7–16.

22 Scott Kelly et al, *Building Performance Evaluation and Certification in the UK: is SAP Fit for Purpose?*, Tyndall Working Paper 155 (Tyndall Centre for Climate Change Research, 2012).

23 GB Murphy et al, 'A comparison of the UK Standard Assessment Procedure and detailed simulation of solar energy systems for dwellings', *Journal of Building Performance Simulation*, 4 (2011), 75–90.

24 Kelly, *Building Performance Evaluation and Certification in the UK*.

25 English Heritage, *Energy Efficiency and Historic Buildings, Advice for Domestic Energy Assessors and Green Deal Advisors* (English Heritage, 2013).

26 Kelly, *Building Performance Evaluation and Certification in the UK*.

27 Heledd Mair Iorwerth, Lannon, Simon, Waldron, Diana, Bassett, Thomas and Jones, Phillip John, 'A SAP Sensitivity Tool and Gis-Based Urban Scale Domestic Energy Use Model', *Building Simulation 2013 (BS2013)*, (2013).

28 E Crobu et al, 'Simple simulation sensitivity tool', presented at *Building Simulation 2013 (BS2013)*, Chambéry, France, 25–28 August.

29 Geographical information system (GIS) is a software that can present and analyse data in a mapping environment.

30 Shady Attia, '"Architect friendly": a comparison of ten different building performance simulation tools', *Eleventh International IBPSA Conference*, Glasgow, Scotland, 27–30 July 2009.

31 T Lannon, Bassett et al, 'Calculating the solar potential of the urban fabric with SketchUp and HTB2', presented at *Solar Building Skins* (Bressanone, Italy, 6–7 December 2012).

32 DECC, *The Government's Standard Assessment Procedure for Energy Rating of Dwellings* (2009 Edition – Incorporating RdSAP 2009)', (2011).

33 Tina Fawcett, 'Exploring the time dimension of low carbon retrofit: owner-occupied housing', *Building Research & Information*, 42:4 (2013), 477–88.

34 Marion Baeli, *Residential Retrofit, 20 Case Studies* (London: RIBA Publications, 2013).

35 Fawcett, 'Exploring the time dimension of low carbon retrofit'.

36 Diana Ürge-Vorsatz et al, 'Appraisal of policy instruments for reducing buildings' CO_2 emissions', *Building Research & Information*, 35:4 (2007), 458–77.

37 Welsh Assembly Government, *The Welsh Housing Quality Standard – Revised Guidance for Social Landlords on Interpretation and Achievement of the Welsh Housing Quality Standard* (Cardiff: Welsh Assembly Government, 2008).

38 Crobu et al, 'Simple simulation sensitivity tool'; Welsh School of Artchitecture, *SAP Sensitivity Tool*, http://www.lowcarboncymru.org.uk/tools [accessed 30 June 2015].

THREE

Retrofitting heritage buildings

....

Peter Cox

INTRODUCTION

The Kyoto Protocol is an international agreement linked to the United Nations Framework Convention on Climate Change, which commits its Parties by setting internationally binding emission reduction targets.

Recognising that developed countries are principally responsible for the current high levels of Green House Gas (GHG) emissions in the atmosphere as a result of more than 150 years of industrial activity, the Protocol places a heavier burden on developed nations under the principle of 'common but differentiated responsibilities'.

The Kyoto Protocol was adopted in Kyoto, Japan, on 11 December 1997 and entered into force on 16 February 2005. The detailed rules for the implementation of the Protocol were adopted[1] at the 7th Conference of the Parties to the UN Framework Convention on Climate Change (COP7) in Marrakesh, Morocco, in 2001, and are referred to as the 'Marrakesh Accords'. Its first commitment period started in 2008 and ended in 2012.

In principle, the meeting of main world powers in Kyoto made decisions to accept the concept of 'Climate Change' and to introduce a number of measures relating to reducing dependency on fossil fuel, reducing primary energy use and reducing our greenhouse gas emissions, and also measures to make buildings more energy efficient. This resulted in an agreement to introduce ambitious targets of reducing CO_2 emissions by 20% by 2020, based on 1990 levels.

Given that the world economy, and in particular China's industrial output, grew during the late 1990s and into the early-mid 2000s, our CO_2 emissions must have increased dramatically

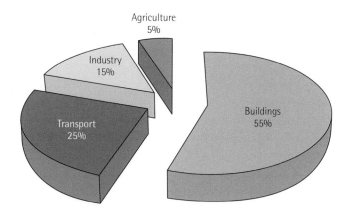

Fig 3.01 Energy
Consumption Pie Chart

in this time, resulting in an urgent need to achieve significantly higher reductions in CO_2 emissions within a much shorter period. In most cases governments have not reacted, and consequently there is a kneejerk reaction to introduce incentives, carrots and sticks, to meet these extremely stiff targets.

BACKGROUND

In 2006 the European Union introduced the first EU Directive on energy end-use efficiency and energy services:[2] 'Reducing energy consumption and eliminating wastage are among the main goals of the European Union (EU). EU support for improving energy efficiency will prove decisive for competitiveness, security of supply and for meeting the commitments on climate change made under the Kyoto protocol. There is significant potential for reducing consumption with cost-effective measures. With 40% of our energy consumed in buildings, the EU has introduced legislation to ensure that our existing building stock consume less energy.'[3]

A key part of this legislation is the Energy Performance of Buildings Directive,[4] first published in 2002, which required all EU countries to enhance their building regulations and to introduce energy certification schemes for all buildings. All countries were also required to enforce inspections of boilers and air conditioning units.

The target of governments across the world, but particularly in Europe, is to use the retrofit of our existing housing stock to achieve a substantial percentage of the reduction in CO_2 emissions required under the Kyoto Protocol – the targets are set at 20% by 2020, based on 1990 levels. This, we believe, will put much pressure on our built heritage and may threaten the fabric and heritage value of many of our older and traditional buildings. The International Council on Monuments and Sites (ICOMOS) recognised this following their annual meeting in Dublin, Ireland, in 2010, and a working group was formed to research the sector and to report back to the annual meeting of 2012 in Beijing, China. As a result of the findings and the concern at international level, an International Scientific Committee (ISC) on Energy and Sustainability (ISCES) was ratified at the meeting in China. Since then, the ISCES has been active in researching and collating hard evidence, research studies and practical case studies on the subject. It is the aim of the committee to act as a catalyst and international information centre for all to access. The research is not confined to Europe and will include opposite climates and the need for cooling as well as heating as a primary use of energy. In general, 'buildings' produce approximately 50% of all greenhouse gas.

WHAT IS A HERITAGE BUILDING?

The word 'heritage' is used in this chapter as a generic typology. It refers to buildings that have been constructed prior to 1945 and in general are vernacular and/or traditional. It does not include listed buildings or protected structures, as these are exempt under current legislation. For the purpose of this section on heritage buildings, the work of the International Scientific Committee on Energy and Sustainability and other European groups, we have referenced and based our information on pre-1945 buildings. It is estimated that there are close to 65 million dwellings in the 28 countries of Europe from this period; listed buildings or protected structures account for 8%, so there are approximately 60 million dwellings with potential historic value at risk. This is roughly 30% to 34% of Europe's total housing stock. If we were to include all other building typologies from the period, such as public, institutional and commercial buildings, it would represent over 50% of our total building stock.

Within this broad genre are buildings from the late middle ages, the 16th and 17th centuries, the Georgian and Victorian periods, when building was prolific, up to the mid-20th century, so we are referring to a diverse range of building fabric, construction methods and styles, and level of heritage value. Many also question why we stop at 1945: why not include buildings of the 1960s, or indeed the early 1970s?

When we refer to a historic building we define this as a building of architectural, historical, cultural and scientific value. Many of the buildings are not listed, protected structures, nor do they have any statutory protection under national or international law or conventions. Under the European Directive 2010/31/EU (introducing Building Energy Rating (BER), or in UK terms EPC – Energy Performance Certificates), there is an exemption for heritage properties and listed buildings; however, the majority of the buildings referred to in this study are not exempt as a building must be listed or have statutory protection to be exempted under the directive. It is now the belief of most heritage professionals that exempting listed or protected structures is perhaps a mistake, and that we should take a more inclusive approach and insist all older buildings comply with a standard of sensible, sensitive and measured retrofitting. Most schemes promoting or encouraging energy retrofit do not require a professional to lead the project, let alone a heritage professional; one is thus relying on the contractor's knowledge and understanding of a traditional building.

The key element of a historic building is that it is of traditional construction, or that the external walls are of solid masonry construction. This can include everything from early mud wall construction through to solid concrete construction, as well as timber frame buildings in some countries. Obviously there are the other elements of any building, such as windows, doors, floors and roofs, that will have an impact on the thermal efficiency of the building. Any drastic changes implemented under the need for energy upgrading will have an adverse effect on the actual and/or potential heritage value of a building.

There is a further consideration that is as important as the heritage value, and that is 'aesthetics'. If a building is a semi-detached or in a terrace the streetscape is as important as the individual building, so when considering external insulation, for example, the impact on the overall street or group of buildings has to be taken into account.

ICOMOS ISCES

ICOMOS – the International Council on Monuments and Sites – is the technical advisory body to UNESCO on world heritage and the built heritage. Within the structure of ICOMOS International are a number of International Scientific Committees (ISCs), one of which is the ISC on Energy and Sustainability (ISCES). In 2010 many ICOMOS National Committees voiced concern over state parties introducing incentives and guidelines on the energy retrofitting of older and traditional buildings. Most of these incentives and guidelines had little or no respect for the historic fabric of such buildings or the impact many interventions would have on the heritage value of older and traditional buildings. The lack of inclusivity of traditionally constructed buildings in such guidelines coupled with the possible negative impact many measures would have on the general building fabric, the aims of the intervention and the likely perceived improvement of energy efficiency or CO_2 emissions and, perhaps most importantly, the negative effect it would have on occupier comfort all point to concern over how these schemes are being designed and implemented. Taking into account the non-financial return on investment, no one will win on any front.

This was discussed at length at the Dublin meeting of ICOMOS International in October 2010, and a resolution was passed to form a working group to investigate this sector with a view to the formation of an ISC. At the Paris meeting in 2011 an ISC was deemed to be required, and it was formally adopted at the Beijing ICOMOS Advisory Council meeting in 2012. The International Scientific Committee on Energy and Sustainability is made up of 56 international ICOMOS members representing some 24 countries, all with an interest in the sensible energy retrofitting of heritage buildings. Since its formation the committee has spent time researching the market and the main issues, and in developing a policy on how to interact with the main actors and influence government and EU policy.

The European Union has recognised the potential, both positive and negative, of the energy retrofit sector. On one hand, they see the need for this action in delivering most governments' commitments on reducing primary energy and CO_2 emissions. They see the potential of this sector for bringing employment, but they have also realised there is a need for control. With this in mind, the EU has asked the Comité Européen de Normalisation (CEN), or in English the Central European Standards Committee, to develop a new European Standard on the subject. The first step is to produce guidelines for improving the energy performance of historic buildings.

The International Scientific Committee on Energy and Sustainability, including Climate Change has a representative on the Central European Standards committee (CEN TC 346 WG8) charged with developing a new European Standard for the 'Energy Efficiency of Culturally, Historically and Architecturally Important Buildings'. The working group has now met five times in 2013 and 2014, and the committee is close to finalising a working document on the subject. Hopefully the standard will become law in early 2016.

MAIN CONCERNS OF ENERGY RETROFITTING A HERITAGE BUILDING

The EU Commission Directive 2012/27/EU refers to 'the obligation on Member States to achieve certain amount of final energy savings over the obligation period (01 January 2014 – 31 December 2020) by using energy efficiency obligation schemes or other targeted policy measures to drive energy efficiency improvements in households, industries and transport sectors'. Since this directive, BER (Building Energy Rating) or EPC (Energy Performance Certificate) has become the norm in domestic and state-owned properties. The assessment criteria are seriously flawed when it comes to older and traditional buildings. Theoretically, a 'protected or listed building' is exempt from the BER or EPC. Research tells us that of the 60 million plus dwellings in the 28 countries of Europe built before 1945, only 8% have statutory protection and therefore are or can be deemed exempt under the EU Commission Directive 2012/27/EU. This leaves 55 million plus dwellings vulnerable to potential irreparable damage of the original building fabric in the name of 'energy efficiency measures'. All indications at present are that the EPC/BER evaluation sheets do not take into account any factors for older or traditionally built buildings with solid-wall construction. This sets the whole process off on the wrong foot as it does not give an accurate U-value of the building being assessed. If the U-value is incorrectly calculated, the proposed methods of intervention will not be correct or conducive to achieving the performance required to meet the targets of the building. Serious consideration needs to be given to the evaluation process, accurately measuring many different types of wall construction and not having default to a narrow range of options.

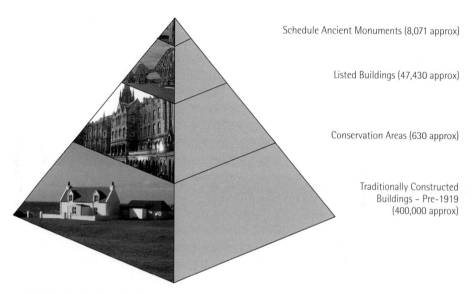

Schedule Ancient Monuments (8,071 approx)

Listed Buildings (47,430 approx)

Conservation Areas (630 approx)

Traditionally Constructed
Buildings – Pre-1919
(400,000 approx)

Fig 3.02 Scottish Traditional Building Stock

The second major threat to our older and traditional buildings is the availability of building materials in the 'retrofit' market and the lack of knowledge among manufacturers, suppliers, professionals and builders about choosing products to upgrade an older or traditionally built home. Many building materials, such as insulations, windows, doors, renders, heating systems and ventilation systems, are designed for use in new construction, and in most cases these

Fig 3.03 Semi-detached
Georgian building

Fig 3.04 Terrace of Georgian buildings

products are not suitable for, or compatible with, older and traditionally built buildings. The majority of older and traditionally built buildings are built using materials that are 'breathable', while most if not all modern building materials are not. Should a non-breathable insulation be installed on a breathable masonry wall, the dew point will be altered and condensation at best, or damp at worst, will cause early decay. The outcome will be a compromised building envelope that will most likely result in a failure of the energy retrofit measures on the building in the short to medium term.

QUALIFICATION FACTORS

One area of concern is the qualification of professionals and/or contractors advising building owners on the retrofitting of older and traditionally built buildings. The majority of 'energy assessors' assessing buildings under the BER/EPC system are not necessarily qualified in this area, or indeed in the construction industry in general. The training given to the assessors is also inadequate and does not include any advice on older or traditional buildings. The contractors engaged in or entering the industry are also not necessarily trained and experienced in the intricacies of retrofitting an older or traditionally built building. This, coupled with a lack of knowledge about the materials they are suggesting or recommending, will lead to many mistakes and disasters for innocent building owners.

There is a strong need to rethink the way we train assessors and accredit contractors in this delicate new industry. The retrofit of older and traditionally built buildings has large potential for the building industry and for employment, as well as helping state parties to meet their committed international targets; but if we do not educate the professionals and building owners and managers, we will not succeed. We should demand a level of qualification and experience for assessors, professionals and contractors on older and traditional buildings so that we do not make mistakes. These mistakes will be costly to building owners and to the buildings, and governments will not meet the targets perceived and necessary in energy reduction and the reduction of CO_2 emissions.

CRITICAL COMPONENTS OF AN OLDER OR TRADITIONAL BUILDING

Key elements of an older or traditional building need careful consideration when potential and suitability for retrofit energy measures are being assessed:

Phase 1
- building envelope including walls, floors, roof, windows and doors
- energy supply
- building services
- condition of all elements
- heritage or conservation value and significance
- authenticity
- integrity
- maintenance
- context and setting

After this initial study has been completed and the information is known, planned interventions and expected new performance should be assessed before a final recommendation is made.

Phase 2
- measures
- reversibility
- product availability and suitability
- possible ill effects on the building fabric
- energy or U-value improvement
- aesthetic impact
- alternative renewable energy sources
- documentation
- final recommendations
- risk assessment
- mitigation

PHASE 1: UNDERSTANDING THE BUILDING

Phase 1 of any assessment to retrofit an older or traditional building must be full understanding of the building in question. This must include the following measures and considerations, and only when this assessment is completed can one decide how to proceed with Phase 2, which should be the planned interventions.

Measured evaluation

Perhaps the most important element in planning a retrofit of a traditional dwelling is to understand the key components – date of the building, construction type, heritage value, materials, *actual* U-value measurements, compatibility of materials to be used in the upgrading, and the aesthetics of the building and/or the streetscape. Most important are the U-value measurements of an older or traditional building. In most cases, no true U-value is measured when a building is being assessed; the U-value is calculated with incorrect baseline information. A number of external wall types and 'calculations' are given, but if the calculation

Fig 3.05 Monitoring of the Fraunhofer test site in Benediktbeuern

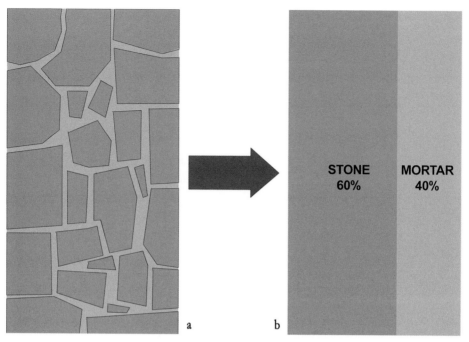

Fig 3.06 Laboratory simulation of traditional construction

is not accurate one cannot prescribe a solution or an intervention to upgrade an unknown. If an incorrect value is given to the U-value of a solid wall, how can one specify a type or thickness of insulation? The practice to date is flawed and will result in a large number of older or traditional buildings having to be re-retrofitted in the short term. If they are not, the interventions will lead to a serious loss of original building fabric through decay mechanisms that, mobilised by these inappropriate interventions, are going on hidden to the owner's eye and will lead to the loss of buildings over time.

A building should be further dissected into the components mentioned above in two phases for the purpose of a proper assessment for energy use and performance, and prior to any decisions being agreed and implemented.

Building envelope
The main elements within the building envelope are as follows:
- **External envelope** – wall construction, its form, condition and components. For example, a solid masonry wall will be made up of local materials in most cases, but a solid masonry wall built of granite will perform completely differently from a solid masonry wall constructed of a soft red sandstone.
- **Windows** – their type, condition and the window-to-wall ratio are of particular importance. Windows are often deemed to be a major source of heat loss when in fact they perform much better than anticipated.

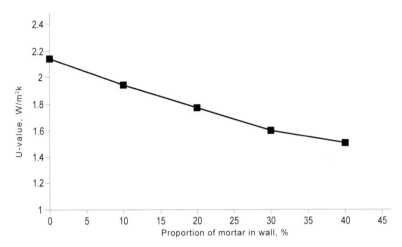

Fig 3.07 Graph showing improvement in lime to stone ratio

- **Doors** – their form, type, originality, airtightness and condition.
- **Floors** – these are of particular relevance as some will be timber with large voids below, while others may be of natural stone or manmade tile set in earth. Many traditional floors are damp, with no moisture membrane. On the other hand, later 19th- or early 20th-century buildings may have concrete floors.
- **Roofs** – on older or traditional buildings these will be functional but not in the least energy efficient, yet this is an area of simple intervention. Pitched roofs are often the source of major heat loss in a building.

Condition of the building

The condition of the building fabric and in particular of the external envelope is a large consideration when evaluating an older or traditional building for an energy retrofit. If a stone or brick building is not maintained, it will not perform positively in a BER or EPC. If the pointing has failed, moisture will penetrate and make the wall damp, thus reducing the U-value; if the pointing is harder than the masonry, this will also entrap moisture and have a similar result. Some people paint masonry, but the majority of paints are non-breathable and on most painted buildings there are multiple coats. Roofs and rainwater goods are also a large contributor to damp in buildings if they are not appropriately maintained and especially if the gutters and drainage outlets are not cleared on a regular basis. Simple and regular maintenance of the external fabric of an older or traditional building can improve its energy performance by as much as 20–30%.

Building services

Building services in older or traditional buildings are often not purposely designed for the geometry or use of the building, resulting in a poorly performing system that produces unnecessary CO_2 emissions. Most older and traditional buildings had open fireplaces as the general heating system, with the kitchen and its cooking fire being central. Later, the method of heating was changed to central heating that was primarily fed by oil-fired heating boilers and larger-than-necessary radiators, as early ones were not efficient. In most cases the boilers may have been upgraded over their relatively short life but the radiators have not.

Controls on the early boilers and radiators were basic, with an on/off control and not much control over the level of heating delivered. Occupiers also became acclimatised to having heat at their fingertips, and in most cases, when oil was cheap, the system was left running longer than required.

It is only in recent times that occupiers and building owners have embraced the use of buildings services design and management systems.

Use of the building

Perhaps one of the most important factors in assessing an older or traditional building for energy efficiency is the occupants and how they use the building. The new maxim is 'Buildings don't use energy – occupants do!' This, of course, is not strictly true as it takes energy to produce the components and to construct the building, but once the building is in existence it is indeed the occupiers who orchestrate and use the energy. Most occupants do not understand how to best use energy, and in particular how to save energy or cope with fuel poverty. One of the other main factors in this lack of knowledge and understanding is the way energy is supplied to most households and appliances such as boilers and central heating systems have been sold to house owners. Boilers and central heating systems are sold by suppliers of such equipment or by plumbers looking to supply and fit them. Historically, such suppliers do not assess the existing performance and heating requirement of the building and go by a 'rule of thumb' calculation to size such equipment. Experience shows us that most of these installations have not been efficient in terms of energy, cost or CO_2 emissions. Education for occupiers in the proper and efficient use of the equipment has also been non-existent.

Historic energy consumption

In assessing an older or traditional building for energy consumption, we need to evaluate the historic energy consumption over a good many years and in particular over a number of seasons. This can be easily achieved by studying the energy bills for a given period and can set a bar for improvement, should a retrofit be chosen. It also gives us extremely valuable information on the performance of the building and of the equipment, and an insight into how the occupants use the building.

Climate

It is also important to assess the macro and micro climate around a building when studying the building's performance. Its orientation – its exposure to wind, rain and wind-driven rain – will be a key factor in any analysis. External and internal temperatures are also important to know and understand, and in most cases they are not fully evaluated. A building of a certain typology will perform completed differently in two dissimilar locations with basic climatic differences.

Heritage value

Heritage value is perhaps the most subjective valuation and will differ according to points of view and interpretations of a particular building's heritage value within its context, which may also include its setting. The issue is made more complex when a building is not listed or deemed a protected structure, as a building with statutory protection will have a professional assessment and category or value given to it. However, as stated earlier in this chapter, 92% of the dwellings we are targeting in the energy retrofit market do not have statutory protection, yet to varying degrees they have an important heritage value.

Heritage value can be architectural, historical, social or scientific, and within each of these categories there can be a range of value from low to very high. However, when one gets to a high value, the building is likely to have statutory protection, so we are essentially dealing with values at the lower end of the scale, which can be more difficult to justify or to get agreement on. Heritage value can also relate to the setting of a building or group of buildings, such as in a streetscape. If one changes the geometry of a building in a terrace by applying an external insulation system, the building and the whole terrace will be compromised and the terrace will lose its heritage value.

Materials and aesthetics also play a large part in evaluating the heritage value of a building or group of buildings. Authenticity is another major consideration. If a building has been greatly altered from its original form in a previous refurbishment, it does not, at worst, have any remaining heritage value, or at best its heritage value is diminished. In cases like this it should also be considered whether a correction can be made to reintroduce some of the original heritage components lost in the previous refurbishment. This will relate mainly to windows and external wall and roof finishes.

Integrity

It is important to consider the integrity of a building, no matter what its level of significance, and this should be assessed as part of the planning of any energy retrofit. Experience shows us that some do not take a building's integrity into account. We see interference of many kinds, such as changing window types, window sizes and doors inappropriately in the name of energy efficiency.

Conservation issues

The main conservation issues will be interference with original heritage features such as internal ceilings, cornices, historic stairs, floors, window surrounds, door surrounds and skirtings, and externally wall finishes, windows, roofs, chimneys, rainwater goods and the geometric relationships of the external facade. As mentioned earlier, the setting of the building and, in particular, the importance of maintaining a recognised streetscape or terrace of buildings can be greatly compromised in the name of an energy retrofit.

The issue of using unsuitable materials in the energy retrofit of an older or traditional buildings is perhaps the most important conservation issue, as most buildings constructed prior to 1945 are deemed 'breathable'. Imposing non-breathable products, such as many insulations and cement-based renders or pointing materials, will have a negative and in most cases a destructive impact on an older or traditional building.

Changing the hygrometry of a traditional masonry building can, and most probably will, in the short to medium term have a detrimental effect on the building.

Reversibility

The primary consideration when implementing any intervention on an older or traditional building is 'reversibility'. This means that interventions must be non-destructive, not changing or removing original fabric; and any interventions implemented must be able to be easily reversed or removed without causing any damage whatsoever to the original material, either internally or externally. This is a tough task and needs considerable knowledge of the building and the materials being used to retrofit, and an even better knowledge and understanding of the materials being used to improve the energy efficiency of an older or traditional building.

Sadly, reversibility is not a consideration in many energy retrofit projects thus far.

Risk assessment

Historically, risk assessment of the impact an energy retrofit has on a particular building or component of a building has not featured, yet this should be a key factor in assessing any interventions in any building, particularly an older or traditional building. The designer, contractor or building owner must understand the building and the existing or original materials they are dealing with and, most importantly, they must understand the effect of introducing new materials to older and traditional fabric.

Setting

The setting of a building of heritage value should also be a consideration at the evaluation stage of a possible energy retrofit project. This can include the grounds of a building, its setting within a complex or group of buildings, or its position within a terrace of buildings, streetscape, town or village. Due consideration must be given to the impact any proposed measures might have on this element of its heritage value.

Professional competence

Professional competence is a major factor when embarking on an energy retrofit project and sadly, to date, little or no compliance is required in many of the schemes being promoted by governments across the world. In the United Kingdom and Ireland, for instance, the incentives offered to energy retrofit your home are contractor led, rather than by a professional architect or engineer. This, in the opinion of the author, is regrettable and will lead to many mistakes and, worse still, the wholesale loss of original fabric and the destruction of much of our heritage building stock. More worrying still is that many manufacturers of products such as insulation are now offering packages with little or no thought to the impact these measures will have on our older and traditional buildings – or even, and perhaps more importantly, the non-performance of such measures in achieving cost reductions for building owners or achieving the bigger picture of government targets for reducing greenhouse gas emissions. This is to say nothing of the costs related to putting these damaging measures right in the decades to come.

Renewable energy opportunities

Little thought, if any, has gone into alternative energy sources in older and traditional buildings. The use of solar panels on visible historic roofs is not considered acceptable due to the effect it has on the 'character' of the building, but many buildings have multi-roof orientations, and solar panels can be placed on hidden roofs. Geothermal energy can be difficult in tight areas or in areas of high value archaeology. However, this could be an opportunity in cases of group schemes and certain typologies of buildings.

Perceived energy performance

When planning and considering an energy retrofit, one must set realistic targets of perceived improvements in the energy performance of a building that must be based on the assessments set out above. Assessors should be professional, have experience in the type of building they are dealing with, and be honest when setting targets to be achieved. Consideration should also be given to assessing the use of the building, the energy required for its proposed or existing use, improving controls, good housekeeping such as closing existing shutters and the use of heavier drapes or blinds, and the possibility of secondary glazing. It will not benefit the building owner, the assessor or the building itself if unrealistic targets are set and not achieved.

Energy savings

Under the existing EU Directive, the target set is to reduce emissions of greenhouse gases by 20% by 2020; this should also reduce primary energy use by the same 20%. When assessing the energy savings that can be achieved, it is necessary to understand the existing thermal performance of the building, the performance of the existing energy systems, and the primary loss of energy in the building.

Embedded energy

No consideration whatsoever has been given to the embodied energy in existing buildings, and there is no allowance in any of the present assessment levels for embedded energy and/or the enormous environmental cost of demolishing existing buildings. There is nothing greener than to reuse an existing building, and the redeployment of industrial buildings, for instance into modern living accommodation, should be encouraged in all jurisdictions. There are many good examples around the world of older buildings being converted to new uses. These are successful from a conservation point of view but should also be successful from an energy efficiency point of view. In the opinion of the author of this chapter, the conversion and reuse of existing buildings should become a credit in the assessment of energy-efficient retrofitting.

Documentation

It is of paramount importance that all stages of an assessment and planned intervention are recorded and documented in as detailed a way as possible. This is important for future assessments of performance and also evaluation of the process carried out.

PHASE 2: PLANNED INVERVENTIONS

Now that the building has been totally and exhaustively examined and understood, Phase 2 can proceed.

Measures

The previous phase will have given the professional or assessor a full understanding of the existing building's performance and shortfalls. A detailed plan of action and worthwhile measures should now be ready for implementation. Such measures may include suitable conservation interventions to the external envelope of the building; boiler replacement; upgrading or replacement of the existing radiators; the possible introduction of underfloor heating; insulation in the floor and roof; upgrading of the windows or the introduction of secondary glazing; if suitable, the introduction of a compatible wall insulation, either internal or external; the introduction of a simple building management system; education of the occupants in the use of modern technology; evidence of the best levels of heat to manage the retrofitted building; and a simple but detailed maintenance manual.

Reversibility

All planned interventions should be reversible and should not damage or replace any original fabric that has heritage value. If replacement of original fabric is necessary, professional evidence should be presented for the reasons for such drastic measures. All measures implemented, and how any particular intervention can be reversed without compromising the original fabric, should be explained.

Product availability and suitability

When considering the use of more compatible products such as natural insulation or breathable membranes, product availability should be a major factor. If specific products are not available, the contractor may often chose an unsuitable alternative.

All products specified should be suitable for the purpose for which they are designed and be completely compatible with the original fabric they will sit beside.

Supervision of the interventions is also extremely important. As designed measures are implemented, there should be a strict sign-off from the designer.

Possible ill effects on the building fabric

Risks of ill effects to any of the original elements of the building should be highlighted to the building owner. Suitable monitoring should be implemented and/or installed so that any ill effects can be identified at an early stage. There should be a section in the maintenance manual on this subject.

Energy or U-value improvement

As mentioned in the Phase 1 discussion, U-value performance should be properly assessed before an improvement is recommended. In many cases the intervention may not be necessary, as older and traditional buildings often perform far better than expected. The simplest measures should be a priority before major interventions, such as wall insulation, are considered. In recent research, a 40mm cement-based render that had been applied to the external facade of a Victorian building in the 1950s was carefully removed and replaced with a lime/hemp render of a similar thickness. This improved the U-value of the solid wall construction by 30%. The solution had no visual or aesthetic impact on the building and increased its heritage value as it was seen as putting back what would have been original to it.

Aesthetic impact

From a heritage value or setting point of view, any aesthetic change to the building under retrofit should be of a minimal impact. If there is a change, it should be fully explained and justified. In the case mentioned in the previous paragraph, replacing a cement-based render, which would be dark grey in colour, with a lime-based product would have an aesthetic impact as the lime would be white or ochre in colour. However, this can be justified by the historic knowledge that the Victorians would have used lime originally and the cement was a later intervention. If windows or doors are to be changed, historic evidence should again indicate what they should be replaced with. There is no reason why a modern high-performing window or door to the original design cannot be used. This said, it is best conservation practice to retain as much original fabric as possible.

Assess alternative renewable energy sources

The use of alternative renewable energy should be encouraged in all situations. The author believes this should be a priority, and more incentivised when dealing with older and traditional buildings. Conservation purists often say you cannot put solar panels or mini wind turbines on heritage buildings. But why is this? In all cases these interventions are reversible and do minimal damage to the original fabric, yet they could lessen the need for more intrusive energy-reducing measures on such buildings. With improving technology, alternative energy sources can be more discreet and effective. We now have small solar panels in the shape of natural roof tiles, and in most cases older and traditional buildings have outhouses that are less precious and can be used to host alternative renewable energy sources.

Mini CHP (combined heat and power) units can cover the needs of a single domestic property. For groups of buildings such as local authority housing estates or housing associations, multi-unit buildings which include the use of a central boiler and a district heating system can be beneficial.

The author believes that there needs to be a sea change in conservation circles regarding the use of modern technology in heritage buildings. We must accept solar panels and moderate wind turbines on the roofs of historic buildings.

Documentation

Once again, documentation at assessment stage and implementation stage is essential so that professionals, home owners and authorities can have access to hard case studies and factual information on successful energy retrofit projects in older and traditional buildings. The construction industry in general, but perhaps more importantly the conservation sector, needs to drive the importance of sharing information. This same documentation can also be essential when evaluating the performance of older and traditional buildings within the short and medium term and should lead to the development of better practice and products.

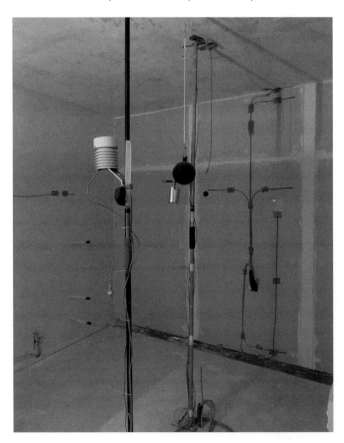

Fig 3.08 Monitoring various insulation systems' performance

FINAL RECOMMENDATIONS

Before making final recommendations on the energy retrofitting of an older or traditional building, one must fully understand the building and the actual U-value of the external envelope, and consider the use of renewable alternative energy sources. One must also consider the suitability of all products to be specified for a breathable building and respect the heritage value of such a building.

We as an industry should not be afraid of energy retrofitting older, traditional or indeed historic buildings, but we need an agreed methodology and set criteria for assessment and implementation of measures and we need, as a matter of urgency, an education and accreditation system for professionals in the energy retrofit industry. We also need the acknowledgement of all authorities that this industry should be professionally led and not led by contractors and/or manufacturers.

Planning

In the field, we are finding a lack of knowledge and understanding in the planning sections of our local authorities. This is a high-risk area for refusal or conditioning-out measures of sensible energy retrofit in older and traditional buildings. Again it comes down to education, and national and international planning institutions should take this on board and hold or promote courses in energy efficiency in traditional buildings. As a sector, we should all promote such education and assist organisations in delivering a basic knowledge to their members.

Research

There is still not enough hard-evidence research. Yes, we as a sector are making strides in this area, but there are large gaps in the research knowledge, and governments and sector institutions should be promoting and funding such research. The more hard evidence we can get on the performance of existing older and traditional buildings, the better our understanding will be in delivering a sensible energy retrofit for our older building stock.

The leader in this area is Germany, with the Fraunhofer Institute of Building Physics carrying out extensive laboratory and field evaluations on buildings and new potential products for use in the sensible retrofit of older and traditional buildings. Historic Scotland is using its own stock of buildings as live test sites for evaluating the existing performance of a wide range of traditional buildings and is carrying out an increasing number of actual retrofit projects. This research and the results of the Fraunhofer research will contribute greatly to advancement in the sector.

Many good projects are being carried out well, but we have no way of including these in our available hard-data information bank. A positive step would be for state parties to give small incentives to building owners and professionals to record best practice in live projects and submit the data to a central information base.

Fig 3.09 View of a 1940s terrace

Fig 3.10 External insulation

Passivhaus vs LEED: a false dichotomy

Should older and traditional buildings be considered for Passivhaus or Leadership in Energy and Environmental Design (LEED)? This will increase the challenge for the professional, and most probably require a specialist more qualified in either Passivhaus or LEED, but it should be achievable.

Passivhaus is the world's strictest standard for building energy performance, and the most effective path to achieving new zero energy-use buildings. Unlike other green design standards, Passivhaus applies a laser-like focus on operating energy, which over the lifetime of a traditional building quickly exceeds embodied energy.

LEED is widely used in the certification of large commercial projects, and is now being used and promoted in new house building and also in some retrofit projects.

There are two recurrent misperceptions of high-performance buildings: first, that one certification is as good as the next; and second, that all green buildings use less energy. The first misperception could not be further from the truth. Many certifications are available to an owner and each has both pros and cons. By employing a well thought-out holistic strategy towards a high-performance building, the synergies within the competing systems can be revealed and certification in several systems achieved, if required. The second misperception is also not true. Just because a building wears a green label, it does not mean lower energy use. In fact, some green certifications have been shown to deliver little in terms of real world energy savings, with some green projects actually using more energy.

In new construction one should combine Passivhaus and LEED certificates to achieve the very highest results. In order to apply LEED to a traditional building, it is necessary to carry out a deeper study of the existing building and invest in a more in-depth design of interventions.

Summary

The experience and findings to date are that all governments are panicking with 2020 fast approaching, and different departments within governments are issuing guidelines and incentives to drive a major assault on the energy retrofitting of our existing building stock. This is at best not thought out, and at worst will cause serious damage to our older, traditional and historic buildings in the short to medium term.

The international community needs to lobby all governments and influence policy in this area, or we will spend a serious amount of money and commit home owners to financial commitments that will not pay off. We will also cause a serious amount of damage to our existing building stock, which will result in the loss of our built heritage. Finally, we will not help our governments achieve the targets set to reduce CO_2 by 20% by 2020, leading to financial penalties for non-conformity.

NOTES

1 United Nations, 2012, Framework Convention on Climate Change. http://unfccc.int/kyoto_protocol/
items/2830.php [accessed 30 July 2015].

2 The European Parliament and the Council of the European Union, 2006. *Directive 2006/32/EC of the
European Parliament and of the Council of 5 April 2006 on energy end-use efficiency and energy services
and repealing Council Directive 93/76/EEC (Text with EEA relevance)* in: UNION, T.E.P.A.T.C.O.T.E. (Ed.),
DIRECTIVE 2006/32/EC. *Official Journal of the European Union.*

3 EPBD, Concerted Action EPBD. http://www.epbd-ca.eu/ [accessed 30 June 2015].

4 The European Parliament and the Council of the European Union, *Directive 2002/91/EC of the European
Parliament and of the Council of 16 December 2002 on the Energy Performance of Buildings* (EC, 2003).

FOUR
Containing the questions

....

Douglas D Kent

INTRODUCTION

Global climate change and the conservation of non-renewable energy resources are widely held to be among the most pressing challenges facing humanity. In the United Kingdom, old buildings have become a particular focus for action to cut the use of fossil fuels. There are serious questions within the heritage sector, however, about how appropriate much of the resulting energy-saving work is. While perhaps suitable for modern buildings, it takes little account of the different needs of older properties. There is a concern of harm to both old buildings and their occupants' health. Carbon reductions could also be less than expected.

A major difficulty until recently has been the lack of guidance for those endeavouring to upgrade the energy efficiency of old buildings. Despite the laudable drive to save energy in them, surprisingly limited research has been conducted in this field. Assumptions about their thermal performance have tended to be based on little more than anecdotal evidence. This has led to conflicting views on the best ways to reduce carbon emissions from old buildings. Research is now in hand, however, to fill the knowledge gap. It has been commissioned by the country's oldest building conservation charity, the Society for the Protection of Ancient Buildings (SPAB).

This chapter sets out the context of the research that the SPAB has under way into the energy efficiency of old buildings and discusses the results so far.

THE SPAB AND ITS TECHNICAL ACTIVITIES

The designer and polymath William Morris (1834–96) and his associates founded the SPAB in 1877. It is the oldest, largest and most technically expert pressure group in the UK that campaigns to save old buildings from harm. The Society's main concern has always been the nature of work carried out on old buildings. Misguided work, in the Society's view, can be extremely destructive.[1]

The SPAB exists, above all, to promote 'conservative repair'. This is the philosophy behind all it does. Conservative repair refers to an abstemious approach towards work on old buildings – doing as little as possible but as much as necessary. The Society believes that the value of old buildings lies in the feelings their antiquity evokes. It argues that old buildings are best protected by maximising the retention of their historic fabric while minimising any disturbance affecting the overall essence. This idea of conservative repair has shaped the approach to work on old buildings not only in the UK but also in many other parts of the world.

The SPAB contends that conservative repair is achieved by adhering to the following key principles:

- carry out work essential to the long-term wellbeing of an old building
- employ compatible methods and materials
- obtain sound information about the history, construction and condition of an old building before making any serious interventions.

Conservative repair is the antithesis of restoration, which the SPAB was formed to oppose. The word 'restoration' is often used loosely to mean all aspects of work on old buildings. In the strictest architectural sense, though, it refers to work aimed at returning a building, or a component of one, to a perfect state. At its worst, it can entail the unnecessary renewal of features that are worn, damaged or unoriginal, and the hypothetical reconstruction of missing elements, or an entire building. Tidy reproduction is achieved at the expense of genuine but imperfect work.

Over 6,000 churches and cathedrals in the UK were restored between 1840 and 1870 during the Gothic Revival. The purpose, far from a desire to conserve material fabric, was to rebuild them to achieve stylistic purity and stimulate greater piety. Morris claimed that restoration created 'a feeble and lifeless forgery'. John Ruskin, the art critic and an early member of the SPAB, was equally forthright: 'Do not let us talk then of restoration. The thing is a lie from beginning to end.' Restoration can come from an overly scholarly approach. This explains why, historically, the Society made little pretence of being academic.

The Society's work has long had a strong technical dimension. This originates from, and is guided by, its philosophy. Morris was the SPAB's great visionary and communicator. It was architect Philip Webb (1831–1915), though, who first showed how the Society's principles could be put into practice. Webb, Morris's friend, was a co-founder of the SPAB. Through Webb, and the younger architects he inspired, the SPAB developed a body of knowledge based on extensive practical experience (Fig 4.01). The Society became what has been called a 'school of rational builders'.[2]

Fig 4.01 Repairs to the tower at St Mary's Church, East Knoyle in Wiltshire were devised by Philip Webb and supervised on site for him by Detmar Blow

The SPAB's technical activities still follow this tradition. Today, there is a small, dedicated technical staff supported by an advisory body, the Technical Panel, and the SPAB offers technical advice through various means. These include a telephone helpline, courses and publications. This technical role lies at the heart of the Society's work. It also complements its training provision. Central to this are the Lethaby Scholarship and William Morris Craft Fellowship programmes. These are for building professionals and craftspeople respectively.

The knowledge the SPAB has accumulated over many years has led it to appreciate the important differences between old and new buildings. This is not merely in terms of their appearance but also behaviour. A prime concern of the Society is the extent of work carried out on old buildings that fails to take into account their 'traditional' construction. Traditional buildings make up no less than a fifth of the UK's building stock.[3]

A traditionally constructed (pre-c1919) building has solid walls of permeable or 'vapour-open' materials. In other words, its walls must 'breathe' to stay dry and are analogous to an overcoat. By contrast, buildings of 'modern' (post-c1919) construction have cavity walls and are 'vapour-closed'. They rely on barriers and air spaces to keep out water and are more like a raincoat. Old buildings often become damp, therefore, when barriers to moisture are added. New buildings, on the other hand, become damp when such barriers fail. Old buildings also require greater ventilation to remove the 'structural moisture' generated by their breathing fabric.

The SPAB's fears over the use of inappropriate methods and materials on old buildings grew with the ever-increasing pressure to upgrade them thermally. Standard building industry practices were being widely imposed, such as the use of impermeable wall insulation and excessive draughtproofing. Such work risked not only aesthetic harm to old buildings but also physical damage. This included the loss of authentic features and degradation due to condensation, timber decay and mould growth. The result would reduce the longevity of buildings and cause more incidences of asthma and other health problems for building users.

There was anxiety that the government's flagship Green Deal to improve the energy performance of the UK's stock would unintentionally compound problems further on a large scale. The SPAB's previous experience with the introduction of energy performance certificates (EPCs) exacerbated this unease. EPCs had become a requirement when properties were built, sold or rented but prompted many unsuitable recommendations for traditional buildings.[4] The subsequent Green Deal was announced as the biggest home improvement programme since the Second World War. It would give loans and cash backs for work intended to improve the energy efficiency of existing buildings in Britain.[5]

Serious concerns over the Green Deal were expressed in a letter sent to *The Times* by the SPAB and a dozen co-signatories.[6] In response, they were invited to contribute to a series of workshops run by the Department of Energy and Climate Change. The Green Deal was also an impetus for the Society and other organisations to come together and form the Sustainable Traditional Buildings Alliance (STBA). The STBA works to promote a better understanding of traditional buildings in the UK.

In the meantime, greater realisation arose within the SPAB that on-site research could benefit the technical advice it gave, nowhere more so than in the field of energy conservation. The SPAB became less reticent about adopting a more academic stance. The view now was that some basic scientific monitoring could complement, not conflict with, the Society's traditional practical approach. This was because old buildings are more complex and diverse than they often at first appear. Good information for their successful repair can be hard to obtain from general observation or laboratory investigations alone.

Three areas of research are being carried out which will be examined in the following sections.[7] These examine:

- fabric heat loss through traditionally constructed walls
- fabric heat loss, airtightness, moisture behaviour, indoor air quality, comfort and fabric risk both before and after renovation (the building performance survey)
- tests to compare results against established hygrothermal modelling systems.

FABRIC HEAT LOSS (U-VALUES)

SPAB building

The SPAB's research began at its own traditionally built headquarters building in London's Spitalfields. The property is Grade II-listed and originated as a silk merchant's house in about 1740 (Fig 4.02). Glasgow Caledonian University monitored heat loss through the rear wall for the Society. The aim was to establish the thermal performance of the solid brickwork as part of a wider energy audit. This would inform decisions on work to make the building more energy efficient.

The study determined the *in situ* U-value of the wall. A U-value is a measure of heat loss through a building element, such as a wall, roof or window. It is expressed as watts per metre squared kelvin (W/m²K). The higher the U-value, therefore, the worse the thermal performance of the building envelope. By contrast, a low U-value usually indicates high levels of insulation.

Fig 4.02 The SPAB's Georgian headquarters at 37 Spital Square, London

Fig 4.03 Air and surface temperature sensors on the rear wall of the SPAB building

In situ U-value monitoring is a non-destructive way of measuring the thermal transmittance of existing, site-specific building elements.

The monitoring procedure conformed to the principles set out in ISO 9869 *Thermal Insulation - Building Elements - In-Situ Measurements of Thermal Resistance and Thermal Transmittance.*[8] Heat flow through the wall was measured with a calibrated heat flux sensor. This was mounted on the internal surface. The results were combined with air temperature measurements inside and outside to obtain a U-value for the wall (Fig 4.03). Monitoring took place over the winter season to maximise interior and exterior temperature differences. This improved the accuracy of the final U-value obtained.

The *in situ* U-value was compared with the calculated figure. This is the reciprocal of all the resistances of the constituent materials in the building element:

U (element) = $1/(Rse + Rsi + R1 + R2 ...)$

where *Rse* is the fixed external resistance, *Rsi* fixed internal resistance and *R1* ... is the sum of all the resistances of the building materials in the element.

The resistance of a building material is derived by the following formula:

$R = (1/k) \times d$

where *k* is the conductivity of the building material and *d* the material thickness.

The result for the SPAB's building was groundbreaking. While the calculated U-value was 1.27 W/m²K, the *in situ* measurements gave a significantly better actual figure of 0.6 W/m²K.

The wall, therefore, lost only half as much heat as the calculated figure suggested. This was the first exercise to use calculated and *in situ* data to prove that an old wall can perform better than previously thought. In doing so, it provided evidence to support what some in the building conservation world had long suspected.

This outcome had far-reaching implications. U-values are just one factor that affects the overall energy profile of a building. Their calculation, though, forms the basis for energy reduction standards and associated legislation. These can apply to existing, as well as new, buildings. The use of inaccurately high U-values, therefore, could suggest misguided priorities for energy-saving measures in traditional buildings. This might lead to unnecessary and harmful interventions. Given that traditional buildings in the UK number in the millions, the scale of potential damage was huge.

Wider survey

The results of the initial research on the SPAB's building raised the question of how other older, traditionally constructed walls performed. The Society, therefore, decided to commence a wider programme to investigate the U-values of traditional walls of varying materials across the country. For comparison, some walls of cavity construction or retrofitted with insulation are also being measured. Once again, the study compares *in situ* figures with calculated ones. This research is being carried out by Dr Caroline Rye and Cameron Scott, guided by Glasgow Caledonian University. So far, individual walls in 78 buildings have been studied.

Various building owners have volunteered solid walls in their houses for monitoring. These include walls comprising a variety of stone types, unfired mass earth construction, and timber framing with different infills (including wattle and daub, as well as modern alternatives). The measurements are normally taken from walls with their internal and external finishes intact. The work complements independent studies by Historic Scotland and Historic England that focus predominantly on sandstone and brick respectively. The results of the study to date are varied, reflecting the varying materials and wall thicknesses.

The findings can be classified according to whether the walls are of homogenous or heterogeneous construction. Homogeneous walls are built of a single material. Heterogeneous walls have a body consisting of more than one material and/or incorporate some form of air gap within their build-up.

Homogeneous walls of high-density materials – for example, stone, brick or cob (mass unfired earth) – give U-values that decline in proportion to their thickness (Fig 4.04). It is possible to begin to identify a consistent range of *in situ* figures for particular materials, such as limestone and granite (Fig 4.05). This indicates that it might be possible to provide U-values that are more accurate for other, similarly built walls by extrapolating from these *in situ* results.

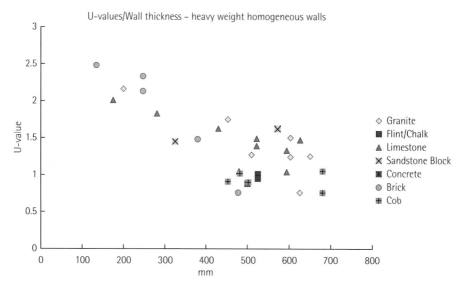

Fig 4.04 U-values for heavyweight homogeneous walls measured *in situ*

The SPAB study has produced an average *in situ* U-value of 1.31 W/m²K for all 39 heavyweight homogeneous walls monitored so far. This figure lies at the lower end of the range of U-values for unfilled brick cavity walls measured by Hisschmöller (1.4–1.9 W/m²K).[9] The SPAB has obtained a further average *in situ* U-value of 1.36 W/m²K solely for the solid stone and brick walls studied. The averages returned for each material are 1.42 W/m²K for the stone walls and 1.24 W/m²K for those of brick.

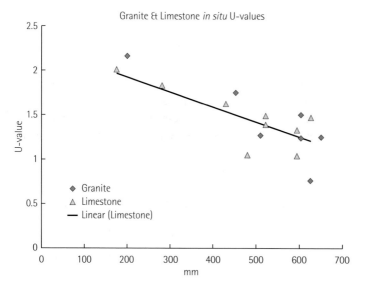

Fig 4.05 U-values for granite and limestone walls measured *in situ*

Homogenous walls constructed of less dense materials yield lower U-values in comparison. This is because they incorporate more trapped air that reduces their thermal conductivity. Therefore, the link between wall thickness and decreased U-values found among heavyweight walls is not replicated here. The lightweight homogenous walls comprise materials that are often not typical of traditional walls. Examples of the U-values for such walls are 0.28 W/m²K for straw/clay construction (398mm); 0.14 W/m²K for polyisocyanurate (PIR) (168mm); and 0.87 W/m²K for hempcrete (174mm).

The heavyweight or lightweight distinction becomes more difficult with heterogeneous walls. Various combinations of heavyweight and lightweight materials exist. The lowest U-values inevitably come from walls that are entirely of lightweight construction or include a substantial addition of a lightweight insulating material. An example is the figure of 0.16 W/m²K for a 580mm granite wall with 100mm of PIR insulation. On the other hand, wattle and daub infill panels for timber-framed walls, which are of thin section and mainly of a heavyweight material (clay), inevitably exhibit high U-values of 1.69 and 2.03 W/m²K.

A secondary layer within a wall that traps a layer of still air is also found to reduce the U-value. For instance, whereas a solid limestone ashlar records an *in situ* U-value of 2.01 W/m²K, a similar wall in the same building dry-lined with standard plasterboard gives a figure of 0.97 W/m²K.

While these results assist in quantifying heat transfer through different forms of traditional wall construction, they do not indicate the consequences for building performance of adding insulation, particularly any increased risk of dampness. This aspect is being considered separately as part of the building performance survey.

In situ versus calculated results
A further exercise has compared the U-values from the 78 walls measured *in situ* with figures calculated using BuildDesk U 3.4, a software program widely used within the construction industry. The basis of this software is BR 443 *Conventions for U-Value Calculations*.[10] This provides the methodology for evaluating U-values in a whole-building energy performance under the Standard Assessment Procedure (SAP) or Reduced SAP (RdSAP), which underpin the Building Regulations and EPCs.

A significant discrepancy has been found between the figures produced by the two different U-value estimating methods. In 77% of cases, the software indicates greater heat loss through walls than the measurements taken on site. This, therefore, supports claims that standard calculating methods underestimate the thermal performance of traditionally built walls (Fig 4.06). The heat loss measured through walls of vernacular materials can be as low as one third of that calculated. The discrepency is largest for stone walls and less pronounced with infill panels to timber-framed walls. Contrary to the results from

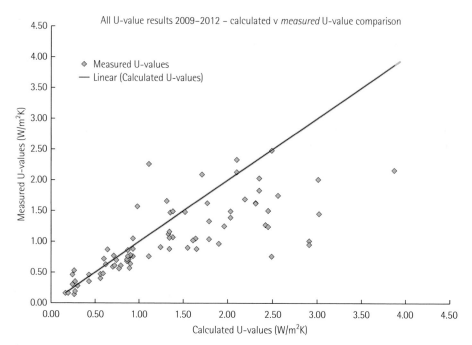

Fig 4.06 Comparison of U-values measured *in situ* and calculated using BuildDesk

calculations, heat loss through the solid walls sampled is less than that of the majority of unfilled modern cavity walls.

It is important to note that the research does not challenge the validity of the U-value modelling software but highlights the difficulty in assessing the thermal performance of traditional walls using conventional calculation methods. BuildDesk is a respected, class-leading software program designed for use with modern buildings. It is also, however, widely used to calculate U-values for traditional buildings in the absence of more tailored software. The main reason for the discrepancy between measured *in situ* and calculated U-values in the SPAB study seems to be the fundamental problem of inputting accurate data for an existing wall.

Various difficulties exist when inputting data to calculate U-values for existing walls. The overall thickness of a wall may be known but the exact materials and their proportions frequently defy accurate description. Mortar, voids and other hidden characteristics, for example, can be hard to define and quantify, so simplified data is inputted. The lack of thermal conductivity data for most UK vernacular building materials, which are diverse and can be location-specific, further increases the inaccuracy of calculations.

A calculated U-value figure tends to correspond better with the *in situ* figure, therefore, when more information is known about the build-up of the wall being assessed and its specific thermal conductivity can be given. When a wall construction conforms more closely to modern methods of construction, such as the build-up of discrete layers found in timber frame infills, and/or utilises modern materials with more robust thermal conductivity data, a good correlation between calculated and *in situ* U-values is found.

A U-value figure calculated from an *in situ* test is likely to represent the actual thermal performance of a particular wall better than its calculated equivalent. This is because the *in situ* figure includes all the elements in that wall construction that affect its conductivity (ie the mortar, voids and other unknown elements), unlike the calculated values. It is also determined over time in a non-steady state, dynamic environment – the real world, where the direction heat flows can reverse – and therefore takes into account thermal mass (the heat storage effect of mass walls) and the influence of temperature change and other climatic conditions.

Building performance survey

A new programme of U-value research forms part of the SPAB's building performance survey. This set out to examine seven traditionally built owner-occupied houses scheduled for renovation and assess them according to a number of parameters both before and after work. The additional components of this further research project – airtightness, moisture levels, indoor air quality, comfort and fabric risk – are discussed separately in the sections that follow. ArchiMetrics Ltd, a building performance research company, is undertaking this project for the Society. Historic England and the Dartmoor National Park Authority have assisted with funding.

The desire to improve energy efficiency has been cited as one of the primary reasons for renovation work at all of the seven properties. Post-renovation monitoring is yet to take place at three of the sites. The upgrades adopt a range of methods and materials not necessarily advocated by the SPAB. The properties are quite widely distributed across England, with a cluster in the south-west due to the funding from the Dartmoor National Park Authority.

Internal wall insulation was used on the walls of three of the four properties monitored to date:

- Drewsteignton, Devon: 100mm of PIR insulation (with an air gap and plasterboard lining) to a 603mm granite wall
- Shrewsbury, Shropshire: 40mm of woodfibre board insulation (with an 8mm lime plaster finish) to a 357mm brick wall
- Skipton, North Yorkshire: 35mm of hemp/lime plaster (with 5mm lime plaster finish) to a 540mm gritstone rubble wall.

External wall insulation was applied on the remaining building:

- Riddlecombe, Devon: 50mm of insulating lime-based render (with lime scratch and finish coats) to a 655mm thick cob and stone wall.

Table 4.1 Measured and calculated U-values for the walls pre- and post-renovation

Location	Measured uninsulated W/m²K	Measured insulated W/m²K	% reduction	Calculated uninsulated W/m²K	Calculated insulated W/m²K	% reduction
Drewsteignton	1.24	0.16	87	2.45	0.19	93
Riddlecombe	0.76	0.72	4	0.95	0.56	41
Shrewsbury	1.77	0.56	68	1.62	0.61	62
Skipton	1.63	1.00	39	2.31	1.72	26

The U-value results obtained for these houses pre- and post-renovation are shown in Table 4.1. Reductions in heat loss are noted with all four renovated buildings. No direct comparisons can be made between the figures, since the original walls are of different widths and insulated with dissimilar products applied in various thicknesses.

The walls at Drewsteignton and Shrewsbury show considerable average percentage reductions in measured heat loss. The figures for the wall insulated with hemp/lime plaster at Skipton show a smaller decrease, which is understandable as this product is not exclusively an insulating one but combines the roles of an internal finish with some thermal benefit. The higher percentage reduction for the wall at Drewsteignton is a result of the additional width of the insulation material used and its lower thermal conductivity.

Table 4.1 also shows that there is a tendency for calculated post-renovation U-values to overestimate the heat loss of the walls. This is probably due to the thermal resistance of the original part of the walls not being fully accounted for within the calculations. There is not always, however, better correlation between the measured and calculated U-values post-insulation. This is because the degree of correlation is determined by a number of factors, principally the contribution of the new insulating layer to the overall thermal transmissivity of the wall. This insulation is of known quantity and conductivity, so where its contribution to the thermal profile is significant, the calculation is more likely to be aligned with the measured U-value post-insulation.

The thermal performance of the original wall at Skipton still exerts significant influence on overall thermal transmissivity. This contribution continues to be underestimated within the calculation. Furthermore, the thermal conductivity of the additional insulating layer of hemp/lime plaster may not be particularly well defined within the calibration.

The wall at Riddlecombe provides the only example where the post-insulation calculated U-value is lower than that the measured result and where little change is shown between pre- and post-renovation *in situ* figures. The reason is suspected to be the high moisture content of this wall, as discussed later.

AIRTIGHTNESS

Airtightness refers to the degree of air leakage through the fabric of a building (for example, via gaps in floors, walls and windows). Airtightness testing is a way of quantifying this. In addition to providing an overall indication of airtightness, such testing can apportion the contribution made by leaks from different sources in a building. This is particularly helpful for pinpointing elements that would benefit from draughtproofing.

Airtightness may be expressed as m^3 of airflow per hour per m^2 of building enclosure ($m^3/(h.m^2)$) where there is a 50Pa difference between the air pressures internally and externally. Rather than relating airflow to the surface area inside a building, airflow is often related to the building's volume and expressed as air changes per hour (ach @ 50Pa), since this can be easier to comprehend. If this figure is divided by 20, it gives an approximation of air changes per hour at normal pressure.

Testing of the properties in the SPAB building performance survey is being carried out by Green Footsteps of Cumbria in line with the methodology set out in the Air Tightness Testing and Measurement Association's (ATTMA's) Technical Standard L1 (2010).[11] The procedure involves temporarily covering or closing any deliberate points of ventilation, such as fireplaces, boiler flues or extractor fans. A pressure difference of 50 Pa is created between the inside of the building and outside using a fan/fans inserted into a suitable external opening (for example, a doorway). The airflow through the fan(s) is then measured.

Testing assists in identifying individual paths of air leakage since it exaggerates the normal cooling from air infiltration on the building fabric. Either infrared thermal imaging or smoke is used to locate leaks, depending, respectively, on whether the fan is depressurising or pressurising the building. It is possible to apportion the approximate air leakage associated with a particular element by comparing the airflow readings for it sealed and unsealed.

The airtightness results for the three buildings tested so far as part of the building performance survey are shown in Table 4.2. The tests have yielded a wide range of results before and after renovation. Some compare favourably with the limiting airtightness for new

Table 4.2 Airtightness before and after renovation

Location	Pre-renovation		Post-renovation	
	Airtightness $m^3/(h.m^2)$ @ 50 Pa	Air changes ach @ 50 Pa	Airtightness $m^3/(h.m^2)$ @ 50 Pa	Air changes ach @ 50 Pa
Drewsteignton	-	-	-	-
Riddlecombe	5.5	7.2	5.4	6.9
Shrewsbury	11.4	15.7	8.5	11.7
Skipton	16.9	14.8	10.9	8.6

build dwellings under Part L1A of the Building Regulations (2010), ie 10m^3/(h.m^2) @ 50Pa, and are lower than orthodoxy.

The post-renovation airtightness tests for Skipton and Shrewsbury display significant improvements from the pre-renovation results. They reflect the unrenovated state of the properties, including areas without plasterwork, although some work was yet to be completed in both at the time of re-testing. At Shrewsbury, it was possible to identify the effect of the secondary glazing installed as part of the renovation by comparing results when it was opened and when it was closed. When opened, it increased airflow through the whole property by 11%.

The improvement in airtightness at Riddlecombe after renovation is less significant because the building was already relatively airtight beforehand and the scope for draughtproofing measures limited. The estimated air change rate at ambient pressure (rather than 50Pa), is just over 0.3 ach. It is generally considered that occupants and their activities require a rate of 0.4–0.5 ach and that traditional buildings require roughly 'twice the normal level of ventilation' to remove the moisture generated by their breathing fabric.[12] The figure of 0.3–0.4 ach may present a problem, therefore, without further purpose-provided ventilation, particularly given a reasonably high occupant density.

A modern extension at Riddlecombe also appears to be less airtight than the building as a whole. Conversely, an extension at Shrewsbury has a result superior to that of the building overall.

The airflow through some chimney flues has been measured at the properties. The results do not equate directly to the airflow through the chimneys in practice (as they ignore passive stack and convective effects) but show considerable variation between properties and flues. The ATTMA's Technical Standard L1 procedure excludes flues. They are included in SAP calculations, however, where the use of a single ventilation rate for chimneys is now shown to be questionable.

Thermal imaging during depressurisation at all three properties has shown air leakage via the junctions of walls and ceilings to beams, at sills, around loft hatches and through floors. Ingress through closed windows and around casements (in the extension and due for replacement) was evident at Shrewsbury and through some windows and doors at Skipton, despite these being recently installed.

SURFACE AND SUB-SURFACE MOISTURE

Moisture readings have been taken from the internal surface and sub-surface of the walls at Drewsteignton, Riddlecombe, Shrewsbury and Skipton before and after renovation. The readings were obtained by measuring the electrical resistance and capacitance of the walls.

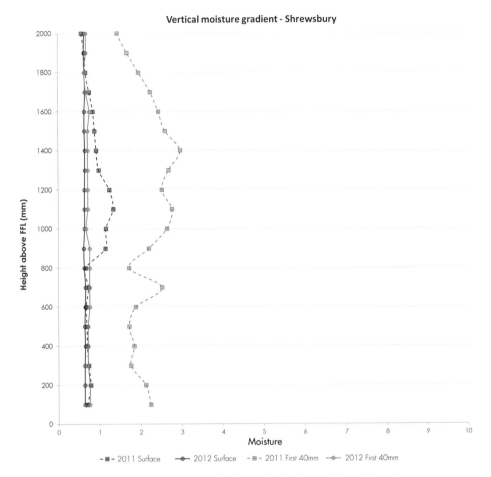

Fig 4.07 Pre- and post-renovation measurement of surface and sub-surface moisture at Shrewsbury

All four walls show a general decline in surface and sub-surface moisture levels following renovation. The readings for both Drewsteignton and Shrewsbury, which were insulated internally with sheet materials (PIR and woodfibre board), suggest dry and stable conditions at surface and sub-surface level (Fig 4.07). Before renovation, the sub-surface readings were a little more dynamic and indicated the influence of groundwater and/or rain. The insulation has moved the points of moisture measurement away from this zone of greater fluctuation in moisture levels.

The internal hemp/lime plaster at Skipton, however, still shows differentiation between the surface and sub-surface readings. Although both are broadly lower than prior to renovation, the latter show less stability. This could be partly because the new plaster has not fully dried out. It is also likely to reflect the continued coupling of the plaster to the masonry, unlike the isolation from it that resulted from the application of discrete forms of insulation at Drewsteignton and Shrewsbury. The readings for

Skipton seem to show, therefore, the influence of external forces, such as groundwater, before and after renovation.

The figures for Riddlecombe, an externally insulated wall, also show a general declining trend for surface and sub-surface moisture. Here, however, sub-surface readings above 1,400mm remain little changed. The elevated moisture content within the depth of this wall has been ascribed to the continuing presence of water from rain penetration through the previous, cracked cement render, significantly compounded by the necessary wetting down of the wall face prior to application of the new lime render.

INTERSTITIAL HYGROTHERMAL CONDITIONS (INCLUDING HYGROTHERMAL MODELLING)

Interstitial hygrothermal gradient monitoring

Long-term interstitial hygrothermal gradient monitoring (IHGM) is another important component of the building performance survey. IHGM refers to the measurement of temperature and humidity at the same location within a wall. The aim is to assess the risk of interstitial condensation, ie condensation occurring within the wall. This may happen with moisture-laden air diffusing into a wall if the temperature is lower on the other side. Alternatively, it may occur where moisture condenses from the air present within the structure due to low temperatures.

Measurements of temperature and humidity are taken through and either side of each wall section. The monitoring entails embedding four interstitial temperature and humidity sensors into the body of the wall at different depths, depending on its overall thickness. The sensors are numbered 1 to 4 from the inside to the outside. Moisture and temperature at various points through a cross section of the wall are monitored using prototype gradient loggers. Interior and exterior relative humidity and air and surface temperature measurements are used in combination with the values reported from the interstitial sensors to produce profiles of temperature and dew point through the wall sections.

Conditions within the walls are examined in a number of ways, namely through an analysis of relative and absolute humidity over time, cross sectional averages of absolute humidity, temperature and dew point, and also the dew point margins (the temperature drop required for condensation to occur at a certain location).

Relative humidity

Relative humidity is the proportion of water vapour held within the air at a certain temperature in relation to what it would contain if saturated. This is given as a percentage. Relative humidity is a temperature-dependent quantity. It indicates the risk of water vapour affecting building fabric. Relative humidity readings from the four interstitial sensors are

Table 4.3 Annual average relative humidity for all interstitial sensors

Location	Year	Annual average relative humidity (%)			
		Sensor 1	Sensor 2	Sensor 3	Sensor 4
Drewsteignton	3	68	85	90	96
	4	64	87	92	97
Riddlecombe	3	72	91	98	100
	4	78	91	99	100
Shrewsbury	3	66	72	75	83
	4	66	71	77	81
Skipton	3	71	74	79	81
	4	-	-	-	-

plotted along with the measurement of internal and external temperature and relative humidity for each of the four properties in the survey.

During the warmer spring and summer months, the relative humidity at all four sensors for both Shrewsbury and Skipton is similar as the temperature difference across the walls is less acute than in winter. During the autumn and winter, the greater difference in relative humidity levels at the sensor locations in each wall is due to the effect of central heating and increased internal/external temperature gradients. Lower relative humidity is found largely towards the warmer internal side of the wall, away from the colder external conditions.

Despite the more volatile responses found near to the external wall faces at Shrewsbury and Skipton in comparison to the Devon buildings, the annual average relative humidity readings appear to be quite stable and largely below the 80% threshold for mould growth (Table 4.3).

Sensors 1 and 2 at Shrewsbury also show a coupling of responses. This indicates that vapour exchange is taking place through the woodfibre insulation between them, as well as possibly a hygroscopic buffering of the internal room relative humidity in proximity to sensor 1 behind the internal wall finish.

By contrast, the wall at Drewsteignton records a more muted response and higher average relative humidity values that show an overall rising trend for this wall post-insulation. There is a period during the summer when relative humidity falls at sensors 3 and 4 but this 'recovery' does not occur at sensor 2. Averages at sensors 2 to 4 are considerably above the 80% mould growth threshold.

An unusual summer peak in relative humidity at Riddlecombe may be due to solar gain causing the evaporation of the moisture introduced into the cob during its re-rendering as part of the renovation work. It remains to be seen whether the high moisture levels in this wall decline or become a cause for concern.

Absolute humidity

This occurs when the water content of air expressed as grams per cubic metre (g/m^3). Absolute humidity for the interstitial sensors at the four properties in the building performance survey has been monitored over six to 12 months, along with measurements of internal and external temperature and absolute humidity at each property.

Table 4.4 Annual average absolute humidity for all interstitial sensors

Location	Year	Annual average absolute humidity (g/m^3)			
		Sensor 1	Sensor 2	Sensor 3	Sensor 4
Drewsteignton	3	8.53	8.76	8.96	9.13
	4	9.24	10.04	10.24	10.17
Riddlecombe	3	9.47	12.66	12.74	12.27
	4	12.10	12.96	12.72	11.75
Shrewsbury	3	9.01	8.80	8.95	9.18
	4	9.56	9.42	9.69	9.65
Skipton	3	10.46	9.99	9.68	9.54
	4	-	-	-	-

Absolute humidity increases at each location over the summer months due to the capacity of the warmer air to hold more water vapour, and this is mirrored within the walls. There is a fall in absolute humidity from the external to internal side of walls but this pattern reverses in winter because of indoor heating. The rise in absolute humidity at Riddlecombe in the summer far exceeds that of the external absolute humidity values in comparison with the other properties. This supports the suggestion above that there is an additional source of vapour for this wall coming from moisture vaporisation caused by solar gain.

There is an increase in the quantities of vapour within the walls at both Shrewsbury and Drewsteignton over the most recent year. At Shrewsbury, this could be explained by the extremely wet weather encountered during this monitoring period and the fairly thin, south-facing wall. The wall at Drewsteignton is thicker and faces north–west. The vapour gain is about twice that at Shrewsbury and seems likely to have resulted from a lack of drying opportunities at this location and/or the application of impermeable insulation. The insulation has cooled the masonry and restricted vapour movement.

Riddlecombe, however, has the highest amount of vapour found within the four walls (and also, perhaps as a result, the highest relative humidity averages). Rather than a year-on-year increase at all four sensors, a decrease is noted at sensors 3 and 4 that suggests vapour has been able to evaporate from the external surface during sunnier periods.

Hygrothermal sections

All walls monitored show the same pattern of temperature gradient across their sections over an annual cycle. The gradients are approximately level though the summer when there is little difference between internal and external temperatures. These gradients increase from inside to outside during the autumn due to interior heating. There are differences, however, regarding the dew point margins observed in the walls.

All four walls have experienced a narrowing of dew point margins post-insulation. The readings for the walls at Riddlecombe and Drewsteignton, though, also appear to show a continued narrowing post-insulation.

The extent of change pre- and post-insulation is much greater within the masonry part of the wall at Drewsteignton (sensors 2 to 4) (see Table 4.4). This may result from the trends of rising relative humidity and year-on-year increased absolute humidity. The narrowest dew point margins are seen during the winter but persist until early summer (Fig 4.08). They possibly reflect the slow response time of the granite wall, which may be exacerbated because of excess damp material (and associated vapour) and a lack of drying opportunities. This could be the case especially for sensor 2, which lies between the insulation and the masonry. Vapour may continue to accumulate at this point deep within the wall during the summer because of evaporation from damp material or vapour that has evaporated elsewhere in the wall. Results suggest that vapour may be moving from an area of high concentration at sensor 3 to one of lower concentration at sensor 2 over much of the year.

Riddlecombe is found to experience 100% relative humidity at sensor 4 throughout the year and narrow or no dew point margins during the summer for reasons previously explained. Margins increase during the winter months but stay much smaller than those for the other buildings studied. This reflects the continuing extremely high vapour profile for this wall.

Hygrothermal modelling

The SPAB's building performance survey includes a study to evaluate the practical application of BS 15026-compliant hygrothermal modelling software for predicting condensation risks within walls using the house at Shrewsbury.

The software currently used by the building industry for assessing condensation risks is based largely on the methodologies presented in BS EN ISO 13788 (often referred to as the Glaser method).[13] This has limitations, though, when used for assessing traditionally built walls. It is known that condensation risk analysis of capillary-active solid walls in contact with driven rain requires the evaluation of additional factors, such as liquid moisture transfer.

To evaluate the risk of condensation in traditional walls, more progressive areas of the building industry have migrated towards sophisticated simulation methods conforming to BS EN ISO 15026: 2007.[14] The BS 15026-compliant computer program evaluated as

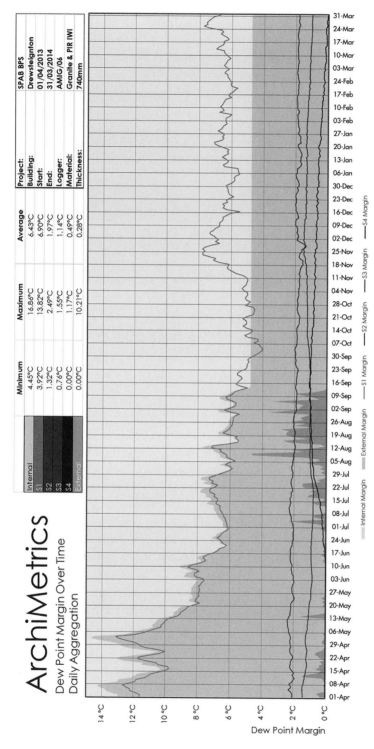

Fig 4.08 Dewpoint margins over time at Drewsteignton, year 4

part of the SPAB's research is WUFI (Wärme und Feuchte Instationär (transient heat and moisture)) version 5.1. This was developed by the Fraunhofer Institute for Building Physics (IBP) in Germany.

Although the advanced software used here has proved its accuracy in field trials over many years, the problems associated with the inability of the user to refine inputs mean the results still present uncertainties. For numerical simulations to improve confidence in internal wall insulation investigations, basic materials testing must be undertaken in conjunction with research into critical limits of driven rain and standards expressing highest likely levels of internally produced moisture.

The findings of this study also suggest that urgent investigations are needed into the issues surrounding the insertion of vapour control layers (VCLs). This standard solution is frequently arrived at through BS 13788 software. According to the WUFI simulation of the wall insulated with woodfibre board at Shrewsbury, though, this would lead to complete failure of the insulation. The VCL would also create conditions conducive to mould growth, as well as wet and dry rot.

INDOOR AIR QUALITY

The building performance survey has logged measurements of carbon dioxide levels, temperature and relative humidity at the four properties before and after their renovation.

Averaged values for these over a two- to three-week period are given in Table 4.5. The Drewsteignton figures show little change because no substantial renovation work has taken place in the part of the building where measurements were taken. At the other three properties, average levels of carbon dioxide post-renovation all lie within the range deemed 'acceptable', ie below 1,000 ppm.[15]

This only describes the average condition of the rooms monitored, however; a better indication of air quality is found through an examination of peak measurements for each. Air quality at

Table 4.5 Average pre- and post-renovation conditions for indoor air quality

Location	Pre-renovation averages			Post-renovation average		
	CO_2 (ppm)	Temperature (°C)	Relative humidity (%)	CO_2 (ppm)	Temperature (°C)	Relative humidity (%)
Drewsteignton	581	16.8	55.13	553	15.8	59.7
Riddlecombe	1,097.5	19.5	60.4	950	18.4	64.1
Shrewsbury	702	15	50.6	595	17	66.1
Skipton	554.5	16.2	63.3	540	16.56	58

Riddlecombe is seen to be appreciably poorer than at the other locations, with carbon dioxide levels frequently peaking above 1,500 ppm and even 2,000 ppm. The maximum recorded quantity is 2,824 ppm. This poor air quality can be ascribed to a combination of low air permeability, high occupancy and low volume areas for the house.

In addition, levels of carbon dioxide at Shrewsbury, Skipton and Riddlecombe since renovation are all slightly lower than those recorded pre-renovation. This is surprising because airtightness at all three properties has improved and it might be expected that reductions in air leakage/air change rates would result in increased carbon dioxide in these rooms. The reduced averaged measurements of carbon dioxide reflect slightly lower room occupancies over the reported period. In the case of Skipton, an alternative or additional reason may be the enlargement that has taken place to the kitchen/dining area where the greater area and volume of the room results in lower concentrations of carbon dioxide.

COMFORT AND FABRIC RISK

Indoor air temperature and relative humidity readings have been logged at five-minute intervals in each of the four properties and plotted to give an indication of comfort and risk to building fabric.

Fig 4.09 shows a typical plot. 'Acceptable' and 'ideal' comfort levels are indicated by two polygons. Risk to building fabric (and human health) is indicated by three temperature and humidity gradients, called the limiting isopleths for mould (LIM).[16] The gradients represent different levels of ambient humidity required for the start of mould growth on different substrates: LIM0 for a substrate comprising an ideal culture medium; above this, LIM1 for biodegradable materials, such as timber; and LIM2 for porous materials of stone-like character, such as brick.

Conditions before renovation indicated poor levels of comfort, which is unsurprising given that the occupants had identified the need for renovation. The temperature and relative humidity clusters sit in proximity to the LIM0 line, indicating a possibility of mould growth on an 'ideal' medium, but none of the properties appeared to provide the conditions required.

Average temperatures following renovation have risen in all cases. The readings were gathered over a longer and warmer period, whereas pre-renovation measurements were all conducted in the winter months. Relative humidity measurements at each location have also increased post-renovation. Once again, however, this increase may be a reflection of the larger data sets. It could also reflect the influence of new plaster drying out in the rooms being monitored.

With regard to the comfort polygons, the majority of temperatures and relative humidity measurements at all four properties lie within the 'acceptable' and 'ideal' comfort zones.

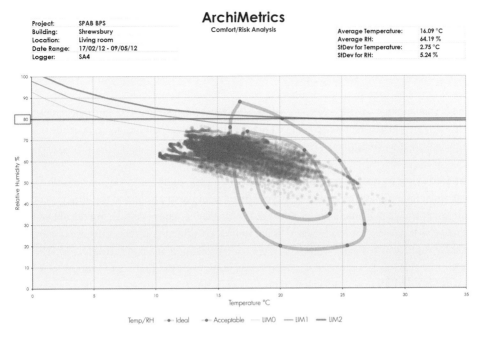

Fig 4.09 Comfort/risk analysis for Shrewsbury post-renovation

A proportion of post-renovation temperature measurements fall below this range at Shrewsbury, Skipton and Drewsteignton but still indicate a long-term improvement since renovation. The extent to which the readings reflect occupant preference is unclear.

Measurements of relative humidity pre-renovation rarely cross the limiting isopleths for mould growth. Post-renovation a proportion of measurements intersect these isopleths, although Shrewsbury would seem to remain at little risk. The proportion of measurements that cross all three isopleths at Skipton and Drewsteignton is small. A greater proportion of indices cross all the LIMs at Riddlecombe. No evidence of mould growth is visible, however, perhaps because it is retarded by the alkalinity of lime-based internal wall finishes.

PROGRESS AND THE FUTURE

The SPAB's research into the energy efficiency of traditional, pre-c1919 buildings is revealing some fascinating and useful findings. This work is still in progress. It is, however, already challenging orthodox views within the building sector about how traditional properties perform. At the same time, the research is also enabling the Society to develop credible alternative strategies for improving carbon savings from traditional buildings without imperilling them or the wellbeing of their occupants. The decision by the 'grandfather' of UK building conservation to commit itself to direct involvement in a carefully targeted programme of cutting-edge site-based investigations, therefore, looks like being vindicated.

Traditional buildings differ from modern ones in important ways. Standard methods of assessing and modelling the energy performance of traditional buildings may give misleading results because of this. Crucially, the research being conducted by the SPAB signals that in many cases heat loss through solid walls is less than calculations suggest. The airflow measured through chimneys in traditional buildings also varies considerably and is commonly at variance with the single ventilation rate used for standard calculations. Such shortcomings must be overcome if energy efficiency interventions are to be made that complement the existing fabric.

The SPAB research has far-reaching implications, not least where the installation of solid wall insulation (SWI) is being considered, ie where the prospect of harm to the special interest of an old building does not rule it out. When SWI is judged suitable for retrofit work, starting with an improved base case U-value will not only identify carbon and cost savings more accurately. It will also cut the chances of over-insulation and potentially broaden the range of viable insulation materials. In particular, it increases the chances of vapour-open insulation being used, which is more compatible with the construction of traditional buildings. The research supports the argument that vapour-open insulation is better able to regulate moisture levels within solid walls. Improvements to modelling software are required, though, to predict more accurately the distribution of moisture and temperature in a traditional wall when changes such as the addition of insulation are made.

The research findings have allowed the SPAB, STBA and others to advise the government on more effective ways to implement its schemes to improve the energy efficiency of the nation's large stock of traditional buildings. Notwithstanding this, one unresolved concern is the adequacy of provisions for traditional buildings in the new energy efficiency regulations for the private rented sector due to come into force in 2018. This issue has been raised with the government. The Society is also in dialogue with software providers regarding modifications to their products so that they produce more accurate predictions for traditionally built walls. Additionally, continuation of the monitoring in hand is aiding the SPAB with clarifying trends and defining links between energy-saving renovation work and long-term building performance.

The SPAB's research, while addressing specific questions, has inevitably prompted a series of supplementary ones that could form the basis of possible further investigations. There will be a need for ongoing, high-quality research to inform future decisions about appropriate interventions to older, traditional buildings. Such buildings have continually evolved over their lives to meet changing needs, and this has assisted their survival. The knowledge necessary to sustain our heritage of older buildings must also be accompanied by suitable skills and values. The SPAB's philosophy of conservative repair is as relevant today as it ever was.

NOTES

1 SPAB Manifesto, 1877. See William Morris, *The Manifesto of the Society for the Protection of Ancient Buildings*, http://www.spab.org.uk/downloads/The%20SPAB%20Manifesto.pdf [accessed 30 June 2015].

2 Society for the Protection of Ancient Buildings (1982), 3.

3 The English Housing Survey (2013) shows that 4.5 million dwellings in England (19.7% of the housing stock) pre-date 1919 and the proportion in the rest of the UK is similar.

4 See, for example, Ross Clarke, 2009. The need to obtain EPCs for listed buildings was withdrawn in 2013.

5 The Green Deal was launched in 2013 but its funding ended abruptly in 2015.

6 Published on 2 August 2011.

7 Society for the Protection of Ancient Buildings, 2011–2014 https://www.spab.org.uk/advice/energy-efficiency/ [accessed 30 June 2015].

8 International Organization for Standardization, 1994.

9 In Hugo Hens et al, 'Brick cavity walls: a performance analysis based on measurements and simulations', *Journal of Building Physics*, 31:2 (2007), 95–124.

10 Brian Anderson, *Conventions for U-Value Calculations 2006 Edition* (Watford: BRE Scotland, 2006).

11 Air Tightness Testing and Measurement Association, 2010.

12 Chartered Institution of Building Services Engineers (CIBSE), *Guide to Building Services for Historic Buildings*, ed Richard Oxley and Peter Warm (London: CIBSE, 2002), 18.

13 British Standards Institution, 2002.

14 British Standards Institution, 2007.

15 As defined by CIBSE.

16 These are based on work by Klaus Sedlbauer, 2001 and cited by Hannu Viitanen, Anne-Christine Ritschkoff, Tuomo Ojanen, and Mikael Salonvaara, 2003.

PART 2

Responses

In this section, a range of contributors discuss their responses in practice to the questions of sustainability and conservation. Two of the contributors discuss the long-term strategies developed while working with academic buildings in the UK and the US respectively. The other chapters offer examples and discussion in the context of domestic and ecclesiastical buildings.

FIVE

An integrated approach to heritage and sustainability:

four academic building projects in the US

···

Tom Hotaling

INTRODUCTION

This chapter presents four projects in the US designed by Ann Beha Architects (ABA) of Boston, Massachusetts, reflecting an intersection of building heritage and sustainability. Each is located on the campus of a private, not-for-profit academic institution. The first is a completed project at the University of Pennsylvania, the second a project currently in construction at the Massachusetts Institute of Technology, the third a completed project at the University of Chicago, and the fourth a master-planning and renovation project for Louis Kahn's library building at Phillips Exeter Academy in New Hampshire.

Each project gives new life to what is loosely considered a 'historic' building in American parlance. A historic building may or may not be listed on an official historic register, though it typically has a significant amount of extant original building fabric and is representative of a specific era in the spectrum of American architectural history and/or important to the heritage of its place. Quite often its original purpose is no longer relevant and an adaptive reuse is appropriate.

The impetus for each of the four projects was driven by an institutional mission. A high value was placed on heritage, with the inherent costs and challenges of adapting historic buildings for 21st-century academic needs clearly recognized from the start. Each of the four institutions has a campus-wide environmental sustainability policy, targeted at responsible building practices that seek to minimize energy use and the impact of construction on our environment, and to promote healthy buildings and sites. More often than not, these policies were in line with preservation approaches, and where they were not, creative interfaces resulted between the two.

Preservation

This term is used in the US much like the term 'conservation' is in the UK. It is an umbrella term, covering four distinct approaches to the treatment of historic properties, as defined by the National Park Service, the agency of the US Department of the Interior that maintains the National Register of Historic Places:[1]

Preservation – applying measures necessary to sustain the existing form, integrity and materials of a historic property. Work, including preliminary measures to protect and stabilize the property, generally focuses upon the ongoing maintenance and repair of historic materials and features rather than extensive replacement and new construction.

Rehabilitation – making possible a compatible use of a property through repair, alterations, and additions while preserving those portions or features that convey its historical, cultural, or architectural values.

Restoration – accurately depicting the form, features, and character of a property as it appeared at a particular period of time by means of the removal of features from other periods in its history and reconstruction of missing features from the restoration period.

Reconstruction – depicting by means of new construction, the form, features, and detailing of a non-surviving site, landscape, building, structure, or object for purpose of replicating its appearance at a specific period of time and in its historic location.

Typically no single category can be applied exclusively to a project involving a historic building, but rather some combination of the four is appropriate. The *Secretary of Interior's Standards* also provide guidelines for the four approaches, not intended to be technical or prescriptive.[2] They form a useful checklist and provide a clear and shared basis of understanding among those designing, reviewing, and administering historic properties.

Review of historic buildings and control of changes made to them can occur at federal, state, and local levels, through agencies empowered by legislature. Every state has a State Historic Preservation Officer (SHPO) guiding preservation within the state. Layered over these agencies may be advocacy groups, many of which have decidedly influenced building preservation in the US. Most American academic institutions – including the four presented here – have internal campus standards as well. As the depth and breadth of historic building control can vary enormously, a thorough understanding of the processes and parties involved is of paramount importance before undertaking any project.

Sustainability

This term is used in the US much as it or the term 'resilience' is used in the UK. When applied to buildings in the US, 'sustainable' broadly refers to green technologies, products, and building/site approaches, all geared at protecting our natural habitat, promoting clean and renewable energy, and sponsoring a healthy environment for building occupants.

Achieving the highest level of sustainability possible in site and building renovation/ construction is becoming a normative goal for building and community design, construction, and maintenance in the US. In many areas of the country these goals are now reinforced by legislation in the form of building codes that stipulate requirements for such characteristics as thermal efficiency, water usage, lighting and indoor air quality.

A number of standards are used in the US, perhaps the most universal being Leadership in Energy and Environment Design (LEED), a building certification program developed by the United States Green Building Council (USGBC).[3] The LEED system ranks buildings in four ascending categories – Certified, Silver, Gold, and Platinum – and has become a recognized benchmark for construction and renovation on many US campuses. As there can be significant costs associated with the LEED process, it is not unusual for some academic institutions to use LEED standards as construction and renovation guidelines, but not actually file for LEED status.

Format

Each of the four projects presented in this chapter begins with a short summary project description. This is followed by information organized by Background (the academic institution, existing building, and project brief), Description (existing conditions, rehabilitation, renovation, new construction, building systems, sustainable design), and Design team (architects, consultants, construction managers).

UNIVERSITY OF PENNSYLVANIA, PHILADELPHIA, PA – LERNER CENTER, DEPARTMENT OF MUSIC

A contemporary building is paired with a revitalized 1892 building to create the Lerner Center for the Department of Music at the University of Pennsylvania. The 25,000 sq ft complex merges campus-wide departmental resources in one location, providing music students, faculty, and administrators with a new community setting for teaching, learning, and collaboration. The Lerner Center was the University's first LEED Gold on-campus building, balancing preservation and contemporary design to create a sustainable result. Design began in 2006 and construction was completed in 2010.

Background

Benjamin Franklin, a founding father of the United States and an innovative thinker, had a vision for an institution of higher education that taught not only the arts but also practical skills. This translated into the Academy and Charitable School in the Province of Pennsylvania, which opened in 1751 to educate the children of both gentry and common people. The School prospered and in 1779 became the first American institution of higher education to be named a university.[4] Outgrowing its first location in downtown Philadelphia, the University of Pennsylvania moved to another in 1802, and in 1872 to its present location in West Philadelphia. Today its property portfolio includes more than 180 buildings set in an urban campus of over 300 acres.[5]

Foulke and Long Institute Buildings

In 1900 the University purchased the Foulke and Long Institute, adjacent to its campus (Fig 5.01) and built as an industrial home for orphan girls, the daughters of Philadelphia firemen and of soldiers who had served in America's 1860–65 civil war.[6]

Constructed in 1892, the two connected buildings of the Institute were designed by the Philadelphia firm of Cope and Stewardson in a loosely Italianate aesthetic. The firm went on to design buildings for the University of Pennsylvania, Princeton University, and after winning an international competition, the entire campus of Washington University in St Louis, Missouri.

The buildings served a wide variety of academic uses for the University, including as offices and classrooms, and at one point housed a Van de Graaff generator, or 'atom smasher'. In 1967 the north building was transferred to the University's Department of Music, its interior largely demolished and renovated, and two contemporary annexes constructed. The building was renamed the 'Music Building'.[7]

Project brief

The Music Building (Figs 5.02 and 5.03) no longer met the space needs of the growing Department of Music, and following an invited competition to propose design solutions, Ann Beha Architects (ABA) of Boston was selected in 2006 and given a directive to:

Fig 5.01 The Engineering Annex, c1910

1 Music building (1892)
2 Serviced wing (c1896)
3 Music annexes (c1968)
4 Morgan building (1892)

Fig 5.02 Plan of first floor, existing conditions (2006)

1 Lerner Center
2 Seating Terrace
3 New Walkway
4 Morgan building

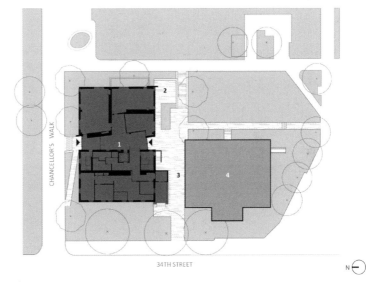

Fig 5.03 Plan of first floor, completed (2010)

- consolidate all departmental teaching and learning spaces, then dispersed throughout
  the campus
- provide an acoustically appropriate environment for the teaching, study, and practice
  of music
- create a setting to bring departmental faculty, students, and administrators together as a
  community, on a day-to-day basis and for special events
- establish a dialogue between the old and new, through the revitalization and expansion of
  the 1892 building, connecting it to the surrounding campus landscape.

ABA's work began with simultaneous space programming and existing conditions analysis, progressing to the rehabilitation and renovation of the 1892 Music Building and the design and construction of a new companion building.

Description

The 1892 building is listed on the Philadelphia Register of Historic Places and on the National Register of Historic Places, and is designated as 'contributing' to the University of Pennsylvania Campus Historic District. The project came under the review purview of the Philadelphia Historical Commission and State Historic Preservation Officer. And as the University's 'Design Guidelines' apply to all renovations and new construction on the campus, the review process also included the University architect, the University Design Review committee and its Cultural Resources sub-committee.

Demolition

The building comprised three floors, an attic, a partial basement, a rear service wing, and two annex buildings constructed in the late 1960s. The majority of the original exterior building fabric was extant; the majority of interior fabric had been removed and replaced in 1967–68. Historic research yielded information on the building's context, original design, and chronology of change, and following a thorough examination and documentation of existing conditions, a preservation strategy was developed.

Design work began with an approach targeted at retaining all of the main building, the service wing, and two annexes, to minimize the amount of additional new construction needed to meet the Department's spatial needs. However, it became apparent that the two annexes compromised planning due to their complicated internal layouts, level changes, and blockage of campus footpaths. Further research indicated that the rear service wing (originally housing support functions for the orphanage) had not been built in precise conformance to available historic documentation, and was therefore arguably of lesser contributing value to the building complex. It was successfully demonstrated through diagrams and dialogue with the historic agencies that its removal would improve the function of both the original building and its proposed expansion as a music facility. Approval was granted to demolish all three appendages, with the stipulation that the design of the expansion 'respect the massing, materials, and rhythms of the main building.'[8] These removals left the Music Building with a rectangular footprint, and its three stories, attic, and partial basement totaling 11,300 sq ft of area (Fig 5.04).

Exterior preservation and interior renovation

Cleaning and repair methods for exterior materials were tested through mock-ups. The building's bluestone water table was patched, repointed and cleaned, as was the exterior decorative brickwork and terracotta, returning the latter to their original bright red/orange color. The slate roof supported by a wood truss system in the attic was repaired, with new

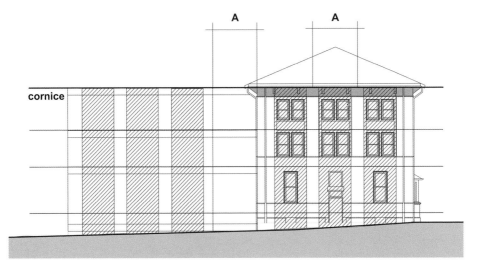

Fig 5.04 Datum line study for New Building (2006)

gutters and downspouts installed. The decorative wood brackets supporting the extended roof eaves and wood soffits, a significant contributing factor to the building's design, were repaired and restored. Following microscopic paint analysis, the wood window and door surrounds, window sash, and porch columns were painted their original red-brown color, and the roof and porch soffits their original black-green.

A range of options was considered, from repair to replacement, for the building's original windows set deeply in punched masonry openings in carefully arranged patterns across its facades. The decision was made to insulate wall cavities at window/masonry junctions, repair sashes and frames with epoxy resin consolidation, maintain their operability, install new acoustic gaskets at the top and bottom of the sashes, and add operable interior glazed panels, to improve both thermal and acoustic performance.

Existing wood floors were reinforced with additional wood joists, and the existing double-loaded corridors on each floor maintained. As original interior fabric had been previously removed, the building's interior was completely renovated. Selected columns and loadbearing interior walls were removed and replaced with steel structure to allow modifications to interior layout suited to programmatic needs.

New Building
A new 13,700 sq ft three-story building with a partial basement and concrete floor and framing structure was constructed adjacent to the existing building and connected to it (Fig 5.05). With a footprint only slightly larger than that of the 1892 building, the new building is both referential and individual. It extends the existing building's massing, materiality, rhythms and proportion. The horizontal datum lines of the brick belt courses,

Fig 5.05 New Building
concrete frame construction
(2008)

window heads, window sills and cornice are transferred to the new building. However, instead
of brick, the new building is clad with a terracotta rain-screen panel system, custom-colored
to match the brick and terracotta of the original building (Fig 5.06). Exterior sunshades and
louvers temper direct sunlight, and a metal cornice and extended eaves reference those of
the 1892 building. Because the Music Department desired a building where music is not only

Fig 5.06 New Building
exterior envelope mock-up
(2008)

Fig 5.07 View from north–east (2010)

heard but seen, its windows are large expanses of glass, providing a transparency unlike that of the punched masonry window openings of the 1892 building. Angled projecting walls on the building's east facade set a new pattern, control daylighting, and improve the interior acoustics of the practice rooms and studios located here (Fig 5.07).

Interior planning

The completed Lerner Center provides a total of 25,000 sq ft. The disposition of the functions it houses was the collective result of acoustic needs, activity zoning, existing structural constraints, and opportunities presented by new construction. The more cellular layout of the 1892 building, with its double-loaded corridors, lent itself to office needs. Despite the difficulties of creating new vertical shafts within existing structure, building services, restrooms and the elevator were located in this building, freeing up planning options in the new building for spaces requiring larger and more open footprints. A five-stop hydraulic elevator masters the lack of floor alignment between the new and old buildings. The entire building complex was made accessible per the requirements of the Pennsylvania and Philadelphia building codes, and the Americans with Disabilities Act. Mechanical systems in basement and attic spaces use hot and chilled water from the central campus system. HVAC is delivered throughout both buildings via a combination of hydronic baseboard and forced air systems, with extended ductwork to mitigate air flow sound. Both buildings are fully sprinklered with a wet system.

The most student-centered functions were located in the new building. These include three recital/classrooms, six practice rooms, computer teaching lab, graduate student room, professional/performance offices, faculty lounge, and computer lab. The glazed connector joining the new and old buildings serves as both an entrance and commons on the first floor. Additional common gathering spaces are placed on each upper floor, encouraging the interaction between students and faculty that is a pedagogic hallmark of the University of Pennsylvania.

Site design

The removal of the two annexes and service wing from the 1892 building opened vistas through the immediate campus, and made possible new footpath connections within the University's pedestrian-oriented campus. The siting of the new building frames a new campus green, a setting for gatherings and events. A south-facing terrace at the glazed entrance connector extends the campus tradition of intimately scaled transitional spaces between buildings and larger open areas on the campus. As a campus amenity, it invites others to join departmental activities, and helps heighten the visibility of the Department of Music within the University community.

Acoustic treatments

The acoustic strategy for the Lerner Center placed the most acoustically critical spaces – recital/classrooms, practice rooms and recording studios – in the new building, where the exterior envelope and interior partitions could be purpose-built to meet strict acoustic criteria. Acoustics were a significant factor in specifying a concrete floor and framing system for

Fig 5.08 Third floor Commons Space at junction of New and Old Buildings

the structure of the new building. Partitions extend from slab to slab, and for those spaces with particularly sensitive acoustical needs, double partitions with an air space between were constructed. Practice room partitions have a total of eight layers of gypsum wall board on metal studs. Audio/visual systems in the large classroom are designed to accommodate multiple functions, including instruction, performance, recording, and events.

In the existing building, acoustic interventions were designed to meet teaching and research demands, while preserving building character. Vibration isolation in walls, floors, and ceilings and new interior glazed panels in the original wood windows temper vibrations and sounds from the heavily trafficked street in front of the building. Concrete topping and new plywood subflooring were applied to existing floors to diminish sound transfer vertically. These measures, along with enhanced partitions between offices, allow faculty to do research, play instruments and hold music tutorials within their offices with minimal external sound interference (Fig 5.08).

Sustainable design
The University of Pennsylvania endorses the United States Green Building's LEED system of green building certification. The goal of LEED Silver was set initially but surpassed, making the Lerner Center the first building on Penn's central campus to receive a LEED Gold rating. Specific features of the design that contributed to its LEED status include:

Sustainable sites

- urban location; connections to public transport and pedestrian networks
- bicycle racks
- rainwater infiltration basin servicing new and existing buildings.

Water efficiency

- groundcover planting requiring no irrigation
- rain garden, and smart controllers for reduced irrigation demand
- high-efficiency restroom plumbing fixtures.

Energy and atmosphere

- post-occupancy commissioning
- 35% of electrical power usage from sustainable sources.

Materials and resources

- building reuse
- recycling/salvaging of 95% of non-hazardous construction debris

- brick, terracotta, and bluestone salvaged from demolition of service wing
- total amount of recycled content of all construction materials 10% by cost.

Indoor environmental quality

- mechanical system designed to increase ventilation to 30% above ASRAE standard 62.1
- monitoring and control of outdoor air and associated ventilation in classrooms via CO_2 sensors
- materials selected to enhance air quality of building; all adhesives, coatings, paints and carpet certified for low VOC emissions; no urea-formaldehydes in wood and fiber products
- individual lighting controls, including occupancy sensors for 90% of building occupants
- direct daylight views provided for at least 90% of building occupants
- operable windows in the 1892 building.

Other

- sustainable cleaning materials and methods implemented by the University
- sustainable furnishings.

Design team

Ann Beha Architects, Boston, MA	architects
Keast & Hood Co., Philadelphia, PA	structure
AHA Consulting Engineers, Lexington, MA	MEP
Hunt Engineering Company, East Malvern, PA	civil
Stephen Stimson Associates, Boston, MA	landscape
BCA, Inc, Philadelphia, PA	materials conservation OK
Ripman Lighting Consultants, Inc, Belmont, MA	lighting
Kirkegaard Associates, Chicago, IL	acoustical and audio visual
AHA Consulting Engineers, Lexington, MA	LEED
Wojciechowski Design, Somerville, MA	signage and graphics
Kalin Associates Inc, Newton, MA	specifications
Van Deusen & Associates, Cherry Hill, NJ	elevator
Ingersoll Rand Security Technologies, Needham, MA	hardware
The McGee Company, Chester, PA	cost estimator
Daniel J Keating Company, Narberth, PA	construction manager

MASSACHUSETTS INSITUTE OF TECHNOLOGY, BUILDING 2

The 119,000 sq ft Building 2 is part of a series of connected buildings known as the 'Main Group', MIT's historic campus core completed in 1916 (Fig 5.09). Building 2 is currently undergoing extensive exterior envelope rehabilitation as well as a comprehensive interior

Fig 5.09 Aerial view with Building 2 (2014)

renovation for the Department of Mathematics and Office of the Registrar. A rooftop addition will add 13,500 sq ft of space. Building 2 is the first of the Main Group buildings to undergo this degree of work, and will help guide future work to remaining Main Group buildings. A LEED Gold rating is anticipated. Design began in 2012 and construction will be completed in 2016.

Background

MIT is a private university founded in 1861, with a strong focus on science, engineering, technology, and associated research. Originally located in Boston's Back Bay, MIT moved across the Charles River to its new consolidated campus in Cambridge, MA, in 1916. The design of the new campus was a combination of aesthetics and pragmatics, a successful outcome attributable to two professionals – Architect William Welles Bosworth (1869–1966), and John Ripley Freeman (1855–1932), a civil engineer and member of MIT's corporate board.[9]

Beaux-Arts trained Bosworth was selected to design MIT's new campus in 1913, and developed an axial scheme with a large open courtyard facing the Charles River, surrounded by low-winged buildings focused on a central domed building. Importantly, this scheme looked to the future, providing a framework for other buildings to be added as needs evolved. The Classical Revival buildings were clad with limestone veneer, punched with distinctively tall openings for steel-framed windows and spandrels, behind which was a cast-in-place concrete structural frame. Non-loadbearing interior partitions, tall ceilings, and wide double-loaded corridors created a flexibility of plan that has served MIT well for almost 100 years.[10]

The 1916 campus plan was an unusual one. At most US academic institutions, campuses typically grew as independent buildings, as needed and purpose-built for their departments, forcing students to pass outside from one building to another.[11] The MIT campus was conceived at one time as a whole, with all buildings connected by what is known at the Institute as the 'Infinite Corridor'.

Building 2

The 119,000 sq ft building is C-shaped, with a basement and three floors, plus a small fourth floor area in a pavilion structure which is the terminus of its south wing (Figs 5.10 and 5.11). The building stands in the south–west corner of the Main Group, surrounding an outdoor courtyard and adjacent to the Charles River. The Department of Mathematics and Registrar classroom spaces together occupy 93,000 sq ft of the building, with the remaining area used by the Department of Chemistry. The majority of the Mathematics area is dedicated to offices for faculty, postgraduate, and graduate students, all of whom use their offices both for research and for teaching. The remaining Mathematics areas serve administrative and shared departmental seminar, meeting, and commons needs.

Project brief

Following a 'Request for Proposal Process', ABA was selected for the project in 2012 to address two primary goals:

- rehabilitation of the exterior building envelope, including its roof, limestone exterior cladding, and steel windows
- full interior renovation of all interior spaces, with specific goals of office size standardization, consolidation of administrative staff, consolidation of research groups, and creation of formal and informal spaces to foster intra-departmental collaboration.

1 Undergraduate Lounge
2 Classroom
3 Administrative Offices
4 Registrar Classrooms
5 Offices
6 Flat Floor Lecture Room

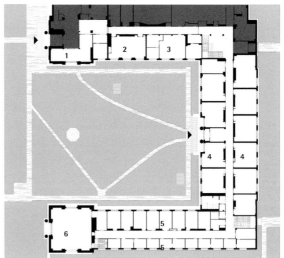

Fig 5.10 Plan of first floor, existing conditions (2012)

1 Undergraduate Lounge
2 Department Chair
3 Administrative Offices
4 Registrar Classrooms
5 Seminar Room
6 Corridor Breakout Area
7 Offices
8 Tiered Lecture Room
9 New Staircase
10 Accessible Entrance
11 Acessible Restrooms

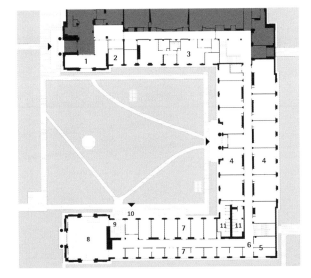

Fig 5.11 Plan of first floor, proposed renovations (2013)

Work began with a space programming and conceptual design phase, progressing to full design and construction services and the selection of all furnishings for the project.

Description
Exterior preservation
The general approach has been to preserve all building elements and features that contribute to the aesthetic and institutional heritage of the Main Group, to restore deteriorated historic elements, and to employ for all new construction a contemporary design aesthetic that is clearly differentiated from the historic aesthetic (Fig 5.12).

Exterior limestone veneer cladding and mortar joints were in need of significant repair due to natural weathering and cracking from building settlement, the use of Portland cement mortar

Fig 5.12 View of South Wing from north–west, existing conditions (2013)

Fig 5.13 Section through South Wing with proposed new fourth floor and renovated lower floors (2013)

instead of lime mortar during more recent repairs, and exfoliation and rust-jacking of steel angles attaching limestone to its brick backup (Figs 5.13 and 5.14). The steel windows had experienced varying degrees of degradation due to failed glazing, exterior water infiltration, and interior condensation.

A separate 'Facade and Window Project' had already been completed by MIT. Its purpose was to assess envelope issues prior to the rehabilitation of the exterior of Building 2 and ultimately of all Main Group buildings. A 'mock-down' phase of the project removed the original single-glazed steel windows in three of the most climatically exposed bays of Building 2. This revealed existing conditions and allowed exterior, as well as interior, conditions of adjacent masonry to be assessed.

Based on the information gathered in the mock-down, a 'mock-up' was completed with three window options ranging from restoration of an original window to replication of the original

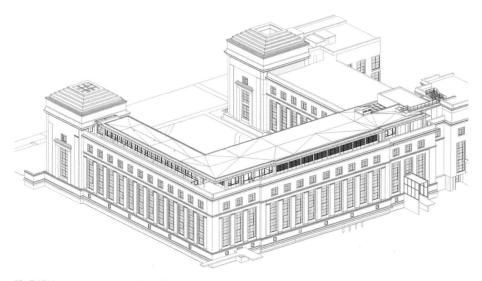

Fig 5.14 Axonometric with new fourth floor

design with a new window, using galvanized steel attachment angles that transferred wind load to the structure, per the latest Massachusetts building code. The new window option was selected, with vacuum glass panels. Sashes remained operable, to allow building occupants to temper the amount of fresh air, an MIT prerequisite and key component of the sustainability approach for the project. Masonry repair standards were developed and codified, and moisture sensors installed, to assess the impact of seasonal change on the building envelope. Ultimately, no additional insulation was added to the exterior walls. The results of the mock-up have set the standard for all subsequent limestone rehabilitation, and the replacement of all windows for the Main Group.

Interior renovation
The original and pragmatic corridor treatment creates a memorable experience in all buildings in the Main Group. Concrete structure is exposed, as are building utilities running at high level. Floors and bases are terrazzo, and walls are plastered with doors and frames painted black. Translucent glass, mostly original, in doors, transoms, and adjacent clerestory panels provides a high level of natural light in the corridors. The approach for Building 2 is to maintain the historic finishes and off-white paint color, with doors reconditioned with their traditional black paint, and fitted with new accessible hardware. As the original light fixtures had been previously replaced, new LED fixtures will be installed. Accent paint colors in selected locations, new graphics and artwork will help identify the Department of Math as its own place within the Infinite Corridor. A new sculpture by Antony Gormley will be installed in the north–east staircase of Building 2, through MIT's 'Percent-for-Art Program'. Interventions include the removal of an original staircase and the installation of a new one for improved egress, and the removal of offices at the end of the north–south corridor on three floors, providing vistas to the exterior and breakout/gathering spaces outside new corner seminar rooms.

Demolition of intermediate room partitions has been minimized. New finishes have been chosen for their low emissivity and recycled content. The new thermally improved windows, with solar shading integral in their glass, will receive new interior venetian blinds, of similar design to those installed in 1916. New LED lighting on occupancy sensors and individual HVAC controls in each office will optimize occupant comfort. Existing slate blackboards have been salvaged and will be reinstalled. Full furniture mock-ups using two different vendors were provided, to test the assumptions of interior layouts for faculty offices. A desk system using locally sourced furniture made from native cherry wood has been selected and will be installed in all faculty offices (Fig 5.15).

A large new Faculty Commons will be located on the second floor of the Pavilion at the west end of Building 2 (Fig 5.16). The original concrete structure of the floor above will be exposed above floating wood 'cloud' ceilings that will carry recessed lighting. New maple wood wall paneling and new cherry wood floors will be installed. Additional new meeting spaces on every floor will provide space for graduate students to tutor undergraduates and to carry out collaborative study and research.

Fig 5.15 Mock-up of proposed faculty office furnishings (2014)

Rooftop expansion

Space programming at the start of the project identified a square footage need for the Department of Mathematics greater than could be provided by Building 2. Reducing MIT's office size standards, as well as reconfiguring existing interior layouts, were investigated. The introduction of a mezzanine level – found space within the tall first floor – was proposed. After a full-scale mock-up was created, this concept was ultimately rejected as too intrusive on the building's interior ambience.

As neither lateral nor underground expansions were practical, vertical expansion was investigated. Structural calculations revealed that a fourth floor could be added on the

Fig 5.16 Proposed second floor Faculty Commons (2013)

Fig 5.17 Mock-up of proposed new fourth floor exterior envelope (2014)

building's roof (Fig 5.17). Design studies and negotiations with the City of Cambridge Historical Commission resulted in a new floor with 13,500 sq ft of additional space, sufficient to meet the Department's anticipated future space needs without increasing the building footprint. The resultant design, with its low profile roof and solar shading, will provide faculty offices, seminar room, commons space and connection to renovated graduate office space in the west pavilion, a space whose occupants were previously disconnected from the rest of the Mathematics community. A large mechanical room will hide rooftop equipment, while corridors and a roof terrace will provide superb views of the Charles River and Boston skyline. The expectation is that the new fourth floor on Building 2 will serve as a prototype for future rooftop expansions on other Main Group buildings.

The renovated building and new fourth floor will provide the Department of Mathematics with 131 office spaces for a total of 270 faculty, postgraduate and graduate students, and administrators. In addition to new informal gathering spaces along corridors, the Department will have an undergraduate lounge, 2 seminar rooms, 18 meeting rooms, a faculty commons, faculty seminar room, and departmental commons. Ten renovated classrooms and a new 134-seat tiered lecture hall will be shared by Mathematics and other departments at MIT.

Building systems
MIT's central utility plant will continue to provide electricity, steam, and chilled water to existing basement mechanical spaces in Building 2 and to the new mechanical space on the fourth floor. Offices and other perimeter spaces will utilize passive or active chilled beams, heat recovery and variable speed ventilation. Hot water radiation is provided along the building's perimeter, under the new operable windows. New accessible restrooms with high-efficiency water-saving fixtures will be provided on all floors.

Sustainability
MIT endorses the United States Green Building's LEED system of green building certification. The goal of LEED Gold has been set for Building 2. Some of the specific features of the design that will contribute to this LEED status include:

Sustainable sites

- public transportation access
- bicycle storage and changing rooms
- replanting of landscape with native species
- heat island effect (roof and non-roof).

Water efficiency

- low-flow and sensor-activated fixtures
- 35% water reduction.

Energy and atmosphere

- replicated steel windows, thermally-broken with glazing and infiltration improvements
- chilled beam cooling
- enhanced commissioning
- LED fixtures
- sub-metering for departmental electrical usage
- occupancy sensors for lighting in all workspaces
- heat rejection louvers at skylights.

Materials and resources

- building reuse
- construction waste management (75%)
- recycled content (10%) and regional materials (10%)
- salvaged wood doors and interior glazing.

Indoor environmental quality

- outdoor air delivery monitoring and increased ventilation
- indoor air quality management
- low-emitting materials
- daylight-responsive lighting
- increased daylight and improved views
- enhanced ventilation.

Other

- green housekeeping
- educational programming.

Design team

Ann Beha Architects, Boston, MA	architects
Stephen J Wessling Architects, Inc, Waltham, MA	exterior envelope
Robert Silman Associates, Boston, MA	structure
WSP, Boston, MA	MEP/FP, tel/data
Nitsch Engineering, Inc, Boston, MA	civil
Halvorson Design Partnership, Inc, Boston, MA	landscape
Speweik Preservation Consultants, Inc, Chicago, IL	masonry
Horton Lees Brogden Lighting Design, Boston, MA	lighting
Acentech, Inc, Cambridge, MA	acoustics
RDK Engineers, Boston, MA	audio/visual
Wil-Spec, LLC, Lynnfield, MA	specifications
The Green Engineer, Inc, Concord, MA	sustainable design
Hughes Associates, Inc, Marlborough, MA	code
AM Fogarty & Associates, Hingham, MA	cost
Campbell-McCabe, Waltham, MA	hardware
Bond Brothers Construction, Waltham, MA	construction managers

UNIVERSITY OF CHICAGO, CHICAGO, IL – SAIEH HALL FOR ECONOMICS

Saieh Hall has created a new setting for interdisciplinary economics research, teaching, collaboration and global outreach. It combines the University's Department of Economics, the Becker Friedman Institute for Research in Economics, the Energy Policy Institute at Chicago, and the Center for the Economics of Human Development. The 150,000 sq ft complex incorporates the adaptive reuse of an existing Gothic Revival building (previously the Chicago Theological Seminary) (Fig 5.18), above-ground and below-ground additions, two adjacent existing houses and a new research pavilion wing. Extensive site and landscape design included the rerouting of a city alley, as well as the conversion of a city street to a pedestrian way that joins the new Center to the adjacent University campus. A LEED Silver rating is anticipated. Design began in 2010, Phase 1 was completed in 2014, and Phase 2 was completed in 2015.

Background

The University of Chicago's founding in 1890 was an initiative that combined both religious and private investment interests. It was the creation of the American Baptist Education

Fig 5.18 Aerial View, c1957

Society and John D Rockefeller, founder of the Standard Oil Corporation, who described his donation as 'the best investment I ever made'.[12] Land in Hyde Park, south of Chicago's central Loop area and west of Lake Michigan, was donated by Marshall Field, the owner of the Chicago department store of the same name. The vision of the University's first President, William Rainey Harper, was for 'a modern research university, combining an English-style undergraduate college and a German-style graduate research institute'.[13]

The University's charter incorporated a commitment to gender equality for both undergraduate and graduate education and a commitment to non-sectarianism and equal opportunity. Students were initially drawn from the Midwest, mostly the children of merchants and professionals. Chicago-based architect Henry Ives Cobb was selected to design the new campus. Working with President Harper, Cobb designed a series of quadrangles in the English Gothic style, an implied link to English academic precursors for this new institution with no heritage, located on the edge of a large city in a Midwestern state.[14]

The Chicago Theological Center Building
Affiliated with the United Church of Christ, the Chicago Theological Center (CTS) was founded in Chicago in 1855, with the mission of training ministers to serve on what was then America's western frontier. The CTS chose a site in Hyde Park for its new headquarters and the Chicago architectural firm of Herbert H Riddle, completing its building at 5757 South University Avenue in three phases between 1923 and 1928. The University purchased the CTS building in 2008 (Figs 5.19 and 5.20).

Project brief
The building, referred to hereafter as the '5757 Building', occupies a site geographically strategic for the University on the edge of its campus, surrounded by the Booth School of Business, the Oriental Institute, and Frank Lloyd Wright's Robie House. The project required repurposing of this ecclesiastic building,[15] with specific criteria from the University:

1 Chicago Theological
  Seminary (West)
2 Chicago Theological
  Seminary (East)
3 Nursery School

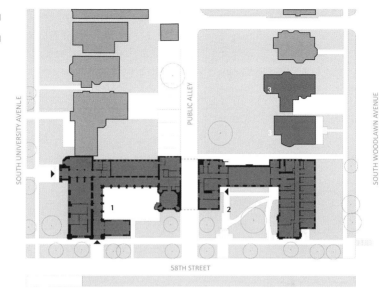

Fig 5.19 Plan of first floor, existing conditions (2010)

1 Main Lobby/Saieh Hall
2 Research Pavillion
3 Below Grade Classroom
4 Below Grade Mechanical
  Space
5 5749 South Woodlawn Ave
6 5740 South Woodlawn Ave

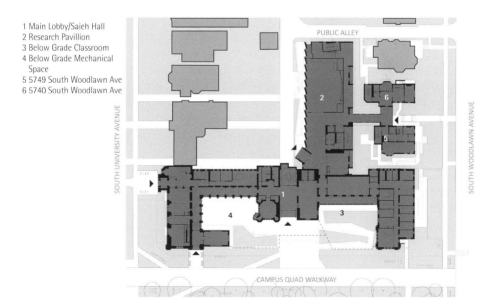

Fig 5.20 Plan of first floor, completed (2014)

- Renovate, adaptively reuse, and expand the 5757 Building to provide a physical home for the Milton Friedman Institute for Research in Economics and for the Department of Economics.
- Create an environment to promote connectivity with other programs in the University's Booth School of Business, Law School, Harris School of Public Policy and Stevanovich Center for Financial Mathematics.

Ann Beha Architects of Boston, in association with Gensler of Chicago, were selected for the project in 2010. Work commenced immediately with space programming, followed by full design and construction services, including the selection and specification of all furniture.

Description

The four floors (plus attic and basement) of the 5757 Building provided a total area of 77,000 sq ft. Constructed of reinforced cast-in-place concrete, the building has multi-wythe masonry walls and a roof of precast concrete planks supported by built-up steel trusses. Selected areas of its first floor are constructed with loadbearing vaulted tile systems manufactured by the Guastavino Fireproof Construction Company.[16]

Much of the building's exterior design – a mélange of Gothic, Jacobean and Tudor interpretations – referenced nearby structures on the University of Chicago campus. The interior of the building offered some highly crafted and distinctive ecclesiastic and academic spaces, while the remainder of the building was dedicated to classrooms, offices and dormitory rooms, all with basic finishes and low ceilings.

The building footprint is distinguished by its length – essentially a full city block long – and by its narrow width. Single-loaded corridors run along the length of most floors, with double-loaded corridors on upper floors leading to dormitory rooms in the wider wing at its east end. The building's narrow width, while offering ample natural light for interior spaces, had always been problematic, forcing passage through rooms on the first and second floors to get from one end of the building to the other. Furthermore, the building had no single entry, and due to the public alley running through its center, there was neither connection nor disabled access between its east and west sides on the lower floors.

Exterior and interior rehabilitation

The 5757 Building is not listed on the National Register of Historic Places but is within a National Historic District, the Hyde Park–Kenwood Historic District. As well, the Chicago Historical Commission designated the building as 'a place that has some architectural feature or historical association making it potentially significant in the context of the surrounding community'.[17]

Exterior rehabilitation focused on all aspects of the building envelope. The existing slate roof was removed and a new roof of Vermont slate was installed. Exterior masonry was assessed, and while the bricks were generally in good condition, mortar was replaced comprehensively and selected limestone coping, cornice caps and headers repaired and replaced. Building energy modeling revealed that the greatest source of wintertime heat loss was not through the masonry walls but through the windows. Ultimately, no insulation was added to the walls, and thermal improvement of the windows was prioritized. The windows on the building were original, mostly single-glazed steel casements with lead caming. As a significant contributing attribute to the building's aesthetic, the initial plan was to restore and retrofit them with interior storm panels, leaving their exterior appearance the same. Three other options were explored, including replacement of the existing windows with new thermally broken, double-glazed ones of similar appearance. Options were weighed from sustainable, historic, cost and operability standpoints, and the replacement strategy was selected for steel windows in rectangular openings. Those in openings with arched and other geometries were repaired and interior storm panels added.

The building's 82 stained glass windows were fabricated by the Willet Studio of West Philadelphia.[18] Providentially, they had been installed originally as panels in rabbeted grooves within the frames of the windows, with the anticipation of removal at some point for cleaning. Those with the more secular messages and several with religious motifs were removed, cleaned, re-leaded as required, and reinstalled with clear glass exterior panels and solar film. The remaining windows were removed and reinstalled in CTS's new building and in the chapel of a local medical center. These were replaced with new windows of similar muntin pattern but with clear or translucent glass, adding significantly to natural light levels within the building and to occupant comfort.

The interior rehabilitation prioritized the most character-defining spaces in the building – the distinctive spaces mentioned above with the most extant detail and highest level of contributing craft (Figs 5.21 and 5.22). Finishes were cleaned and, where necessary, repaired. This included cleaning and selected in-color painting of the Guastavino vaulted tile ceilings. The majority of remaining spaces in the building, especially at its east end – originally meeting rooms and dormitory rooms – were deemed to be non-contributing to the architectural character of the building, and therefore malleable and eligible for change as required by the needs of the University.

Renovation and new construction
The initial space programming phase of the project determined that roughly twice the amount of square footage of the original CTS building was needed to meet the demands of the Department of Economics and the Becker Friedman Institute. Options were developed with the goal of minimizing the amount of new construction. The resulting solution was a combination of 'found' space in the attic of the original building, new underground and aboveground additions, the incorporation of two adjacent houses owned

Fig 5.21 Second floor
Graduate Commons,
previously the Chapel (2014)

Fig 5.22 Second floor Tiered
Lecture Room, previously the
Library (2014)

by the University, and the construction of a research annex wing to the north of the seminary building:

5757 South University Avenue Building	77,000
Build-out of attic at 5757 Building	3,600
New aboveground area at 5757 Building	9,600
New underground area at 5757 Building	9,800
House (5750 South Woodlawn Avenue)	6,300
House (5740 South Woodlawn Avenue)	6,100
New Research Pavilion	38,000
Total GSF	150,400

The building complex provides 107 offices, 54 administrative spaces, 207 graduate student and research workspaces, and 22 instructional spaces (Fig 5.20). The large chapel was repurposed as student commons (Fig 5.21), the small chapel as a conference room, the cloister as a graduate student lounge, and the library as a tiered classroom (Fig 5.22). The awkwardness of passing through primary spaces to get from one end of the building to the other in the original plan was corrected by adding new glazed passages to the exterior of the building that double as informal seating areas. The attic, previously unoccupied, was renovated as a shared graduate student office space (Fig 5.23). An area in the front of the building was excavated to provide a new underground top-lit tiered classroom space, too large to fit within the confines of the existing building's narrow footprint. Permission was granted to close the public alley that ran through the center of the building, bifurcating the first and second floors. The space occupied by the alley was infilled with a vestibule, generous lobby, cafe and open staircase connecting all floors. This gave the building the primary central entrance that it had never had, as well as much-needed clarity of exterior and interior way-finding and disabled access. Other than renovations for new restrooms and building support spaces, the remaining areas of the building were renovated with new partitions and finishes as offices and meeting spaces.

Fig 5.23 Fifth floor Graduate Lofts, previously attic storage (2014)

Fig 5.24 View from south–east (2014)

The exterior of the renovated and expanded 5757 Building remains recognizable as the original CTS building, while changes to it are clearly stated, in line with the *Secretary of Interior's Standards for Rehabilitation* (Fig 5.24).[19] New construction is referential to the massing, detail, and materiality of the original building, though distinctly contemporary and of its time.

Research Pavilion wing

This new building is placed in the interior of the city block, behind a row of existing houses, thus preserving the residential scale and cadence of South Woodlawn Avenue (Fig 5.25). It is a reinforced concrete structure with three stories and a basement. Its contemporary

Fig 5.25 View from north, proposed New Research Pavilion (2013)

exterior is clad with a combination of aluminum composite panels and glazed curtainwall system. Angled terracotta panels on its west wall temper strong afternoon sunlight and animate the facade, while three large roof monitors provide top-lighting to interior office spaces on the third floor.

The Research Pavilion connects the 5757 Building and two houses, and offers additional exterior entrances and connections to the surrounding campus. The floors of the annex align with those of the 5757 Building, for full accessibility. Interior circulation is selectively diverted to the sides of the annex to double as light-filled gathering spaces, supporting the collaborative intent of the department. The remaining space in the building is used for classrooms, seminar rooms, offices and research spaces. The basement provides more space for research assistants and mechanical areas.

Houses (5740 and 5750 South Woodlawn Avenue)
Constructed in 1895 and 1896, two adjacent houses on the north side of the 5757 Building had been serving as a nursery school for the children of University employees. These have been repurposed for administrative and research purposes for the Center for the Economics of Human Development, a program within the Department of Economics. Each house has three floors and a basement, with exterior masonry bearing walls. Their wood-framed floors and roofs were reinforced with sistered wood joists and steel. Interior layouts, staircases and historic fabric remain largely intact, with an egress staircase added in each. A new glazed ramped corridor connects them to the Research Pavilion and also serves as the entrance to the two buildings.

Building systems, life safety and accessibility
The existing steam radiator heating system, as well as plumbing and electrical systems in the 5757 Building, were antiquated and removed in their entirety. As there had never been central air conditioning in the building, unsightly and inefficient window units had been used throughout. Building systems in the two houses were also antiquated and were removed (Figs 5.23, 5.24 and 5.25).

Hot and chilled water are provided by plants located on the University campus. The renovated 5757 Building and Research Pavilion utilize a combination of two HVAC systems, active chilled beams with supplemental perimeter radiation, with select areas of both buildings on a VAV system. The houses utilize a VAV system with units in the basement of each. All restrooms are new.

All spaces were made accessible via elevators and/or ramped walkways. The buildings were fully sprinklered, though in select historic spaces, where the installation of sprinklers was not possible without serious loss of historic ceiling fabric, a compliance alternative was negotiated with the Chicago Fire Department to install infrared cameras and alarms for fire detection.

Site design
The city alley behind the building was rerouted, so that it no longer runs through the center of the building. The street in front of the building was closed to traffic and repaved, and now serves as a block-long pedestrian way and outdoor events space, connecting and extending the reach of the campus. New plantings were selected for their hardiness and appropriateness for the climate, and trees removed due to new construction were replaced with new trees.

Sustainability
The University has established a policy that supports sustainability in its building construction and renovation projects, and utilizes the United States Green Building LEED Certification System to guide sustainable renovation and construction on its campus. LEED Silver certification is pending:

Sustainable sites

- public transit access
- bicycle storage and changing rooms
- site open space (over 20%)
- storm water management system (under 58th Street)
- heat island effect/non-roof reduction (light-colored pavers)
- vegetated roofing on Research Pavilion roof monitors.

Water efficiency

- water reduction (over 35%/ Phase 1, 20%/Phase 2)
- water-efficient landscaping.

Energy and atmosphere

- chilled beams
- building envelope upgrades (new and restored windows, new roof)
- enhanced commissioning
- enhanced refrigerant management.

Materials and resources

- building reuse
- storage and collection of recyclables
- construction waste management
- materials selection (20% recycled content, 20% regional, low-emitting).

Indoor environmental quality

- outdoor air delivery monitoring
- construction indoor Air Quality Plan (during construction and before occupancy)
- controllability of systems
- controllability of lighting.

Other

- double transit ridership
- Green Housekeeping
- reduced mercury in lamps
- diverted waste management (over 95%)
- green power (35%).

Design team

Ann Beha Architects, Boston, MA	lead architects
Gensler, Chicago, IL	associate architects
Thorton Tomasetti, Inc., Chicago, IL	structure
dbHMS, Chicago, IL	MEP
OLIN, Philadelphia, PA	landscape
Burnham/The Code Group, Chicago, IL	code
ArchiTech Consulting, Inc., Mt. Prospect, IL	specifications
CCS International, Inc, Oakbrook Terrace, IL	cost estimator
Terra Engineering Ltd, Chicago, IL	civil
Superior Engineering, Hammond, IN	steam system
Harboe Architects, Chicago, IL	exterior envelope
BCA Inc, Philadelphia, PA	materials conservation
Mary Clerkin Higgins, New York, NY	stained glass conservation
John Weiler & Associates, Chicago, IL	pipe organ
Schuler Shook, Chicago, IL	lighting
Kirkegaard Associates, Chicago, IL	acoustical
Shem Milson Wilke LLC, Chicago, IL	audio-visual
Gensler, Chicago, IL	FF&E, signage and graphics, LEED
Syska Hennessy, Chicago, IL	elevator
Turner Construction Company, Chicago, IL	construction manager

PHILLIPS EXETER ACADEMY, EXETER, NH – CLASS OF 1945 LIBRARY

Louis Kahn's library has been a central and cherished place for the Exeter community since it opened in 1971 (Fig 5.26). It is widely considered to be one of the most significant

Fig 5.26 View from south (2015)

20th-century buildings in the US. An Interior Rehabilitation Plan was completed in 2004 following an extensive exterior envelope repair and preservation project. A comprehensive master plan for the Library building was undertaken in 2013 and will be completed in 2015. As part of this plan a series of 'pilot projects' were identified, designed to test proposed renovation assumptions. The first of these, a Library Commons and cafe on the ground floor of the Library, was completed in 2015.

Background

Located in Exeter, 55 miles north of Boston, Phillips Exeter Academy was founded in 1781, and today is a private co-educational high school for over 1,000 boarding and day students. The campus includes more than 100 buildings organized around greens and building quadrangles, many designed by the historicist architect Ralph Adams Cram (1863–1942). His red brick neo-Georgian-style buildings give the campus much of its character and have influenced the design of subsequent buildings on the campus, including the Class of 1945 Library.[20]

The Class of 1945 Library

Having outgrown its Davis Library building designed in 1912 by Cram, the Academy formed a committee in 1964 to develop a program for a new library building and to recommend an architect to Academy trustees. The final design brief published in 1966 by the committee provided an exceptionally comprehensive design intent for the building, and in many ways presaged user-centric trends in library operations today:

> emphasis should not be on housing books but on housing readers using books. It is therefore desirable to seek an environment that would encourage and insure the pleasure of reading and study.[21]

Leading modernist American architects of time were considered – Edward Durell Stone, Paul Rudolph, IM Pei, Edward Larrabee Barnes, Philip Johnson and Louis Kahn.[22] Kahn was selected to design the new Library, which opened in 1971 (Fig 5.27).

Fig 5.27 Rockefeller Hall (2014)

Project brief

After 44 years of sustained use, the library interior is in need of refurbishment, building systems require updating and current standards of disabled accessibility need consideration. Furthermore, the changing ways in which students study and the changing nature of library collections are prompting repurposing of the building's interior. As the task in total is a large one, the Academy's intent is to first study the building, then develop options and finally recommend a phased strategy for the building's renewal and operations. Specific criteria include:

- space programming study that takes into account both changing student needs and the evolving nature of academic libraries
- conceptual design for restoration and renovation that balances change, preservation, sustainability and the original design intent of Louis Kahn
- a scope of work and cost for total building renewal, including all buildings systems, millwork, finishes and furniture
- specific 'pilot projects' that can be initiated immediately, to test the premises of study and serve as prototypes for change throughout the building.

Ann Beha Architects were selected by the Academy in 2013. The master plan will build on ABA's 2004 Interior Rehabilitation Plan and the first completed pilot project, the Library Commons, and be finalized in 2015.

Description

Existing conditions

The Library building has an area of 96,000 sq ft, with a total of nine levels, six of which wrap around Rockefeller Hall, the central atrium space, which is the striking focus of the building's interior (Fig 5.28). Four of these six levels were designated for book stacks, making books very 'present' in the Library, seen through large circular openings in the building's concrete structure. Louis Kahn's 'deeply personal appreciation for the idea of the book drove the design of the library at the deepest level'.[23] Circulation aisles circumnavigate Rockefeller Hall on the upper stack levels. Between the stacks and the building's perimeter, Kahn placed reading areas and study carrels where they had the maximum benefit of natural light: 'Kahn often spoke of the ritual of "bringing the book to the light", and this was an especially graceful expression of the process.'[24]

The exterior is clad with brick masonry, with teak wood window frames and spandrel panels. The interior palette is simple, with the building's exposed concrete and brick structure serving as the primary wall and ceiling finishes. Paneling, doors, and millwork are all white oak. The ground-floor entry, main staircase and Rockefeller Hall have travertine floors, while floors in corner entries and stairs are polished concrete and slate.Floors elsewhere are finished with wool carpet in three different colors. All metalwork in the building has a pewter-colored finish, including the building's exposed air ducts. Original furniture, both built-in and loose, is still in use.

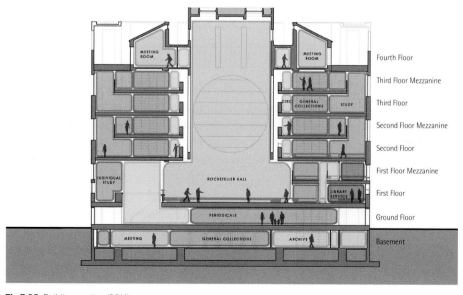

Fig 5.28 Building section (2014)

The Class of 1945 Library and its place in the history of modernist architecture are strongly valued by the Academy. The building has remained essentially the same as it was when it opened in 1971, through ongoing maintenance and repairs. In 2002 a major rehabilitation of the exterior envelope addressed issues caused by water infiltration. New flashing and membranes were installed, windows were removed and reconditioned with new glazing, exterior woodwork refurbished, and oak millwork on the inner side of the exterior walls repaired and reconditioned. Further to ABA's 2004 Plan, the current study recommends re-conditioning of remaining wood millwork, replacement of carpet, and cleaning of all exposed concrete and masonry.

Interior planning recommendations
The Library's interior is a carefully conceived composition of interrelated spaces, reflective of Louis Kahn's vision for the building. Potential changes to room layout are challenging, both for this reason and because most interior partitions are in fact loadbearing concrete or masonry walls. The preservation strategy adopted for the Library is a straightforward one: restore finishes, install new building systems as seamlessly as possible, minimize space changes and make them reversible whenever possible, all with the preservation of Louis Kahn's original design intent a high priority (Fig 5.30). Changes being considered are related to current building operations, to the specific needs of high school students, and to phenomena that libraries all over the world are facing:

- The Class of 1945 Library building is an international destination for architects and visitors. Its main entrance is not clear, as it is located behind the ground floor arcade. Upon entering the building, wayfinding is further complicated by the location of the main information desk and majority of staff a floor above in Rockefeller Hall. No changes to the building entrance are proposed; however, research of the original landscape plan (never implemented) is under way and this may inform a design strategy for guiding building users more clearly to the main entrance. A comprehensive graphics and signage plan for the Library is recommended by the master plan.
- Acoustics are a major issue in the Library, as sound travels easily through the building's open plan. This is in conflict with the increasing emphasis on student group projects that involve dialogue and the need for acoustically separate collaborative spaces. New glass-enclosed group project rooms are proposed for selected locations on upper floors where book stacks can be repurposed due to decreasing print collections. Other enclosed project spaces are proposed for alcoves around the building's perimeter where brick archways can be easily (and reversibly) infilled with glass doors and transom panels, all with minimal impact on existing fabric.
- Most students now prefer to study together at shared tables, not in conversation but 'alone together', versus studying alone at individual study carrels, as was the case when the building was designed. Retrofits to selected carrel areas are proposed, creating shared work areas where students can study together quietly. Elsewhere, simple furniture changes will accommodate shared study.

- A key feature of an Exeter education is the Harkness table, a collaborative learning setting whereby classes of 12 students gather with a faculty member around an oval table for dialogue and interaction. Faculty hold classes in the Library, and additional Harkness table settings are planned. There is also a growing need for teaching spaces that are more flexible and technology intensive. Some of this demand will be met with group project spaces, and elsewhere by the creation of new class areas with tables and chairs that can be easily reconfigured, and a full complement of audio/visual equipment.
- At Exeter – and at most libraries – the role of the librarian is no longer focused on the conveyancing of printed material, but on helping users find information and research. The master plan proposes new technology stations where a librarian and student can work side-by-side, sharing a computer screen, as well as settings for bibliographic instruction classes. Also proposed is the consolidation of reference and circulation at one single service point, the Help Desk, in Rockefeller Hall with additional side-by-side consultation stations.
- The approach to furnishings in the Library is a composite one. Antique furniture currently in the building and part of the Academy's collection will be relocated to be more visible. Selected furniture items that date from the building's opening in 1971 will be refurbished. New furniture will be purchased, compatible with IT needs and on wheels, and reconfigurable in response to changing study and teaching needs. The role of furniture in promoting flexibility of use is especially important in this relatively inflexible building designed for a particular way of operation in 1971.
- Special collections and archives are taking on a new importance in terms of curricula in many academic libraries in the US, and becoming destinations for outside scholars. Unlike general collections, where the trend is toward electronic format, special collections by nature most often grow in print format. This has been the case with Exeter's collections, which are currently stored in several locations in the building and growing. The master plan proposes to consolidate these collections on the basement level, where conditions are dry and the floor structure offers the only opportunity in the building to support the weight of space-efficient compact stacks. A separately zoned climate control system is proposed, to provide consistent humidity and temperature for these collections. Unification of the collections will make a higher level of security possible, consolidate staffing, and, with proposed instructional and exhibition spaces, allow the excellence and breadth of the Academy's collections to be leveraged.

Building systems, life safety and accessibility

Most buildings on the Exeter campus are served by a central chilled water and steam system. The majority of the Library's mechanical equipment is located in the adjacent Elm Street Dining Hall building (designed by Louis Kahn at the same time as the Library) and connected to the Library by means of a utility tunnel leading to four mechanical spaces in the corners of the building in a sub-basement level.

Assessments of all building systems – HVAC, electrical, lighting, and plumbing – generally recommend replacement, as most are beyond their expected useful lives. The challenges of integrating new energy-efficient systems into the building's open plan are significant, and a complete strategy for this has yet to be finalized. The power service to the building is inadequate, and stressed by growing power needs of both Library equipment and laptops now used by all students. Replacement is complicated as most wiring is embedded in concrete structure. Lighting throughout the building is antiquated, and replacement with LED fixtures is recommended. A building-wide wireless data system has been installed, and the routing of wiring has been an ongoing visual issue, given the building's open plan and its interior finishes of exposed concrete and masonry. Closets and telephone booths that are no longer needed have been seconded for equipment, and exposed wiring and apparatuses will be reorganized for minimal visual impact.

Life safety and accessibility requirements for academic libraries have changed significantly since 1971. The building's code challenges have been identified, and chief among these are the lack of sprinklers and the open interior plan. The building is 'grandfathered' – that is, protected to a degree by its age and the codes in place at the time of construction. A strategy is being developed that takes into account this status as well as the Academy's campus-wide program for code upgrades.

Pilot projects
As a means of testing the assumptions and recommendations of the master plan, a series of trial projects were developed for immediate implementation. These involve prototypical building interventions that include changes of use in selected areas of the Library building and corresponding renovations, new furniture and upgrades to finishes (Figs 5.29 and 5.30).

Fig 5.29 Ground floor periodicals room (2014)

Fig 5.30 Library Commons (2015)

The first of these pilot projects, the Library Commons, has been completed (Figs 5.31 and 5.32). Originally designed as a reading area for the periodicals collection, the ground floor has been transformed as an informal student hub, with collaborative study and teaching spaces, lounge seating and a coffee area. The layout of the floor has remained the same, with the majority of the change accomplished with new carpeting and furnishings, rehabilitated finishes and millwork, with some created from sustainable wood products and recycled content.

1 Entrance Lobby
2 Reading & Lecture
3 Periodicals
4 Office
5 Work Room

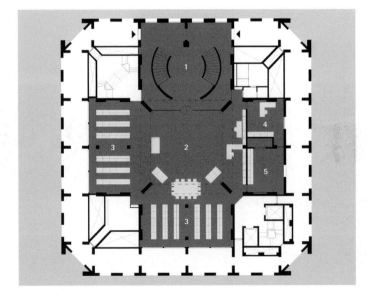

Fig 5.31 Ground floor plan of Periodicals Room, existing conditions (2012)

1 Entrance Lobby
2 Reading & Lecture
3 Open Classrom
4 Cafe
5 Harkness Classroom
6 Work Room

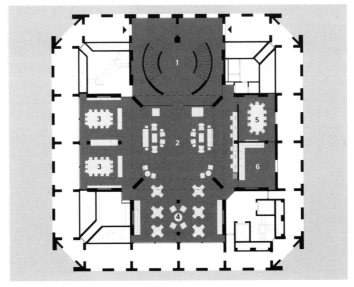

Fig 5.32 Ground floor plan of proposed Library Commons (2014)

An office has been repurposed as a Harkness classroom. A storage space has been reserved as a future kitchen support space, in expectation that the current simple coffee service will prove popular with students and faculty, and evolve as a cafe.

Existing fluorescent lighting fixtures hung below concrete ceiling coffers have been replaced with LED fixtures raised into the coffers, to help increase the sense of height in this low-ceilinged space. These new fixtures have reduced the draw on power, a significant step toward building-wide energy savings, and serve as a potential prototype for future lighting elsewhere in the building (Fig 5.33).

Fig 5.33 LED Lighting (2014)

Sustainability on the Phillips Exeter Academy campus
The Academy has developed an Environmental Mission Statement committed to integrating sustainability and environmental stewardship into all aspects of school life. The Academy's goal is to create for the campus a more sustainable environment that reduces energy use and cost, improves the health and wellness of students, faculty and staff, and provides effective environmental and sustainability education for the Academy community.

The Academy has developed a LEED-based policy, 'Guiding Principles for Sustainable Construction', for all renovation and new construction on its campus, as well as a Green Cleaning Program that uses third-party cleaning products and a sustainable purchasing policy. Recent actions include:[25]

- conversion to natural gas from oil in its central plant, resulting in a reduction in greenhouse gas emissions of 63%
- installation of 40 geothermal wells for heating and cooling classroom buildings
- campus-wide recycling; elimination of use and sale of plastic water bottles; composting at the Dining Hall
- energy audits of key high-use buildings and plans for campus-wide metering
- a curriculum of environmental education through science, technology, mathematics, economics and humanities
- Academy programming; 'E-Proctors' in every residential dormitory; and a full-time safety and environmental compliance manager to monitor indoor air quality and efficiency of campus and building systems
- partnerships with local, state and federal entities on best practices for sustainability and environmental stewardship; outreach to the community through environmental education with speakers, film series and campus events.

The Academy's policies for sustainability continue to inform the preservation goals and proposed renovations for Class of 1945 Library. A full LEED checklist and sustainable goals for the Library building are being developed for the Master Plan.

Design team

Ann Beha Architects, Boston, MA	architects
Robert Silman Associates, Boston, MA	structure
Rist-Frost-Shumway, PC Engineering, Laconia, NH	MEP/FP
RW Sullivan Engineering, Boston, MA	code
Brightspot Strategy LLC, New York, NY	organizational strategy
Sladen Feinstein Integrated Lighting	lighting
Crabtree McGrath Associates, Georgetown, MA	food service
Wayne Towle, Needham, MA	wood restoration
Shawmut Design and Construction, Boston, MA	estimating and construction manager

CLOSING

While the intent of this chapter is to present four independent building case studies that speak to heritage and sustainability, comparisons yield some common threads shared by all:

- While institutional mission was the engine of change for building transformation, heritage and sustainability were at the forefront. Excellent clients, for whom these issues matter deeply, certainly facilitated design and implementation. Their clear visions for outcome and their openness to collaborative design processes are defining the success of these projects.
- The existing buildings are all authoritative in design, built for specific purposes, tangible products of their eras, each with a distinct history. A shared goal of both clients and architects was to ensure that this history remain visible and not be eclipsed by transformation. Detailed archival research, the development of building chronologies and preservation approaches supported this goal, as did extensive existing conditions analysis conducted by teams of consultants well versed in the issues posed by contemporary interventions in historic fabric.
- Initial space planning began with the approach of 'working with the building' – attempting to fit program into the existing square footage through spatial efficiencies, found space, shared space and underground space. Only when this approach proved infeasible were other options involving new construction considered, all targeted at minimizing footprint expansion.
- Well-articulated policies for sustainability exist on all four campuses, so there was a shared basis of sustainable practices between clients and architects. Actions included early workshops to assess sustainable opportunities, to establish sustainable goals, and to draft LEED checklists that served as benchmarks throughout design and construction. Sustainable goals informed building design at all levels – building layout, specification of materials and building systems.
- Cost estimators and construction managers were part of the design processes from the start, advising on the financial impact of options and issues of constructability, helping to keep scope and cost on a parallel track. Mock-ups tested the operational and visual impact of a wide variety of design issues, especially in cases where their impacts were repetitive and potentially expensive. The Exeter Library project takes the concept of mock-ups further, with the actual construction of pilot projects designed to test effectiveness of design concepts through day-to-day use, before full-building implementation.
- The designs of the four projects share trends that are occurring in academic settings throughout the US. As more and more group assignments are made by faculty, new group study and collaborative spaces for students are provided. Acknowledging that learning happens in many ways, a wide of variety of informal spaces – often within building corridors and lobbies – allows for serendipitous student-to-student or student-to-faculty conversations to happen in seamless ways. Healthier settings, with better ventilation and

daylighting, and comfortable places for work breaks and interaction, are all intended to make long hours of work each day more palatable. They may also help strengthen and sustain community in academic settings.

The original intentions for the existing building use at MIT and Exeter are not changing: pedagogies have certainly evolved, but Building 2 at MIT will continue to house the Department of Mathematics and the Class of 1945 Library at Exeter will carry on as a library (Fig 5.33). The 1892 building at the Lerner Center at Penn, while a music building previously, was not designed for music. Adapting and expanding it as the venue for a first-class music program involved significant change and expansion. Saieh Hall at the University of Chicago is the only full-fledged example of adaptive reuse. However, like the other three projects, it will always be recognizable for what it was, with its heritage apparent. All four buildings will go on to serve useful lives, adjusted to serve contemporary needs. They will continue to manifest basic tenets of sustainability by the simple fact that they continue to exist as physical structures, retaining the majority of the embodied energy of their original material fabric. Hopefully, their performance will have a lighter impact on the environment in the future, their occupants will benefit from settings designed with their health and wellbeing in mind, and their planning and fit-out will prove to be flexible enough to sustain the changes they will inevitably experience in the future.

NOTES

1 *The Secretary of Interior's Standards for the Treatment of Historic Properties* http://www.nps.gov/tps/standards/four-treatments.htm

2 Ibid.

3 USGBC, *United States Green Building Council*, http://www.usgbc.org/ [accessed 30 June 2015].

4 Steven Morgan Friedman, *A Brief History of the University of Pennsylvania* (Philadelphia: University of Pennsylvania Archives & Records Center, 1998).

5 http://www.upenn.edu/about/heritage.php [accessed 30 June 2015].

6 George E Thomas and David B Brownlee, *Building America's First University: An Historical and Architectural Guide to the University of Pennsylvania* (Philadelphia: University of Pennsylvania Press, 2000).

7 Ibid.

8 Johnathan E Farnham PhD, Acting Preservation Director City of Philadelphia Historical Commission, 27 July 2007.

9 Mark M Jarzonbek, *Designing MIT: Bosworth's New Tech* (Boston: Northeastern University Press, 2004). The interaction between William Welles Bosworth and John Ripley Freeman, as well as the fascinating story of how the design of the MIT campus evolved, is well documented in the publication.

10 Ibid.

11 Ibid.

12 *History: The University of Chicago*, http://www.uchicago.edu/about/history/ [accessed 30 June 2015].

13 Ibid.

14 *Architecture: University of Chicago*, http://architecture.uchicago.edu/ [accessed 30 June 2015].

15 *Partners for Sacred Places*, , www.sacredplaces.org, a non-profit advocacy and consulting organization in Philadelphia, is an excellent source for information and case studies for adaptively used ecclesiastic structures.

16 John Ochsendorf, *Guastavino Vaulting: The Art of Structural Tile* (New York: Princeton Architectural Press, 2010). Designed to be the both floor structure and finished ceiling surface, this system had been used at the University of Chicago's Harper Library (1911) and for a number of churches in the Chicago area. Other notable buildings using the Guastavino system include the Boston Public Library (1890) and, in New York, Carnegie Hall (1891), Grand Central Station (1913) and the Registry Hall at Ellis Island (1917).

17 http://www.cityofchicago.org/city/en/depts/dcd/supp_info/landmarks_commission.html [accessed 30 June 2015].

18 Mary Clerkin Higgins, 'Stained glass report: Chicago Theological Seminary', in *Stained Glass Report* (Brooklyn 2010). William Willet (American, 1867–1921) studied with the painter William Merritt Chase and worked with the stained glass artist John Lafarge in a neo-Gothic style that incorporated, according to the Corning Museum of Glass, Pre-Raphaelite motifs inspired by the work of Dante Gabriel Rossetti and Edward Burne-Jones. The windows at the CTS were designed specifically for the Seminary, and conceived as liturgical works of art, where their message was intended to reinforce a religious message, and to educate and inspire viewers.

19 *The Secretary of Interior's Standards for the Treatment of Historic Properties* http://www.nps.gov/tps/standards/four-treatments.htmStandard 9, 'New additions, exterior alterations, or related new construction shall not destroy historic materials that characterize the property. The new work shall be differentiated from the old and shall be compatible with the massing, size, scale, and architectural features to protect the historic integrity of the property and its environment.'

20 'Design of the Library', http://www.exeter.edu/libraries/553_4375.aspx [accessed 30 June 2015].

21 *Program of Requirements for the New Library Recommended by the Library Committee of Faculty*, Phillips Exeter Academy, 1966, p6.

22 Carter Wiseman, *Louis I. Kahn: Beyond Time and Style: A Life in Architecture* (New York; London: WW Norton, 2007). Chapter 7, 'A temple for learning: the Phillips Exeter Academy Library 1965–1972', details the process that led to the selection of Louis Kahn as the architect for Exeter's new library building.

23 Ibid, p187.

24 Ibid, p198.

25 Thomas E Hassan, Principal, Phillips Exeter Academy, 're. U.S. Department of Education's Green Ribbon Schools Program', letter to Dr Judith D Fillion, Division Director, New Hampshire Dept of Education, 4 Feb 2013.

SIX

New Court, Trinity College, Cambridge:

continuing a legacy of inhabitation

··

Oliver Smith

INTRODUCTION

In the course of most listed buildings applications, the discussions of the relative heritage significances of historic buildings or settings are dominated by a number of factors such as the significance of a particular historical association, traditional building typology or details of construction, fabric and finish. Such discussions tend to lead to a heavily 'conservation normal' approach to the adaptation or refurbishment of listed buildings.

In the project for the sustainable retrofit of the Grade I-listed buildings at New Court for Trinity College, Cambridge, it was successfully established that of the various components of the heritage significance of New Court, the most important lay in the unbroken use of the court and its buildings for their original purpose; and, consequently, the need to adapt the court to make it continue to be fit for this purpose might override the perceived and potential 'harms' to other heritage significances.

As Fig 6.01 illustrates, the works involved in the New Court project included not only local replanning to create facilities relevant to 21st-century college life (bathrooms, accessible suites, etc) but also major improvements to the thermal performance, airtightness, and energy and carbon efficiency of the building, and its insulation, double-glazing and renewable energy generation.

After a three-year process, listed building and planning applications were submitted for an integrated package of works to the buildings of New Court that are conservatively modelled

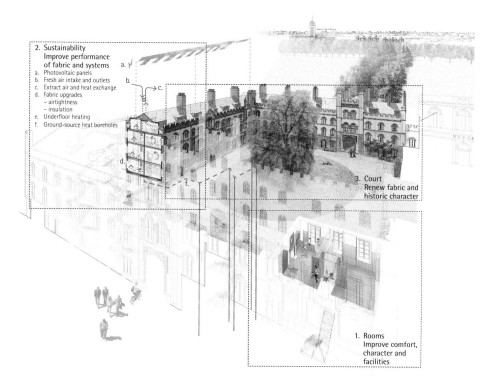

Fig 6.01 Project overview

to reduce the existing energy consumption and carbon emissions of New Court by c.75% and 88% respectively. These proposals were approved by the local authority in January 2013 and endorsed by the Secretary of State for Communities and Local Government in February 2013. The building works commenced in spring 2014 and are due to complete late in 2015.

This project provides a precedent (for process – the analytical, modelling and design work that underpins the proposals – rather than for the project-specific outcomes) for the refurbishment not only of college buildings but also of other historic buildings where the continuity of occupation can be shown to be a prime consideration, and where significant improvements to environmental and economic sustainability of the historic spaces and fabric are required to make such occupation viable. The New Court project demonstrates that the benefit to the legacy of occupation together with wider public benefits, such as the reduction of carbon emissions, can be shown to outweigh the potential, perceived 'harms' to the other significances of the building.

The project development process brought together the client body, in the form of occupants, maintenance staff, technical review and building committees, and active college governance, with an interdisciplinary team comprising architects, planning and heritage consultants, structural, mechanical and electrical engineers, building physicists and industry experts to work on the design, research and negotiation process. While demonstrating that the proposals would not cause harm to the building fabric or character – through a thorough exploration of the existing and future building character and the detailed monitoring and modelling of existing and future fabric conditions – the team explored the existing and emerging heritage and environmental policies to identify a coherent policy approach that prioritised an understanding of both heritage values 'in practice' and local policy concerns.

The landscape of policies and guidance on heritage and environmental sustainability included the then newly issued National Planning Policy Framework (NPPF), British Standards and local plan policies as well as guidance from English Heritage (EH) and other related bodies.

This chapter describes the role of building physics and design in this process and will argue that these are essential components of any strategy to resolve the critical gaps between – and oppositions in – the policies addressing heritage and environmental sustainability. It also identifies the critical case for the allocation of appropriate resources (time, money and intellectual rigour) by all parties involved in such projects – clients, design team, local authorities and statutory consultees – to ensure that the nuanced judgements at every level in building physics, design and policy interpretation are made in a fully informed, and hopefully collaborative, manner.

BACKGROUND

5th Studio is a practice of architects and urban designers with studios in Cambridge and London. The work of the practice combines building and urban design projects with research. Current project work ranges from individual new buildings and refurbishments to large-scale strategic, landscape and master planning, while research covers a range of subjects from the conditions of incipient urbanism and infrastructure-led regeneration to the development of strategies for sustainable construction with particular regard to the adaptation of existing fabric.

The application of this latter strand of research has led to completion of a number of award-winning projects for the sustainable refurbishment of notable college and other residential buildings of the 1960s and 1970s. Most of these projects in central Cambridge have primarily addressed the technical and practical issues of increasing thermal performance and the airtightness of existing fabric, of controlling moisture and ventilation, and of educating owners and occupants in the encouragement of sustainable behaviours. Despite their historic settings and, perhaps, because of the age and character of the buildings, there have rarely been onerous heritage or conservation policy constraints on the scope of these projects.

However, such buildings represent only a small proportion of the building stock of central Cambridge, and once these have been addressed there remains the pressing need to improve sustainability and habitability of the more important historic buildings that comprise the larger part of the college estates and the historic core of the City. Here, the 'normal' interpretation of heritage policy and conservation practice has traditionally constrained the scope and ambition of refurbishment projects, severely limiting the viability of these buildings in terms of environmental sustainability, maintainability or economical rent yield.

5th Studio completed the successful reworking of the 1970s Wolfson Building for Trinity College in 2006. As well as local replanning and provision of new social facilities – adapting the building for contemporary student life – this project had addressed the sustainability of the building in a then innovative fashion. The addition of insulated roofing and an insulated dry lining with new double-glazed windows reduced the fabric heat losses. Combining improved airtightness with the introduction of an MVHR plant reduced ventilation losses and provided tempered fresh air to all rooms, significantly improving comfort levels. The electrical load of the MVHR was met by the output from a roof-mounted PV array.

Following the success of this project, Trinity College asked 5th Studio to explore the refurbishment of New Court in late 2009. The college had become frustrated that the 'normal heritage' approach so constrained the scope of refurbishment that it was possible to meet neither the demands of the Building Regulations and environmental health requirements for houses in multiple occupation, nor contemporary student expectations in terms of standards of comfort or energy efficiency. These failures were seen to undermine the habitability and viability of the buildings.

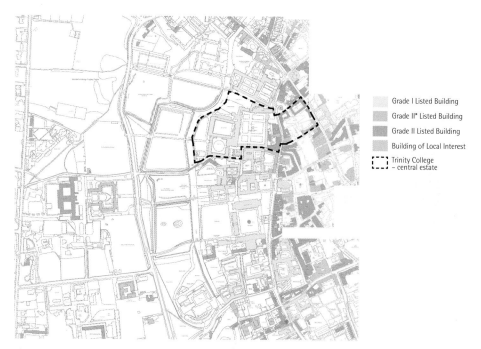

Grade I Listed Building
Grade II* Listed Building
Grade II Listed Building
Building of Local Interest
Trinity College – central estate

Fig 6.02 The College's central estate and listed buildings

As shown in Fig 6.02, apart from the Wolfson Building (see above) the college has few buildings in its central site that are not listed and – beyond demolition and new build – no option other than to continue occupation of these buildings for the residential and teaching purposes for which they were originally designed and built.

The college's brief for refurbishment of New Court asked for provision of levels of comfort, amenity, facilities, services and energy efficiency that would make the buildings viable as a setting for a traditional combination of residential, teaching and administrative uses for the foreseeable future. This future-proofing should also address both issues of climate change mitigation and adaptation to future climate conditions – principally of predicted changes to temperature and rainfall patterns.

NEW COURT

The buildings of New Court were completed in the 1820s by William Wilkins and form part of the complex of buildings at the centre of Trinity College, including Great Court, Nevile's Court and New Court (or King's Court), which were listed as Grade I on 26 April 1950.[1] Fig 6.03 shows

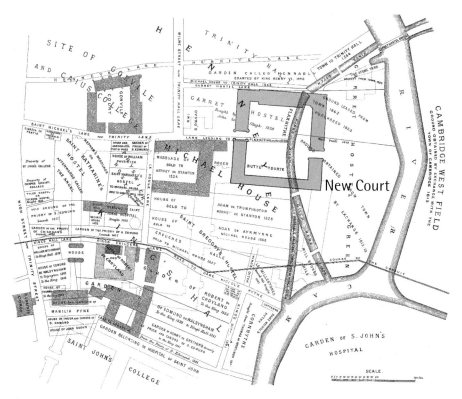

Fig 6.03 The New Court site

Backs Facade in the Graeco Palladian Style – William Wilkins. 1821

Backs Facade in the Gothic Style – William Wilkins. 1821

Fig 6.04 Wilkins alternative proposals

that New Court itself was built on land purchased by the college from the town – partly on the course of the old King's Ditch.[2]

In 2009, the court provided accommodation for approximately 120 undergraduate students, as well as offices for the admissions and senior tutorial staff and a number of teaching rooms and fellows' sets. Fig 6.04 illustrates copies of Wilkins's drawings kept in the Wren Library. These show both the original design in the 'Graeco-Palladian' style and the 'Gothic' style in which the buildings were completed.

The buildings form a three-sided court against the older buildings of Nevile's Court to the north (the south range of this being redressed in a matching Tudor Gothic style). New Court had originally been built on a tight budget and, with the exception of the west elevation – towards the river – which was faced in Ketton stone, was of modest construction and finish, with plain interiors, Wilkins stating in a contemporary letter that the 'interiors may be of very simple architecture'.[3]

The construction was entirely of local brick, with timber floors and roof, and included the innovative use of cast iron window traceries and chimney pots. While the southern elevation, to Garret Hostel Lane, was of bare brick, the court elevations were faced in Roman cement render almost certainly with a lime-wash finish that matched the hue of the Ketton stone.

The buildings had been refurbished a number of times between 1825 and 2009 – to provide, in a contingent fashion, WCs, showers and bathrooms, beneath staircases and in cupboards. At some point – possibly in the late 19th century – the original metal window frames and leaded lights had been replaced with simple timber casements, as shown in Fig 6.05.

The most recent major expenditure in the late 1970s had addressed a significant dry rot outbreak that had followed the introduction of central heating and associated alterations in

Fig 6.05 New Court stone, render and brick elevations

the 1950s. It is thought that by adding warmth to existing damp wall conditions (defective gutters, roofing, etc) and blocking ventilation/draught routes (subfloor voids and chimneys), the 1950s works led to the creation of good conditions for mould growth.

The 1970s works included the replacement of the timber ground-floor structures with concrete slabs, reconstruction of the parapet gutters and the entire third floor and roof structures, and the re-rendering of the court elevations in a Portland cement-based pink-grey render (perhaps matching the tone and hue of the then exposed Roman cement – the limewash having disappeared from all but the most sheltered locations).

In 2009, the interiors were cold, dark and damp. Removal of the pugging from the intermediate timber floors to facilitate installation of central heating had reduced the acoustic insulating properties of these floors, creating issues of acoustic separation and nuisance. Historic interventions had obscured the clarity of the original plan form, with the ad hoc provision of showers, WCs and kitchens also creating fire hazard and means-of-escape issues. As the illustrations in Fig 6.06 show, the simplicity of the interiors was further compromised by boxed-out service risers, surface pipework and radiator installations, and by the addition of an array of blinds and curtains that cluttered the visual effect of the significant window reveals and panelling.

The provision and quality of heating, lighting and power systems was uneven in distribution and efficiency. Fire detection, alarm and means of escape provisions were inappropriate.

Existing rooms vary in quality, character and sense of their original form

Washing and cooking facilities have been added in an ad hoc and contingent manner over the years

Fig 6.06 New Court interiors (2009)

COLLEGE BRIEF

The college brief called for the provision of 180 study–bedrooms, fellows' teaching sets, and tutorial offices, together with shared facilities to meet the statutory requirements for housing in multiple occupation and of the Building Regulations; and the provision of accessible study–bedroom suites and ensuite shower rooms to a third of the rooms, together with all appropriate fire detection and alarm systems and means of escape, new service installations and major reductions in the building's energy use of and carbon emissions. It was important to the college that the project would establish a level of comfort and compliance that would exceed the current requirements and endure through the next 30-year refurbishment cycle as these requirements developed, including adaptation to a range of anticipated future climate conditions.

In early 2010 the college approved a feasibility study that outlined an integrated strategy for the sustainable refurbishment of New Court, and the design team initiated consultation with the local authorities and EH. The agenda and discussion from these earliest meetings was both extensive and intensive, covering a broad sweep of issues in great detail. This dialogue continued through the development of the project to the submission of listed buildings and planning applications in July 2012, and is ongoing through the site stage of the project. Although encouraging and constructive, the character of these early meetings confirmed that the success of any listed buildings application for the radical proposals implicit in the college's strategy would depend upon the college team establishing a close understanding of the planning and listed building policies and management of the pre-application negotiation process.

POLICY CONTEXT

An initial study undertaken by Beacon Planning mapped the policy context within which the project would be developed. This covered statutory and non-statutory policies and guidance related to sustainability and heritage, at both local and national levels. This context changed significantly over the course of the project development, as former Planning Policy Statements (PPS)[4] were superseded by the National Planning Policy Framework (NPPF) and the Localism Act.[5] Indeed, while the project development was initially guided by the relevant PPS, the final negotiations and submissions were framed in response to the then newly published NPPF.

Local planning policies

The principal local planning policy document relevant to this project was *Cambridge Local Plan Policy 4/10 – Listed Buildings*.[6] This policy requires proposals affecting listed buildings to demonstrate a clear understanding of the building's importance in the national and Cambridge context – including an assessment of which external and internal features and aspects of its setting are important to the building's special (architectural, historic or other) interest. The policy also requires demonstration that the proposed works will not harm any aspects of the building's special interest or that these impacts can be mitigated, for example by being easily reversible; and that where there will be an impact on the building's special interest, this is shown to be the least damaging of the potential options and there are clear benefits for the structure, interest or use of the building, or a wider public benefit.

Interestingly, public benefit is defined neither in the Local Plan nor in the NPPF – in which it also forms a significant criteria – but is understood to relate to the delivery of other national and local policy objectives such as the encouragement of economic activity, provision of community and transport infrastructure, and the reduction of carbon emissions. The local plan policies in Cambridge have been cast to reflect particular local priorities, including the reduction of carbon emissions, the conservation of the historic core of the city centre, and the provision of new housing and transport infrastructure. Conversely, the policies necessarily generalise for a wide range of situations and a large number of listed buildings with varying degrees of special interest, from intrinsic qualities of design or fabric to general townscape contribution. This generalisation requires each project to be assessed against both the intent and the wording of the policies. The drafting of the policies establishes both a clear process and a set of criteria to be addressed through design process, consultation and presentation.

National Planning Policy

The National Planning Policy Framework (NPPF) was introduced in March 2012 and was intended to shape the planning system so that this contributed to the delivery of sustainable development through three dimensions of activity: economic, social, and environmental.[7]

The NPPF aims to enable sustainable development by adoption of 12 'core principles', including that planning should 'not simply be about scrutiny, but instead be a creative exercise in finding ways to enhance and improve the places in which people live their lives'.[8] A further principle requires that high-quality design and a good standard of amenity should be secured for all existing and future occupants of land and buildings.

The NPPF expressly supports the 'transition to a low carbon future in a changing climate including conversion of existing buildings' and the conserving of 'heritage assets in a manner appropriate to their significance, so that they can be enjoyed for their contribution to the quality of life of this and future generations'.[9] The framework encourages local authorities not to 'stifle innovation, originality or initiative through unsubstantiated requirements to conform to certain development forms or styles'.[10] Local authorities are advised that they 'should not refuse planning permission for buildings or infrastructure which promote high levels of sustainability because of concerns about incompatibility with an existing townscape, if those concerns have been mitigated by good design, *unless the concern relates to a designated heritage asset and the impact would cause material harm to the asset or its setting which is not outweighed by the proposal's economic, social and environmental benefits'.*[11]

The NPPF (Section 12: 'Conserving and enhancing the historic environment') requires applicants to describe the significance of any heritage asset (designated or otherwise and including the setting) affected by a proposed development. Local authorities are required to take account of *'the desirability of sustaining and enhancing the significance of heritage assets and putting them to viable uses consistent with their conservation and the positive contribution that conservation of heritage assets can make to sustainable communities including their economic vitality'.*[12] The NPPF seeks to establish a planning climate that encourages innovation, initiative and the appropriate, sustainable refurbishment of heritage assets, subject to provision of suitable evidence on the desirability of enhancement and viable use of these assets. These policies establish that the local authority should be responsible for determining the balance between the heritage significance and any harms/benefits to this and other public benefits arising from any proposal.

These policies reinforces the moving of decision-making on the acceptability of perceived harms (to heritage significance) away from purely heritage consideration and into the broader field of economic, social and environmental sustainability policy. The change in emphasis and responsibility is tempered with advice that balances public benefits against the 'great weight' to be attached to the conservation of any asset and the loss of significance and, specifically, the plan emphasises that consent should be refused unless the public benefits derived from the project are substantial and outweigh the harm or loss to heritage significance.

Non-statutory guidance

Sitting beside the statutory policies are a number of non-statutory documents and guidance produced by other – heritage and standards – agencies. Examination of these affords insight into the primary concerns of the agencies and the differences between them, in terms of interpretation and direction, at national and local levels. Principal among these documents is *Conservation Principles, Policies and Guidance for the Sustainable Management of the Historic Environment*,[13] produced by EH in 2008. The primary aim of this document was to strengthen the credibility and consistency of advice offered by EH officers by establishing a clear framework of principles to which the officers can be expected to subscribe and within which they are to make their assessments and offer judgements.

The document identifies four interrelated, high-level heritage 'values' that are to be assessed for each particular building or place under consideration. These values range from the 'evidential', which is dependent on the inherited fabric of the place, through the 'historical' and the 'aesthetic', to the 'communal' – 'those that derive from people's identification with the place'.[14] To protect these heritage values, the document establishes a set of Conservation Principles, and policies and guidance on the application of these in practice. The six Conservation Principles establish the primacy of heritage values in any decision-making process and in guiding conservation as the preferred process for managing the inevitable changes in the historic environment. While this priority is generally reinforced within the sections on interpretation of principles and policy in practice, these also offer useful guidance on the meanings and interpretations of such widely used and misconstrued terms as authenticity, design value, visibility, sustainability, reversibility, monitoring/evaluating and periodic renewal – definitions that can usefully inform project discussions and design-led negotiation.

It is noted, for example, that the 'authenticity' of a place is derived from whatever most truthfully reflects and embodies the values attached to that place and can therefore relate to design and function as well as to fabric. The guidance suggests: 'Retaining the authenticity of a place is not always achieved by retaining as much of the existing fabric as is technically possible.'[15] Similarly, it suggests: 'Design value may be recoverable through repair or restoration, but perhaps at the expense of some evidential value';[16] and that contemporary interventions to a building or place should be subtly different (in style, detail and construction) so as to be legible and capable of discernment and interpretation.

The document acknowledges inevitable competition between heritage values and establishes that prioritisation of 'competing' heritage values should be based on a comprehensive understanding of the values and of the works necessary to sustain them.

In addressing the issue of sustainability, EH promotes those heritage values that can contribute to environmental sustainability, and suggests that the low-energy economy for which many historic buildings were originally designed has imbued them with the qualities and forms necessary for a sustainable future. The guidance identifies that the removal and replacement of historic buildings requires a substantial reinvestment of energy and resources and states that many traditional buildings and building materials are extremely durable and perform well; but it ignores the effects and unintended consequences that the almost inevitable subsequent interventions will have had on heritage assets, their planning and occupancy behaviours, as well as their performance and fabric.

Guidance on 'reversibility' suggests that interventions to improve the energy efficiency of a place should be capable of being reversed if these lead to any unintended and harmful consequences and proposes, to this end, that projects and places should be monitored regularly both to identify unintended outcomes and to provide a growing case history to guide future projects. Finally, the guidance suggests: 'Periodic renewal of elements of a significant place, intended or inherent in the design, is normally desirable unless any harm caused to heritage values would not be recovered over time.'[17]

Balancing conservation and the public benefit

The EH document concludes by addressing the balance between perceived harms to heritage significance and other public interests and proposes that the underlying considerations should always be proportionality and reasonableness. This suggests that the balance to be struck is between retained significance – defined as the sum of the heritage values ascribed at the point of change to something which, if lost, cannot be replaced – and the predicted and potentially short-term benefits of development. The benefits, including strategies to mitigate and adapt to climate change, need to be subject to scrutiny in proportion to their impact on heritage values. It is suggested that this proportionality is fundamental to equitable reconciliation of the public interest in heritage with other public and private interests.

The requirement for predicted public benefit to 'demonstrably and decisively outweigh' the perceived harm to heritage values calls for an objective level of judgement to be applied to necessarily subjective – and scarcely comparable – attributes of any proposal. No parameters or guidance are offered for weighing benefits, harms or values and, in practice, the difficulty of delivering such decisive evidence suggests that the perceived harms can rarely be seen to be outweighed and that, as a result, the default 'normal heritage' approach will invariably prevail.

While this guidance is in broad alignment with the principles embodied in the NPPF, it clearly prioritises the conservation of heritage values above all others, and the language of 'objective weighing', 'proportion' and 'sum' implies the application of an objective reasonableness to the balance of entirely subjective and personal judgements.

Nonetheless, the identification of the function of a space as an aspect of its value and significance critically allows consideration of the viable continuity of function – the legacy of occupation – as a key heritage value of that building and potentially the prioritisation of this where competing heritage values cannot all be sustained.

Other published EH guidance central to the discussion of the New Court proposals includes *Climate Change and the Historic Environment.*[18] This document acknowledges the urgent need to reduce greenhouse gas emissions, increasing energy efficiency, and exploiting low carbon technologies and renewable energy sources 'to avoid the impacts of a changing climate from having major adverse effects on society, the economy and the environment, including our cultural heritage'.[19] It establishes a commitment to research into climate change issues, including where the historic environment can make a significant contribution towards climate change mitigation and adaptation, research on understanding and improving the energy efficiency of historic buildings, and the efficiency and cost-effectiveness of differing options for mitigation and adaptation.

Summary of policy review

It was seen that all the national and local policies aimed at the reconciliation of the concerns of heritage and sustainability, with each sector acknowledging the existence and concerns of the others. However, there was neither identifiable overlap or elision between these, nor identification of potential methods for achieving reconciliation.

The NPPF establishes the notion of a 'golden thread of sustainability' and suggests that heritage benefits might be balanced against other public benefits: social, economic or environmental. The framework places the responsibility for determining the balance with local authorities, and this aligns with the government's localism agenda. The EH policies and guidance acknowledge the inevitability of change but seek to retain the primacy of heritage significance over other benefits. The local authority planning policies simply and usefully identify the basis on which a case for the innovative retrofit of any historic building should be constructed.

DEVELOPMENT OF AN APPROACH TO POLICY

In response to both the above analysis and the initial conversations with the Cambridge City Council and EH, the team adopted a strategy for development of the project that was rooted in close, iterative consultation with these heritage agencies and, on the basis that this would be to the benefit of all parties, securing 'in principle' officer support for the proposals prior to formal submission. Three stages in the project development were established, at the end of each of which the proposals were to be shared with the City Council and EH.

The first stage would establish and demonstrate a broad and detailed understanding of the building in terms of heritage significance and existing character and fabric performance. The key issues identified for study during the first stage were the risks arising from proposed adaptations and interventions. In the absence of established or approved methodologies for building physics and character analysis, it would be necessary to develop these methodologies and establish their credibility by broad review by the 'in-house' teams and appointed external specialists and advisers. The second stage would include the exploration of a range of appropriate responses, ensuring that all sensible alternative options were fairly evaluated in terms of functionality (delivery of required performance, comfort and amenity with ease of operation and maintenance), significance and sustainability. The third stage would then synthesise a package of integrated proposals that were holistically balanced and interdependent in a manner that precluded isolation, and piecemeal rejection, of individual elements.

It was recognised that the fabric, construction and environmental installations of many historic buildings represent the products of a lengthy empirical evolution, and often form balanced systems for management of the environment and comfort of occupants. Until recently, the interconnectedness of historic building fabric and systems had not been commonly understood and previous interventions, unbalancing these relationships, had led to building failure and the undermining, within the heritage community, of credibility of all but original materials, techniques and technologies. The New Court proposals therefore needed to form, and be credible as, a balanced system, addressing the capacities and needs of fabric, service installations and occupant behaviours in an adaptable but holistic manner.

Given the differing timescales of each of these stages of project development, the demands of a real client and the seasonality of some of the monitoring procedures, the development of the project included considerable overlapping of work stages. It was necessary at times for design work to proceed on the basis of provisional monitoring or modelling data, but the presentations of work to the local authority and others adhered to the principle that the work was to be as coherent and comprehensive as possible and all alternative avenues explored, discounted or adopted in a clear and credible manner.

The developed proposals were to be presented within a listed building submission that responded to the above policy analysis and framed the issues as a series of simple questions that responded to, and clarified, the roles of the local authority and the statutory consultees, including EH and the other heritage amenity groups.

UNDERSTANDING THE EXISTING BUILDING

To establish a close understanding of the existing building character and the history, construction and performance of the existing building fabric, the team undertook a comprehensive examination of the building, including the collection of oral evidence of the history of the fabric and interventions from college fellows and staff. Detailed measured surveys of the plans, sections and elevations of the New Court buildings were commissioned along with a detailed photographic survey and a catalogue of internal features (cornices, picture rails, architraves, fire surrounds, etc).

On the basis of the level of architectural detail, elaboration, coherence and condition of each room interior, the team formulated a hierarchy of significance of the interiors. The conditions of each interior space were assessed by identifying both areas of original work and the extent of any subsequent interventions, repair and maintenance, including areas of replastered ceilings and linings. As illustrated in Fig 6.07, a range of techniques was used to establish the existing building fabric conditions and performance. U-values were measured and seasonal variations in relative humidity and temperature monitored, in both rooms and the floor voids between rooms, to understand the heat and moisture levels as affected by the annual cycle of inputs of climate, occupation and heating system. The airtightness of the existing building envelope was also measured and a detailed thermal imaging survey carried out.

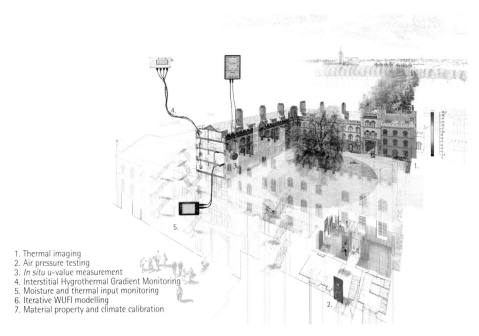

1. Thermal imaging
2. Air pressure testing
3. *In situ* u-value measurement
4. Interstitial Hygrothermal Gradient Monitoring
5. Moisture and thermal input monitoring
6. Iterative WUFI modelling
7. Material property and climate calibration

Fig 6.07 Development stage monitoring

Finally, a significance assessment was conducted that included a review of the listing criteria and appropriate grade of listing, together with a detailed appraisal of the heritage values of New Court. Against the level of detail, survival and quality of the room interiors, the team identified that the 'authenticity' of the buildings lay more in the way in which they provided a robust and neutral setting for collegiate life – unencumbered by either overwhelming architectural expression or the history of specific previous occupation – than in any specific plan form, or historic material or detail. This suggested that the prime historic significance and value of the buildings lay in their continuous occupation for their original intended use and the conservation of this use into the future.

EXPLORATION OF APPROPRIATE RESPONSES

These insights into significance informed the parallel processes that addressed the perceived risks to the historic fabric and character. The first of these focused on the analysis of the fabric. This was based on modelling the moisture and temperature conditions in the external walls, in both their current state and with an added insulated lining. The modelling was undertaken by Max Fordham LLP, using WUFI 5 (an industry standard transient heat and moisture simulation tool for assessing condensation and mould risk that was developed by the Fraunhofer Institute in Germany). An initial plot illustrating the capacity of the WUFI model is shown in Fig 6.08. This compares the possible effects of adding vapour-permeable (breathable) and impermeable insulated linings to the existing walls.

Rather than attempt to establish acceptable limits of harm in term of changes to temperature gradient or absolute or relative moisture or humidity levels, this analysis suggested that the critical indicator of fabric harm might be the development of conditions that fostered mould growth within timber elements in the external walls, and critically those such as wall plates, joist ends and softwood grounds for skirting boards at the interface between masonry and insulation.

All future modelling output was thus related to the Isopleths for mycelium growth or spore germination (developed by Klaus Sedlbauer, also for the Fraunhofer Institute). Fig 6.09 shows the Isopleths related to three categories of substrates for mould growth. These range from Optimum (equivalent to agar culture jelly) to Biologically Very Useable (the paper covering on plasterboard sheets and some contemporary softwoods) and Biologically Hardly Useable (masonry and, arguably, the 185-year-old Baltic pine used in New Court). To ensure a credible factor of safety, proposed constructions were deemed to fail if the conditions created exceeded the germination time for mould spores within a Biologically Very Useable substrate.

The WUFI programme works with a set of default database materials, most of which are of contemporary origin and manufactured to current EU standards of density and uniformity.

Vapour impermeable construction

WUFI®

South-facing wall. No external render. Phenolic foam insulation with vapour barrier

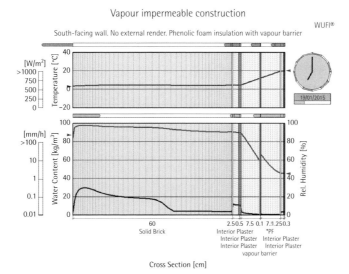

The insulated facade with no external render allows moisture ingress from the external (left) side. The internal vapour barrier prevents moisture from being released into the room and as a result critically high relative humidity levels in excess of 90% occur at the inner face of the brickwork.

Vapour permeable – breathable – construction

WUFI®

South-facing wall. No external render. Breathable internal insulation

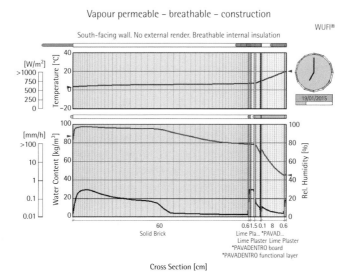

Breathable insulation functions on a wall exposd to a high rain load. The breathable insulation is able to take up and store more moisture without a significant increase in rH. At the same time moisture is allowed to permeate out to the internal environment by vapour diffusion. As a result moisture is drawn away from the surface of the brick and relative humidity stays below 80%.

Baseline comparison of vapour permeable and impermeable constructions for an insulated lining for an exposed south-facing wall.

Fig 6.08 Base case WUFI model

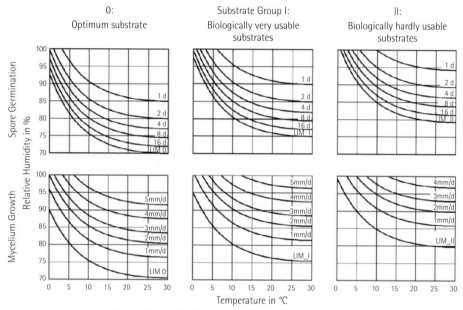

Isopleths published in Sedlbauer showing the required temperature, humidity and duration of exposure for mould germination and growth.

Fig 6.09 Mould Isopleths

To increase the credibility of the model, it was necessary to calibrate this to the historic, uneven and irregular materials of New Court. Samples of the bricks, stone and render were sent to Paul Baker and Chris Sanders at Glasgow Caledonian University for detailed analysis, their porosity and moisture and vapour transport properties replacing those of the database materials within the model. The historic bricks were found to vary enormously in density and transport coefficients. The original building had been constructed on a low budget, and although the facing bricks to Garret Hostel Lane appeared to be of reasonable density and standard, those used in the backings and wall interiors were found to vary from almost burnt to very soft and porous. It was agreed to model all the variants and then base the proposal model on the worst performing brick characteristics.

Similarly – there being no adequate weather data available for Cambridge, and as an alternative to use of interpolated Meteonorm data – it was decided to install a weather station on site to generate weather data for the modelling. These measures allowed computer modelling of the humidity and temperature conditions in the existing wall under real weather conditions. Interstitial hygrothermal gradient monitoring (IHGM), comprising an array of temperature and rH sensors installed at graduated depths through the wall thickness, provided recording of the actual conditions within the external wall. Comparison of these modelled and observed data sets allowed a simple calibration of the model to reflect monitored reality, significantly increasing the credibility of the model and thus its predictions of future conditions.

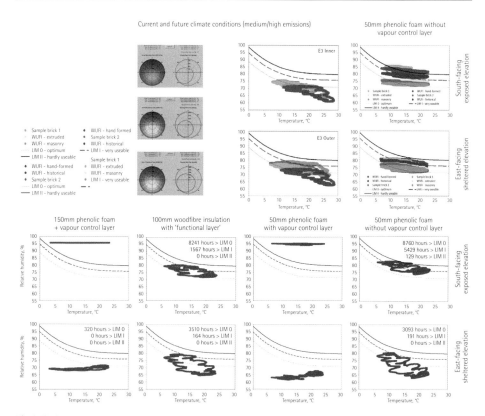

Fig 6.10 Comparative WUFI modelling

Further iterations of the calibrated WUFI model identified the limits on the type and thicknesses of insulation that could be installed without risk, measured against the key mould criteria identified above. These varied with orientation and wall build-up (thickness and finish – stone, render or bare brick) and were found to critically rely on the use of vapour-permeable insulations and finishes. Fig 6.10 illustrates the comparative testing of brick samples, insulation forms and climate conditions.

Fig 6.11 illustrates the mapping of the acceptable insulation thicknesses, which identified as many as four different thicknesses on each elevation.

To avoid this complexity and inherent site coordination risk, it was decided to use a single standard 60mm thickness of vapour-permeable wood fibre insulation throughout. This was set at the lowest risk thickness, and while this did not maximise the potential thermal upgrade, it was found that this level of insulation would improve the existing U-value from an average of 0.685 to 0.25W/m^2°K.

In response to the residual uncertainty over the accuracy of the modelling predictions and the college's natural caution about possible unintended consequences of the proposed

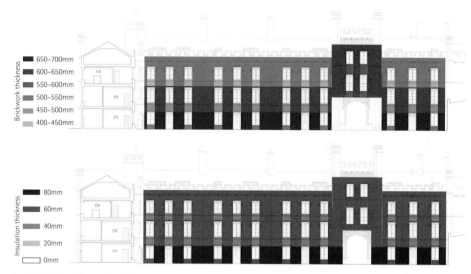

Fig 6.11 Wall and insulation thickness mapping

interventions – caution rooted in their experience and long-term approach to the stewardship of their buildings – it was agreed that a monitoring programme should be incorporated within the works. The monitoring installations would record interstitial hygrothermal conditions as well as the rH and temperature levels of timbers in the fabric at critical locations. Given the thickness and thermal mass of the existing wall construction, it was thought that it would take a number of seasons for these to reach a new steady state and so a long-term (min seven-year) programme was proposed.

This monitoring installation would provide both immediate hazard warnings if conditions exceeded those modelled and long-term feedback on the behaviour of the historic solid walls with internal wall insulation that would be of enormous interest to the college and the wider historic building and heritage community.

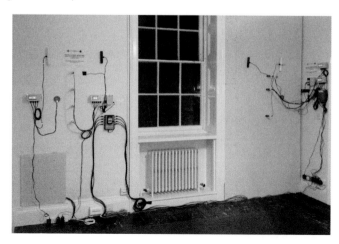

Fig 6.12 HTGM array in I6

As part of the development, a panel of the proposed insulated lining was constructed within I6, a typical room in New Court. IHGM was installed within this and an adjacent 'control' wall, and both were monitored for a period of one year. Fig 6.12 illustrates this installation, which is typical of those that are being installed within the New Court works.

The I6 monitoring identified a number of key results, as shown by the comparative plots for the Control and Test walls in Fig 6.13. The critical monitored level – that of the relative

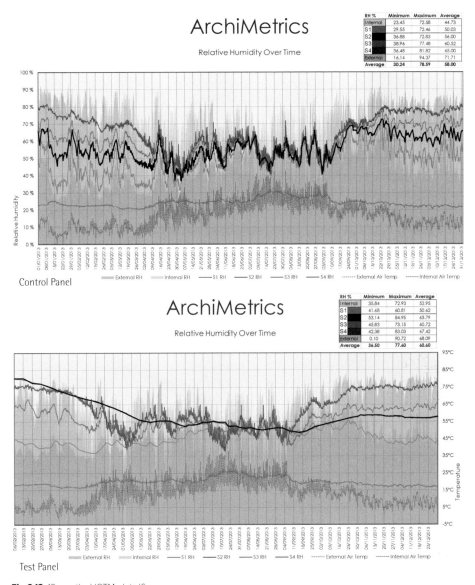

Fig 6.13 12-months HGTM plots I6

humidity at the interface of insulation and historic masonry – is seen to start from an unacceptably high level in the test wall. This was found to be due to the water content of the new lime plaster background to the insulation and, over the monitoring period, this level can be seen to gradually decrease to comparative safety. Moreover, all the temperature and rH levels through the wall are seen to become more steady and less volatile in response to internal and external changes, indicating perhaps that fabric conditions within the wall has become more – rather than less – stable and sustainable as a result of the insulated lining.

DESIGN APPROACHES

The exploration of local, historic and recent precedents, such as the images of St Jerome in his study and of Charles Darwin's sitting room shown in Fig 6.14, and the modelling of a wide variety of options, illustrated in Figs 6.15 and 6.16, led to the adoption of a strategy for the architectural treatment of an interior lining related to Wilkins's own treatment of the original building exterior as a series of linings on a simple brick construction, with the different lining materials corresponding to the significance and outlook of each elevation.

The adopted strategy allowed for the reinstatement of the integrity of the historic form and fabric of the original rooms and complemented this with the addition of a discreet but legible plane of insulation against the internal face of the external wall.

Rather than place a replica cornice onto the insulated lining, the team explored the consequences of stopping the lining short of the ceiling to reveal the existing, retained

St Jerome in his Study. Antonello da Messina.   Darwin's sitting room. Christ's College Cambridge.

Fig 6.14 Precedents: Antonello de Messina, *St Jerome in his Study*

Fig 6.15 Interior Study model

cornice and the extent of the original room enclosure. Careful modelling by Max Fordham and 12 months' monitoring of the installation in I6 by Archimetrics demonstrated that, in this instance, the omission of the insulated lining in front of the original cornice did not form a sufficient cold bridge to lead to condensation and mould formation at cornice level. Further details and shadow gaps formed within the depth of the insulated lining were detailed to accept the existing picture rail (where existing) and skirting boards at junctions with flanking walls.

A second timber lining was designed to accommodate all new service pipework and cable distribution and lighting. This furniture lining, keyed to the height of the original door architraves, would form a subsidiary, inhabited interior within the restored and insulated historic volume.

Fig 6.16 Detail studies

Analysis of the original interiors identified the significance of a number of key elements: fireplace, door/architrave and the deep window reveal, with panelled shutters and soffit, which all project into and inhabit the otherwise simple spaces. The window shutters had been unusable for many years and were painted shut, privacy being provided by an unsightly combination of blinds and curtains that detracted from the simplicity of the interiors. The college wished to repurpose the existing shutters, both as a simple, robust and efficiently maintainable way of providing privacy and enclosure, and in response to Historic Scotland and EH research on the contribution that shutters can improve the thermal efficiency of windows.

It was found that the overhaul of the window casings and shutter boxes and their reinstatement within an insulated reveal would allow for continuity of the insulation and airtightness line through to the window frame and provide sufficient separation of the windows and shutters to allow installation of appropriate ironmongery for contemporary levels of maintenance and security. This detail would also reinstate the key dimensional relationship between the window reveal and the surrounding wall plane.

The window casements themselves had been poorly constructed and required significant overhaul. Many were twisted and warped and would not close satisfactorily, intermediate glazing bars had broken and been replaced in an ad hoc manner, and much of the original glass had been replaced with a mixture of float, patterned and obscured glass. It was determined that while it would be costly to repair the existing windows, the poor thermal performance of the resultant single-glazed casements would not offer good value and did not align with the college requirements of maintenance ease or sustainability. Replacement triple-glazed and high-performance windows were sourced, with sections and sightlines that exactly matched those of the existing casements. These replacement windows were detailed to sit within the re-instated shutter surrounds, offering little evidence of their presence beyond the depth of the glazing spacer bars and minimising any effect on the elevations.

SYNTHESIS OF A PACKAGE OF INTEGRATED PROPOSALS

The outcomes of the building physics and design studies were developed into a set of integrated proposals for the refurbishment of New Court, which were explored and tested through drawings, digital 3D and scale timber models, with full-size maquettes of particular details and a number of iterations of a full-size mock-up room, replicating all the existing details and conditions together with the proposed lining and furniture elements.

The proposals integrated the fabric improvements with the provision of environmental systems, including an MVHR system for extracting moist air, as required by Building Regulations, from bathrooms and kitchens and supplying tempered fresh air to student study–bedrooms. This also provided adequate ventilation to ensure the evaporation of any moisture/vapour that had permeated through the construction, further mitigating the risk of build-up, either at the surface or within the construction.

The modelled reduction of energy loss through the fabric and ventilation system allowed design of an efficient underfloor heating system to run at temperatures that could be sustainably and economically supplied by a ground source heat pump and array of boreholes to be installed within the courtyard. This solution would provide more evenly distributed, efficient and comfortable heating than traditional radiators, was judged more reliable, robust and maintainable by the college's maintenance team, and would allow the removal of the intrusive existing surface pipework and radiator installations. Moreover, the setting of underfloor pipework within an insulated screed between the floor joists would reinstate much of the lost acoustic separation between rooms.

The electrical demand of the pumps to these installations could be partly met by the outcome of an array of photovoltaic panels mounted on the south-facing roof over Garret Hostel Lane. The provision of a GSHP system and a PV array allowed the proposals to reduce the energy demand and carbon emissions of New Court to 25% and 12% of the current levels respectively. Figs 6.17, 6.18 and 6.19 illustrate the design improvements to thermal performance, the integrated package of proposals and the build-up of the reductions to existing levels of carbon emissions.

The integrated proposals were presented and discussed in detail with the City Council and EH on a number of occasions between autumn 2011 and spring 2013. While the proposals were broadly welcomed, particularly in terms of the calibrated modelling and proposals for long-term monitoring, it was clear that the replacement of the existing windows represented an unacceptable loss of historic fabric. On this basis, the team explored a wider range of alternative solutions to retention of the existing windows. As Fig 6.20 illustrates, these ranged

Comparison of U-Values and estimated annual space heating values before and after the works.

	Before	After
U-Value: W/m²K		
External Walls	0.685	
Windows	5.8	
Roof	2.2	
Ground Floor	1.7	

| Air permeability: m³m²/hr@50Pa | 11.0 | |

| Annual Space Heating: kWh | 857,000 | |

Fig 6.17 Thermal performance targets

An integrated approach. Fabric improvements, systems and renewable installations

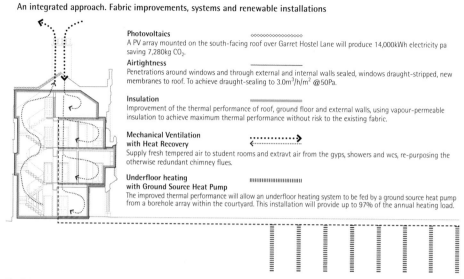

Photovoltaics
A PV array mounted on the south-facing roof over Garret Hostel Lane will produce 14,000kWh electricity pa saving 7,280kg CO$_2$.

Airtightness
Penetrations around windows and through external and internal walls sealed, windows draught-stripped, new membranes to roof. To achieve draught-sealing to 3.0m^3/h/m^2 @50Pa.

Insulation
Improvement of the thermal performance of roof, ground floor and external walls, using vapour-permeable insulation to achieve maximum thermal performance without risk to the existing fabric.

Mechanical Ventilation with Heat Recovery
Supply fresh tempered air to student rooms and extravt air from the gyps, showers and wcs, re-purposing the otherwise redundant chimney flues.

Underfloor heating with Ground Source Heat Pump
The improved thermal performance will allow an underfloor heating system to be fed by a ground source heat pump from a borehole array within the courtyard. This installation will provide up to 97% of the annual heating load.

Fig 6.18 An integrated approach

from doing nothing to the addition of secondary double- or triple-glazing and the reglazing of the existing frames. All of these were assessed against the objective criteria of reduction of heating load, judgements based in the college's experience of operability, and maintainability and subjective assessments of visual intrusion when viewed from inside or outside.

Three-step reduction of carbon emissions

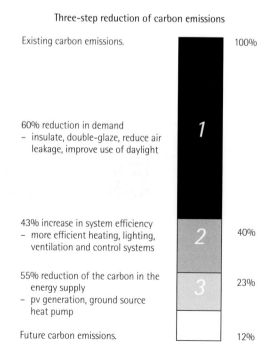

Existing carbon emissions.   100%

60% reduction in demand
– insulate, double-glaze, reduce air
  leakage, improve use of daylight   *1*

43% increase in system efficiency
– more efficient heating, lighting,
  ventilation and control systems   *2*   40%

55% reduction of the carbon in the
  energy supply
– pv generation, ground source   *3*   23%
  heat pump

Fig 6.19 Three steps to
reduced CO$_2$ emissions and
labels

Future carbon emissions.   12%

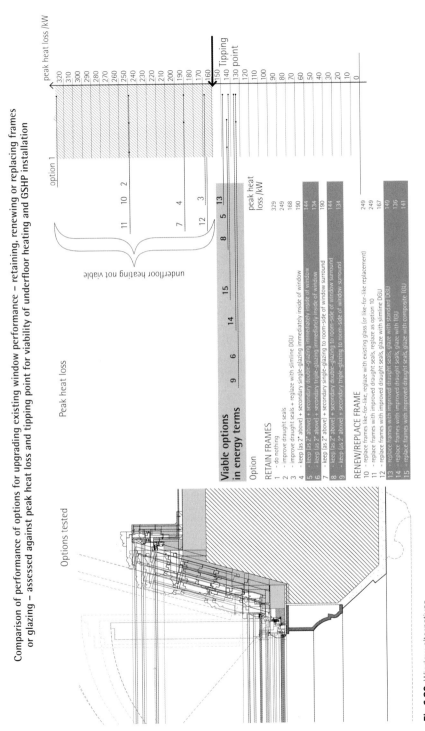

Fig 6.20 Window alternatives

Replica window testing the installation issues and comparative visual affect of historic single glazing (right) and slimline double-glazing (left)

Fig 6.21 Comparison of single or slimline double-glazing in replica window

On the basis of this comparative assessment and range of criteria, the optimum solution proposed the reconditioning of the existing window frames and casements, upgraded with draught and weather seals, and reglazed with slim-profile double-glazed units. An appropriate product called Histoglass had been used successfully in the Tower of London and was also a solution approved by Historic Scotland. This could be fabricated with a drawn-glass outer leaf, replicating the characterful ripple of historic glazing.

Workshop testing showed that the existing frame sections and profiles would accommodate both rebated weather and draught seals and the weight and rebate dimensions required for the double-glazed units. Fig 6.21 shows a replica casement sash, matching the existing profiles, which was produced by the college joiners and glazed with Histoglass. When installed (left) within an existing frame, next to an existing single-glazed casement (right), it was possible to judge the negligible effect of this glazing on the appearance of the window and the wider court.

Although this solution did not maximise the thermal improvement of the existing envelope, it achieved sufficient reduction of the heating load to maintain the viability of the preferred underfloor heating and GSHP solution and had the benefit of retaining the historic frames and reducing planning risk.

During the discussions, it had become clear that the local case officers for both the City Council and EH would need technical support in review of the building physics studies. EH was able to refer the study reports to their internal technical advisers, who had been consulted at interim stages on the methodology and outcomes. The City Council, at some cost, appointed the BRE as external technical advisers.

It was also clear that although the City Council welcomed the ambition, approach and rigour of the proposals, the financial and resourcing constraints under which they were operating precluded the case officers from allocating sufficient time to fully engage with the details of the proposals at a pre-application stage. It thus became necessary to submit a full set of Planning and Listed Buildings Applications to secure appropriate allocation of officer time. The team were instructed to submit a full set of applications in July 2012. Through the formal consultation process, the project was presented to the statutory consultees and amenity groups including City Council Conservation and Design Panel, City Council Accessibility Committee, the Georgian Group and the Society for the Protection of Ancient Buildings (SPAB).

The formal consultation response received from EH confirmed the approval of the technical submissions by their technical officers, but the maintenance of strong objections on the following principal grounds: the insulated linings and their impact on the character of the rooms; the double-glazing of existing windows and the impact of this on the appearance of the court; and the installation of the PV array to the roof over Garret Hostel Lane, and the impact of this on the character of the building and the surrounding historic roofscapes. These objections seemed to be based on a default view of the significance of the buildings derived principally from their existing appearance, form and fabric, rather than use or legacy of occupation.

The EH response stated:

> While we appreciate the importance of conserving energy and reducing carbon emissions, Listed buildings form only a very small percentage of the country's building stock, and buildings Listed at Grade I or II* make up less than 10% of Listed buildings. The contribution that improvements to their thermal performance would make to national efforts to conserve energy, both to conserve resources and to control climate change, would be modest.[20]

The question as to whether it was appropriate to embark on such a project in a Grade I-listed building, rather than developing the appropriate analysis and methodology through projects in less significant buildings, was significant. The default view was that an understanding of the technical issues involved in sustainable retrofit should be developed through projects involving ordinary buildings, this expertise then trickling up to more significant existing buildings and to listed heritage last (if at all).

The college's response to this question – beyond their own lack of an alternative – was that the considerable resources (money, time and rigour) required to develop a methodology for the sustainable retrofit of heritage buildings were perhaps unlikely to be available to many

Figs 6.22 and 6.23 Images of the Phase I interiors - completed September 2015

retrofit projects and that the trickle-up of any useful developments might take so long as to be irrelevant for the immediate needs of the college and the wider heritage building sector.

The college proposed that they develop, through the New Court project, appropriate methodologies and expertise, sharing and disseminating the developed understanding for the benefit of the heritage agencies and other estate and building owners in the private and public sectors (Figs 6.22 and 6.23).

BALANCING HERITAGE VALUES AND SUSTAINABILITY

To assist in the clarification of the local authority's decision-making process on this listed buildings application, the team attempted to de-conflate the consideration of heritage values, harms and public benefits by addressing these issues as the answers to three questions that sought to synthesise the central themes of the local plan policies and the NPPF while recognising the structure of the EH.

The first question asked '*What are the relative heritage significances of the building?*' and clearly required input from the client as well as from all the heritage agencies. Critically, in this case, it was posited that the prioritisation of the significance should reflect the importance of legacy of occupation of the buildings for their optimum viable use: that for which they were originally designed. Response to the second question, '*What are the harms or benefits of the proposals to these heritage significances?*', required recognition of the proposed benefits as well as the perceived harms; these included such works as bringing the shutters back into operational use, the replacement of unsympathetic cement render, and the removal of the surface pipework, radiators and other service boxings. The removal of pendant light fittings and lighting of the rooms with wall-mounted lights would reinstate the original lighting direction and pattern as well as the shadow rendering of the mouldings and panelling.

The third question, '*Are any residual harms outweighed by other public benefits?*', addressed the principal aims of the NPPF and Localism policies. These aims suggest that local authorities should be responsible for judging the balance of harms (to heritage significance) against other public benefits (the reduction of carbon emissions, etc). While informed by officers in every policy department of the local authority, it is clear that this question should be principally addressed by the elected members. The public benefits in this case might include, for example, environmental sustainability and reduction of carbon emissions, advancement of building research and monitoring, and knowledge transfer.

The listed buildings and planning applications were presented to the Planning Sub-Committee of Cambridge City Council on 7 January 2013. The vote was unanimous in favour of the proposals.[21] Referral of the applications to the Secretary of State, through the National Planning Casework Unit, gained endorsement. A letter from the Unit's senior planning manager stated: 'The Secretary of State has carefully considered the impact of the proposal, and the key policy issues which this case raises. In his opinion, the proposals do not: involve a conflict with national policies on important matters; or raise significant architectural or urban design matters.'[22]

CONCLUSION

In gaining consent for an unprecedented package of works to a Grade I-listed building, it is hoped that the methodology developed through the New Court project will inform future project and policy development. New Court should form a useful precedent for the process and adoption of the strategic and tactical measures described to ensure the highest quality of analysis, the most appropriate solutions, and thorough engagement of, and collaboration with, the local authority and other heritage agencies.

It would be inappropriate for the particular building physics and design responses developed for New Court to be adopted for other projects, for which other, individual and specific responses may well prove more appropriate, effective and economical. This project and process have highlighted the complexity of the issues involved in such projects and the nuanced judgements to be made at every level in building physics, design and policy interpretation. There is a critical need for the appropriate allocation of resources (time, money and intellectual rigour) by all parties involved in such projects – clients, consultants, local authorities and heritage agencies – to ensure that all decisions are made in a fully informed and, hopefully, collaborative manner.

ACKNOWLEDGEMENTS

The author would like to acknowledge the enormous role played in the development of this project by the Master, fellows, staff and students of Trinity College and, in addition, to recognise the significant contributions made to the research, design and negotiation processes made by Dr Jon Burgess and Jo Burton (Beacon Planning); Mike Baldwin, Joel Gustafsson and James Freeman (Max Fordham LLP) for the Service Engineering and Building Physics modelling; Bill Bordass (Usable Buildings Trust), Bill Gething (Sustainability and Architecture) and Professor May Cassar (University College London, Centre for Sustainable Heritage) for advice; Dr Phil Cooper and Tyrone Bowen (Cambridge Architectural Research) for structural engineering; Dr Caroline Rye and Cameron Scott (Archimetrics), Diane Hubbard (Green Footsteps) and Neil May, Christophs Zurcher and Fehr (NBT) for building monitoring; February Phillips, Ted Ridge, Beth Lambert and Kieran Perkins (5th Studio) for architectural design, coordination and support.

This chapter was first published as a paper in *The Historic Environment: Policy and Practice. Energy Efficiency and Heritage Values in Historic Buildings.*[23] Thanks are due to Maney Publishing for their permission to publish this version of that paper.

NOTES

1   The building's List Entry Number is 1106371, http://www.historicengland.org.uk/listing/the-list/list-entry/1106371

2   Robert Willis and John Willis Clark, *The Architectural History of the University of Cambridge, and of the Colleges of Cambridge and Eton ... Edited with Large Additions, and Brought up to the Present Time, by J. W. Clark. [with Plans, Etc.]* (Cambridge: Cambridge University Press, 1886).

3   See Letter 39, 12 May 1821, in RW Liscombe, *William Wilkins 1778–1839* (Cambridge: Cambridge University Press, 1980).

4   See, for instance, Department for Communities and Local Government (DCLG), *Planning Policy Statement: Planning and Climate Change Supplement to Planning Policy Statement 1* (London: TSO, 2007), and Department for Communities and Local Government (DCLG), *Planning Policy Statement 5: Planning for the Historic Environment* (London: TSO, 2010).

5   The Localism Act was introduced by the Coalition Government in 2011 to shift power away from central government and towards local people. Its provisions include new freedoms and flexibilities for local government; new rights and powers for communities and individuals, and reform to make the planning system more democratic and more effective.

6   Cambridge City Council, *Cambridge Local Plan Policy 4/10 – Listed Buildings* (2006).

7   Department for Communities and Local Government (DCLG), *National Planning Policy Framework* (London: TSO, 2012) https://www.gov.uk/government/uploads/system/uploads/attachment_data/file/6077/2116950.pdf [accessed 30 June 2015].

8   Ibid, pi.

9   Ibid, p5.

10   Ibid, p15.

11   Ibid, p16 (my emphasis).

12   Ibid, p31 (my emphasis).

13 English Heritage, *Conservation Principles, Policies and Guidance for the Sustainable Management of the Historic Environment* (London: English Heritage, 2008).

14 Ibid, p27.

15 Ibid, p45.

16 Ibid, p45

17 Ibid, p52.

18 English Heritage, *Climate Change and the Historic Environment* (English Heritage, 2008).

19 Ibid, p1.

20 English Heritage, Advice to Cambridge City Council on Listed Buildings Applications, 17 Oct 2012.

21 The Planning Subcommittee of Cambridge City Council stated that 'such Listed buildings, of which there are many in central Cambridge, must evolve if they are to remain in viable use, they cannot all become museums'.

22 Letter from Senior Planning Manager, National Planning Casework Unit, at DCLG to Cambridge City Council, 7 February 2013

23 *The Historic Environment: Policy and Practice. Energy Efficiency and Heritage Values in Historic Buildings*, 5:2 (2014), Maney Publishing.

SEVEN

Four case studies demonstrating the impacts of energy conservation in traditional domestic buildings

....

Oriel Prizeman

INTRODUCTION

This chapter presents two pairs of case studies that deliver performance upgrades, 'seen and unseen', to both built fabric and systems with differing degrees of visibility. The range and contrast between them justifies the need to develop a relational overview of contextual considerations in order to evaluate properly the trajectory of altering building performance for historic buildings. Our methods of evaluating energy use are based on calculation; our methods of evaluating significance are based on comparison and an estimation of rarity.[1] Our presumptions of occupant behaviour for existing buildings are based on typical usage,[2] yet the fact that significant historic buildings are often unusual and will almost certainly have long affected their occupants' behaviour makes such assertions questionable.[3] Taking the UK as a whole, the scale of the problem must be read carefully if historic buildings are not to be put at risk by thoughtless ecological makeovers.

The first principle is to consider the significance of the building at hand – to 'look before you leap', as the Society for the Protection of Ancient Buildings (SPAB) has long advised. It is necessary to identify each element of its character and to estimate its historic value in relation to the building, its setting, local context and use. Much of this assimilation comes instinctively to those used to working with historic buildings, but the challenges of meeting energy reduction targets force us to revisit these assessments.

The expansion of the description of historic buildings to include traditional buildings – all those built up to 1919 – is both helpful and dangerous, as it risks both energising and generalising arguments. Carl Elefante noted that 6% of existing buildings in the US were constructed before 1920.[4] In Europe and the UK this proportion is generally much larger;[5] however, in the US the perceived heritage value of such buildings is proportionately higher. It is possible that this perception shifts the pressure for eco-refurbishment of historic buildings. The European Commission states that the greatest energy savings can be made in existing buildings, which were cited as responsible for 41% of total final energy consumption in 2010.[6] Elefante notes that buildings built between the 1950s and 1980s account for around 55% or 36 bn sq ft of US building stock.[7]

It is important to recognise the scale of the problem. The English Housing Survey 2012–13 Report on Energy Efficiency of English Housing notes: 'Over half of the worst energy efficient homes were built before 1919 (52%).'[8] From a sample of 2,109 of the estimated 4,468,000 pre-1919 dwellings in England, it records that these had a mean SAP rating of 50.3 and CO_2 emissions of 7.2 tonnes per dwelling in 2012. Of these dwellings, 3.9% (175,000 homes) fell into band G, the majority falling into bands D and E (41.6% and 39.7%, respectively). The mean environmental impact rating of such dwellings is 45.9, the majority falling into band E (42.1%) and only 5.1% falling into band G. These figures have steadily improved from 2008.[9] It is important to register the smallness of these numbers; they only comprise 20% of the total English housing stock. The numbers of pre-1919 buildings will not grow, and it is critical to bear in mind that while the ground for the deep renovation of the middle 'traditional' band is actively being fought for, the worst offenders are a diminishing and, to some extent, eccentric group.

The opportunities to improve building performance for refurbishment are conventionally discussed in three distinct terms: fabric upgrades, service upgrades and modifications to occupant behaviour. 'Easy wins' in each area can be gathered before more complex, destructive or expensive approaches are taken. That said, existing contexts are all obviously slightly different. For this reason two pairs of case studies are presented here, each demonstrating a range of alternatives. The range of case studies here is not arranged to present a linear deduction: it aims to provoke an energetic diversification of approach. Kathryn Janda's paper 'Buildings don't use energy, people do'[10] criticises feedback mechanisms on the basis of ignorance and argues for an advanced integration of building understanding. She quotes the ESRC/UK technology strategy board,[11] arguing for a more user-focused architectural education and stating that the role of designers and architects in the historic context is commonly misunderstood. It is important to hold on to the notion of design in this process. A workflow for energy optimisation will help but will not necessarily observe the potential to re-orientate activity within a building. Indeed, the rearrangement of activity may be as relevant as the rearrangement of space. This point, together with the complexity of issues at hand, is key to the discussion of reconceptualising building performance. This position might be extended by calling also for a better understanding of the role of architects in the integration of sustainability and conservation. The technical spectrum of the issues concerned extends beyond the control mechanisms of policy or management bodies. The four case studies here are chosen to present a range of challenges: the thermal insulation of timber framed buildings, the external wall insulation of both terraced and individual houses, the use of renewables to re-cast the potential of a national estate, and finally examples of design used as a tool to modify behaviour. It is arguably as important to recognise the impact of different procurement routes, types of client and final occupant behaviour as it is to read the constructional and material differences between projects.

English Heritage (EH) queries the use of elemental methods of evaluation,[12] yet these are to some extent even more inevitable with historic buildings than with others. Elefante notes the use of an elemental model to develop a practice of life cycle cost analysis.[13] Looking initially at building fabric, as opposed to occupancy behaviour or energy delivery systems, the range of thermal conditions for traditional buildings in the UK is readily simplified to a number of constructional types: solid wall, timber frame, solid floor, suspended floor, tile or slate roof, thatch, sheet metal. This elemental method of calculating heat loss falls into line with SAP calculation procedures; however, it has particular pitfalls in the case of historic buildings whereby the bigger picture must constantly be held in mind. Elemental methods encourage the separation of thermal treatments, and generally their satisfactory thermal continuity cannot readily be achieved without causing significant damage to the fabric. It has been variously argued that heat transfer can only be properly understood with advanced hygrothermal modelling, or on-site measuring that acknowledges seasonal variations and rejects the 'dry-box' assumptions of SAP.[14] The need for traditional buildings to breathe is thwarted by the requirement for a vapour control layer to be installed with almost all forms of insulation. Roof insulation, particularly loose loft insulation, presents a relatively straightforward set of options as to which should be seized upon as the most effective barrier to heat transfer. Floor insulation beneath suspended timber floors is extremely effective in stopping draughts but potentially risks mould and decay;[15] solid floor insulation is likely to be an invasive course of action in a historic building and might only be justified where the building is not listed or has had a concrete floor previously. Junctions to vertical elements without causing cold bridging are tricky in either event. Discounting horizontal elements, this essay focuses primarily on the more debatable vertical elements of walls and openings.

The thermal treatment of windows (predominantly single-glazed and timber but also mullioned and leaded or cast iron) and doors (generally timber panelled) as elements set relatively straightforward categories whose magnitude can be assessed. Research to date has emphasised the need to refine elemental calculations, to recognise the benefits of thicker curtains, shutters and the role of thermal mass in significantly thicker walls, and to recognise the R-value of lime-based mortars and handmade bricks.[16] It also seeks to better comprehend the path of moisture through walls and its impact upon thermal comfort. Nevertheless, when faced with particular situations, architects struggle to assemble paths for best practice. Here, four constructional case studies are used to highlight the pitfalls and opportunities in attempting to reduce, or be seen to reduce, the energy use of historic buildings.

Single-glazed windows with hand-blown or crown glass have survived by luck or through the successful implementation of legislation, yet their potential to enable energy loss is undeniable. These elements of built fabric must be addressed individually. A visual appreciation of the watery effect of hand-made glass can easily fall on deaf ears. Industry pressure to sell replacement windows or sealed units can appeal strongly to householders who suffer from draughts, noise pollution and fly infestations from old and rattling windows. Maintenance of sash windows that have been painted or screwed shut requires more care than can easily be specified. Unlike the familiar and universally skilled car body repairers, few young joiners or decorators can be assumed to have much patience with a putty lamp. The costing of repairs of unknown duration adds uncertainty to contract sums. The incentive to replace single-glazing with slim sealed units professing ever better centre-pane thermal performance is strong. Certainly, windows and glazing that has already been replaced can be upgraded. The EH and Sustainable Traditional Buildings Alliance (STBA) reports and research from Historic Scotland set out the range of energy losses from various types of glazing; they also note the impact of thick curtains and shutters as night-time insulants.[17] These figures are essential to those considering alteration, but it is also important to quantify the area of glazing relative to the external envelope and its orientation. Typically, the window-to-wall ratio is much lower in traditional buildings; this should not be glossed over, and nor should the issue of orientation. Nevertheless, if new buildings can receive BREEAM excellent ratings while clad entirely in an envelope of glass held together with silicone and shipped across the world, historic buildings need to defend their territory in measurable terms. A building composed of local materials that has been continuously occupied for 250 years or more should have a head start over a calculation based on a 30-year payback. Researchers are starting to quantify 'long run measures' of the use of fossil fuels from the start of the Industrial Revolution, weighting CO_2 produced now more highly than that emitted in a (globally) more dilute atmosphere.[18] Related research is using historic analysis to evaluate predictive sustainability by looking at 19th-century records to predict later trends.[19] While such work contributes to wider debates on the social cost of carbon, it is also valuable for the development of strategies for energy use in historic buildings. The fact that there is evidently a business case for companies to specialise in replacing failed double-glazing provides evidence in support of this argument from a commercial perspective.[20]

It has been established that hot box methods upon which the standard values for U-values are calculated are inadequate indicators of the performance of moisture-permeable materials.[21] Elefante mentioned 'common sense' and talked about 'extending service life' for historic buildings.[22] He championed energy use modelling for historic buildings. In 2007, in Norway, Eir Grytli et al have supported the need for more holistic assessment tools.[23] In the UK, Bill Bordass promoted the need for a Heritage 'Triage', which has led to the development of the STBA's 'Green Wheel'.[24] In the US, the Association for Preservation Technologists International are developing OSCAR, an Online Sustainable Conservation Resource. John Cluver pointed out how the costing cycle for refurbishment differs for developers with short-term goals as opposed to long-term investors such as universities.[25] He argues that modelling ensures that cumulative and contributory factors are added up correctly; it is not necessarily a straightforward sum. There is an increasing call for focus on whole life cycle cost, not just energy usage, to become the focus for evaluative debate.[26]

The need to address sustainability in historic buildings as an elemental issue causes us to reconsider the valorisation of buildings and to assess visual risk against measures of performance. The case studies presented here demonstrate how sometimes conflicting conclusions can be drawn from such processes. There is a race to provide numerical evidence, to respond to economies of scale in order to meet targets but also to boost the refurbishment economy. Questions arise that may previously have remained in the domain of the double-glazing salesman. How many single-glazed windows with historic character worthy of retention might there be in the UK? What damage do they do? Can that number be refined? What proportion can usefully fit secondary glazing? To meet goals of economic viability, domestic heat loss is a target for research with regard to historic buildings. Heat loss calculations, predominantly used to size radiators, have targets based on predicted occupant behaviour in various types of room: to what extent might these be given exceptional status?

A TIMBER-FRAMED HOUSE

Timber-framed buildings have been recognised as some of the most challenging to upgrade without causing risk to their fabric, yet they can be exceptionally thermally inefficient (Figs 7.01 and 7.02). Although widespread as a form of construction from Japan to America, both literature and research regarding the deep renovation of timber-framed buildings is limited to a relatively small number of papers over the last 10 years. Current guidance acknowledges that upgrading may only be viable where unsuitable previous alterations are being removed.[27] New breathable technologies developed in France, such as hemp lime, apparently offer scope but it is acknowledged that significant risks may be introduced by renovation works, either through poor detailing or installation. EH guidance notes: 'Very minor errors can lead to serious problems.'[28] Some physical testing surveys are taking place. A pilot project in Germany has tested a range of infill and internal adaptations.[29] Hans Valkhoff has concluded that no single method of insulation is as yet optimal and that hygrothermal modelling for timber-framed buildings is therefore unreliable in this context.[30]

Former owner Dr T Faber's detailed history refers the date of the Old Vicarage to a lease document of 1627 in which the building is described as 'recently built' (Figs 7.03, 7.04 and 7.05).[31] It also notes that although originally two houses, these were joined together in 1881. The house is three storeys high and also has a basement. Massive brick chimney stacks

Fig 7.01 The Old Vicarage,
Thompson's Lane,
Cambridge[32]

Fig 7.02 Back of St Clement's
Old Vicarage, Thompson's
Lane, Cambridge[33]

Fig 7.03 South Elevation
(*c*1930)[34]

Fig 7.04 South Elevation
(2009)

Fig 7.05 South Elevation
(2012)

dominate the rear elevation, which has remained relatively unchanged save for the demolition of the top part of the chimney stacks in the late 20th century. The fenestration of its timber-framed front, however, reveals interventions from a number of different historical periods. The street elevation was apparently clad at ground level in the 1930s with glazed bricks and an applied timber frame motif. The building has been altered to meet changing performance demands, primarily being joined into one and also modernised for the installation of mains drainage in the early 20th century. The colossal chimney stack was tunnelled internally to provide corridors between rooms on the first floor and also bored diagonally, as can be seen in Fig 7.02 for the installation of a clay mains drain. The timber-clad three-storey lavatory extension was replaced with a modified version in 1980, with contemporary materials of purplish brick and asbestos cement slate tile, leaving little of the west gable framework intact.

It is unusual for a building of such scale and age in central Cambridge to have remained in private ownership and inhabited as a house until now. However, its amenity was curtailed by a lack of external space within its own control, causing it to remain on the market for over a year before being sold in 2009. In summary, the house survived an unusual adjacent bombing in the Second World War (Cambridge and Heidelberg were protected under an Anglo-German agreement), the tunnelling for corridors and installation of a diagonal drain through its main structural wall, the re-rendering of the whole timber-framed face in cementitious render, a three-storey extension, and a roof fire in the 1970s.

The house presents a pared-down form of construction typical of the dry but cold East Anglian region. The jettied timber-framed building hugs the south side of its three-storey chimney stack. First- and second-floor rooms are sheltered from the weather by lath and plaster walls internally and externally. Between these approximately 20mm skins there are voids of between 40 and 120mm, with intermittent timber studs and braces at 350–450mm centres and a calculated average steady state U-value of $2.35W/m^2K$. This lean and economical construction is typical of the domestic buildings in the city centre that survived the fire of 1849. In the woodier and more southerly counties of Kent and Sussex, similar constructions are clad in tiles, reflecting a response to heavier rainfall.

The pigmented lime- and often chalk-rich plasters, with their undulating surfaces, are sometimes pargeted, and their jettied upper stories have crooked and mature postures. Their windows sit flush with the external face of the wall (partly because the walls are so thin), and the distortion of the whole, often capped with a thatched roof, is recognised internationally as characteristic of the English vernacular architecture. Indeed, the shelter held up like a stiff blanket surrounding the hearth is fine-tuned to the drier parts of our relatively moderate maritime climate. The tiny windows, originally unglazed or glazed with horn or vellum, have generally all been adapted to hold glass, often 19th-century horizontal sliding sashes or later casements. That so many of these relatively humble buildings survive is miraculous. Concrete floors, damp-proof membranes, polystyrene wallpaper, polyurethane gloss paint, PVC windows and central heating installations do little to help them, yet they survive because the frames themselves are often resistant to rot. Sole plates and wall plates can be replaced and repaired if required, timber windows re-instated, and so on. Above all, they are saved by a form of collective environmental affection that spans a huge section of society. So what can be done to improve their energy efficiency beyond the obvious upgrade of services?

Assuming that a wall with original plaster internally and externally in sound condition should not be pulled to pieces, the options are limited to internal dry lining or external insulation, and cavity-filling with a breathable material. External insulation will be the first to be ruled out from a conservation perspective, as the change in external appearance primarily affects the building's value to society (as opposed to the individual). Internal insulation might be an option if it could be installed in a reversible way, and neither the occupant nor the listed building's officer had any interest in the internal character of the space or it had already been lost. There is another practical concern with this option that is not easily overcome. These buildings were generally humble in scale, their stairs often less than half a metre wide, and their doors often placed in the corner of the room against the outside wall. Reducing the internal space by 200–300mm or even 100mm internally is unlikely to be achievable if circulation spaces are maintained. Finally, the option of filling the cavities (such of them as can be reached between diagonal braces and studs at 300–450mm centres) with crushed newspaper or other breathable insulants is unlikely to be achieved without causing significant damage to the wall, but also, where a wall has only a 40mm cavity to offer, the insulation improvement will be at an absolute minimum.

Where a wall has been modified, however, as in the instance presented here, there is scope for improvement of the fabric but it is not without the compulsion to adopt necessary compromises. As part of a comprehensive refurbishment of the building, it was decided to improve the thermal performance of the external walls, achieving an increased estimated saving of 21% for the areas concerned (Figs 7.06 and 7.07).

Fig 7.06 North Elevation (2009)

Fig 7.07 North Elevation
(2012)

I was consulted by three separate prospective purchasers before my eventual client bought
the house. Although in central Cambridge it was, very unusually, on the market for over a
year before finally being sold. Its site has limited vehicular access and the building, with no
outside land of its own, is sandwiched between restrictive covenants on two sides. Following
14 months of preliminary work, negotiation, drawing and careful specification, work was due
to commence on site in November 2010. The thrust of the project was to make a proposal that
enabled the reuse and enjoyment of the house without entailing further damage to it, this
being the limit of its conservative achievement. However, the greatest dilemma it illustrates
is that of judging at what point ambitions for energy conservation should be abandoned in
the interests of building conservation. In the average architect's conscience, the pendulum
between the two is considerably more weighted towards the former than it was 10 years ago.
The two notions, so easily married in terms of a choice of building materials, are much less
compatible in terms of operation.

The chimney stacks are shown at their full height in a 1938 photograph from the
Cambridgeshire Collection featured in T Faber's book, at a reduced height in the 1978
listed buildings' application and as existing on the drawings. The listing description of
1962 described '5 rectangular shafts set diagonally'. It was proposed to rebuild the stacks
to follow the 1938 image. The detail of the brickwork was designed in accordance with
Nathaniel Lloyd's observations and photographs depicting similar chimneys dated to 1634
at Burwash in Sussex.[35] It was further proposed to remove the cementitious pointing and
repoint in lime the entire rear facade, and also to remove and replace the cementitious render
to the base of that wall and replace it with a lime-based render to improve the breathability
and future weathering of the masonry wall. The location and routing of the pipework proves
problematic for a historic building; the structural, aesthetic, pragmatic and acoustic concerns
it presents are not simply engineered. The drawings here show a range of options, enabling
the benefits and risks of each to be evaluated while taking advantage of various structural
supports (Fig 7.08).

Fig 7.08 Service diagrams

Subject to local investigations, the cracked cementitious render to the three timber-framed elevations was stripped and replaced with a chalk-rich lime and horsehair render. Expanded metal mesh was replaced with sawn timber laths fixed with stainless steel nails. Sheep's wool insulation was installed where feasible to take advantage of any opportunity to improve the building's thermal efficiency while protecting its internal and external character. In addition, all new and replacement windows were designed to incorporate sealed units, since the windows they replaced were not more than 30 years old and their detailing would be more sympathetic to their 19th-century models. The 1980s square-section casement windows in the attic storey would be replaced with horizontal sliding sashes.

The proposal to strip the cementitious render, which was unstable on the east elevation, and to replace it with a lime render with a high crushed chalk content was not difficult (Fig 7.09). It is also obvious from simple calculations that the heat loss of the walls without insulation was going to be significantly worse than with even a minimal installation of sheep's wool. However, the question as to whether the opportunity should be taken to insulate the walls at this point does not have an obvious technical solution. Sheep's wool, although breathable, requires a vapour control layer and a breather membrane to be installed either side of it.

Fig 7.09 The Old Vicarage,
Thompson's Lane,
Cambridge, 2012

On the basis of a modelled projection, I was recommended to use a high-performance, highly breathable material for each, with the inner vapour control layer able to be wrapped around the exposed timber studs and struts, and stapled into position against the rear face of the internal plaster nibs. The sheep's wool could then be fitted in-between the studs and a breather membrane stapled across the face of the whole. In order not to snap the nibs of the external render coming through the new laths, it would be necessary to form a 10mm space using vertical battens. This, in turn, would alter the relationship of the plaster wall face to the existing window reveals, albeit only by 10mm; the external architraves of the old windows on the house were already almost flush with the face of the render.

Despite the calculable benefits, there was still some concern about the proposal. To this end, the most significant design element in many ways was to enable the specification to deliberately allow the process to be open to stalling at any point while having priced for a 'worst (financial) case' scenario. Tests were made before any removal of the render, and the contract allowed omission of the scheme to insulate if this seemed preferable. Ultimately, as the frame was progressively revealed starting with the very damaged west end, some potential to insulate from inside became feasible; a decision was made fairly late on to replace a 1970s oriel window with a straight sash as evidenced in a 1930s photograph. The exposure of the flawed timber framing behind enabled this decision to be made more easily. At the same time, evidence of a second wing turning 90 degrees to the building was also revealed by the stripping work. The permanence of the changes is put in perspective by the fact that render has been removed and replaced twice in 40 years. While it is desirable to presume that the work has longevity, the likelihood that this may happen again within a lifetime is worth noting.

MASONRY WALL

Solid walls, ranging from brick to stone or flint facings, are generally filled with rubble. The thickness of the wall, the porosity of the stone, the quantity and quality of mortar as well as the orientation with respect to solar gain all play significant roles in determining thermal performance. Solid masonry walls of traditional construction contribute considerably to thermal gains, not least because the ratio of glazed to solid wall area is generally relatively modest for structural reasons. In addition, as current research from the Parnassus project at UCL into mitigation and damage related to flood risks in solid walls,[36] EH,[37] SPAB[38] and Historic Scotland[39] have all indicated through *in situ* testing, the role of moisture passing through a solid wall also has a significant impact on its thermal performance. In the absence of onsite measurements, hygrothermal modelling is increasingly used to illustrate this phenomenon in preference to standard condensation risk analysis software. Nevertheless, such tools are not financially viable for many small practices, although to a large extent these are the architects most likely to deal with work of this scale. Beyond the superior R-values of lime-based mortars and handmade bricks, base information for presumed U-value calculations for solid walls is improving and the tables produced by Historic Scotland provide a valuable starting point,[40] demonstrating for example that a 600mm ashlar wall had a measured U-value of $0.6W/m^2K$ as opposed to its calculated value at more than double the figure. It is also worth calculating the wall-to-window ratio and the closest possible U-value of those walls, and considering the orientation of such buildings and other factors, such as internal panelling, shutters or thick curtains, before condemning their fabric as if the same as post-1919 cavity walls.

Options to thermally upgrade solid walls cover internal or external insulation only. The primary concern for buildings with established historic value is one of transforming appearance. Although applying external wall insulation (with properly detailed window reveals and eaves details) to an entire terrace offers far fewer cold bridging concerns than applying internal wall insulation, the loss of historic value to the collective (ie the public domain), as opposed to the private, is likely to evince far more objections. In this case, performance will regularly be trumped by appearance, although arguably, with careful design, external wall insulation could be developed to be a reversible solution. The huge advantage it has over internal wall insulation, beyond its capacity to be seamless, is that of maintaining the building's thermal mass as a resource – something that is completely lost when a building's walls are insulated internally.

However, external wall insulation is subject to attack both from people concerned with the preservation of visual amenity and in terms of its poor performance when badly installed.[41] Recent research has demonstrated persistent problems associated with the application of external board insulation.[42] These include the more immediately obvious concerns of detailing window reveals, verges and eaves to accommodate the extra depth of material. Although it is not impossible to overcome these issues with careful detailing and site controls, the increasing predominance of 'through wall systems' guaranteed only with the use of proprietary sills and drips has significant impact on the design options that respond to contextual issues. The application of a lime render as a finish might be incompatible with the product and require a further superstructure to hold it; the increased depth required of a more naturally resourced product, as opposed to a polyurethane one, to meet regulatory standards might preclude its practical selection. Nevertheless, the potential for external wall insulation to be developed as a reversible adaptation, for the risks of cold bridging to be mitigated and the cohesive upgrade of larger volumes such as terraces accommodated, should still be encouraged.

As has been pointed out with regard to the BRE's showcase refurbishment of a 'terrace' of stables, the design discretion with which apparently minimal interventions are made opens a wide spectrum of value judgements.[43] Taking an example of a detached house built in the 1970s, where a 1/3 extension and complete re-roofing was incorporated into the project, the use of external wall insulation can be seen to play a significant role in the reduction of the energy consumption of the building. The external appearance of the building has been totally transformed (Figs 7.10 and 7.11). The detailing and control of the installation process in this

Fig 7.10 House for adaptation (2006)

Fig 7.11 House adapting (2007)

case was significantly assisted by the scale of the undertaking. Clearly in reinstating the roof wholesale and installing all the windows and doors anew, there is the opportunity to detail junctions effectively. The building was completely isolated, pieced together from economically viable elements such as standard windows and commercial heaters. Cavity wall construction brought the principle of layered construction to the mass market after the Second World War. As a result of being post-1919, the majority of cavity wall buildings are not yet considered 'traditional' although, as time passes, nostalgia refers to later periods. For the majority of buildings of historic interest, however, it is their external appearance that has merited this status and therefore, by definition, the reclothing of these buildings will be deemed inappropriate. In such cases, alternative measures must be adopted.

RENEWABLES AT A GRAND SCALE

Plas Newydd, 'New Place', sits on an ancient strategic site on the edge of the Isle of Anglesey (Fig 7.12). Its dramatic setting lends the sprawling 30-bedroom house a theatrical tendency. Looking over the natural glittery footlights of the Menai Straights below, it faces a changeable audience formed by what Pennant called the 'Snowdonia Alps' on the mainland.[44] The building's medieval origins were expanded in the 18th century to emphasise a castle-like appearance. In the 1890s the much derided fifth 'dancing' marquess renamed the house 'Anglesey Castle', converting its chapel into a 'Gaiety Theatre', which he opened to the village community. During the 1930s, the house was decorated by Sibyl Colefax and a 58ft trompe l'oeil mural by family friend Rex Whistler was added to the dining room, which has dominated as the house's key visitor attraction for much of the ensuing era. Today its manager, Nerys Jones, with the remit of promoting access, seeks to broaden the scope of interpretation,

Fig 7.12 View of Plas Newydd on the Menai[45]

including a complete overhaul of the estate's energy use as a showcase for the National Trust. It is a stated aim of the National Trust to reduce energy use by 20% from a 2009 baseline by 2020, including a commitment that half of the energy should come from renewable sources.[46] Indeed, its widely publicised renewable energy pilot project is known to have increased visitor numbers within weeks of its completion.

The house is said to have been redesigned in a 'very early Gothic Revival' manner by its owner, Sir Nicholas Bayly, in 1751–53,[47] and his son later employed John Cooper in 1783-6 who started refacing the whole in local Moelfre limestone. James Wyatt worked on the house with James Potter from 1793 to 1799. Their 'Gothick hall' is described as 'a *tour de force* of Georgian medievalism'.[48] Since the first Marquess of Anglesey gained the title in 1816 after victory in the battle of Waterloo, the house has been continuously occupied by the same family to date.

The fifth Marquess was bankrupted in 1904 and exiled to Monte Carlo after a 40-day auction to sell the contents of the house. Although impatience with the Marquess's delinquency in terms of the family fortune can be understood, the current manager seeks to highlight his capacity to entertain, the fact that he learned Welsh and his generosity. This seemingly trivial tuning of publicity and communication is highly relevant to the consideration of the changing fortunes of a long-term estate and its requirement to adapt. The sixth Marquess, a cousin from Staffordshire, made the connection with Whistler. He refurnished and modified the building to incorporate numerous bathrooms in 1922–31 under Owen Carey Little, and it would appear that the cast iron radiators and pipework in the house today date from this period. In 1935 HS Goodhart-Rendel removed many of the castellated features from the exterior of the house and notably changed all the sash windows for casements. The seventh

Marquess of Anglesey was an honorary fellow of the RIBA, a military historian, patron of the Friends of Friendless Churches and vice president of the Ancient Monuments Society. His broad interest in conservation is evident. His apparently chaotic ground-floor study bears witness to his foraging mind and is soon to be on show along with the formal military exhibition of his forefathers' effects that he had made.

Until 2014, the whole 3,800m^2 house operated from a single-pipe oil-fired system heating the entire building at a cost of more than £65,000 per year. A Carbon Trust report in 2008 recorded an annual energy consumption of over 129,000 kWh electricity and 1,118,880kWh oil, with 92kg/m^2 CO_2 from two boilers installed in around 1978 and 2006 (Fig 7.13).[49] Indeed, Nerys Jones notes that Plas Newedd was the largest consumer of oil for the whole National Trust estate, which includes more than 350 historic buildings. Retaining her narrative connection to the site, she cherishes a note scrawled by the recently deceased Marquess to the then manager asking her to look at the geothermal installation at Castle Howard featured in an article in *Country Life*.[50] The idea developed in concord with previous reports, which had promoted the

Fig 7.13 View from Study of the late Most Hon the Marquess of Anglesey FSA FR Hist S Hon FRIBA Hon D Litt

use of ground source heat pumps.[51] Keith Jones and Paul Southall intervened at a time when the National Trust were looking for test sites to develop renewable strategies. The seventh Marquess had inherited the estate with a 75% tax bill in the 1940s and the operation was scaled back from having numerous servants to just two members of staff, yet the heating still ran round the entire building as a single loop. During the 1960s a large section of the house and the stable block was leased to HMS *Conway* Naval School, whose rent was in large part used to pay for the oil consumption. In 1976 the house was given to the National Trust, with a flat retained by Lord and Lady Anglesey, who remained in residence until summer 2013. The work to install the heat pump took place between January and May 2014 and its completion, in theory, enables £40k of budget to be re-allocated to conservation on the site.

Secondary glazing has been applied to all the casement windows following early modelling with thermal imaging. The benefit of the geothermal system is that the heat can work more consistently, making use of the building's significant thermal mass. Today 100% of the heat and hot water comes from the heat pump sited under the Menai Straights, with backup from an LPG boiler. Photovoltaic panels on site provide electrical power to run the pump for the house and the turbines. The new boiler room is housed somewhat perfunctorily in the decorative stable block that Potter and Wyatt had erected in 1797. The presence of the nearby 'cromlech', or megalithic structure, posed significant archaeological constraints for the trenching operations. The heating is not yet zoned; it goes into the existing cast iron radiator system, which will be reserviced at a later date with a projected cost of £3m.[52] The whole is managed by a computer-controlled system. Insulation of the 950m^2 of roof space was estimated to have an 8.3-year payback, and a 100 kw wind turbine was proposed at a cost of £230k with a 9.2-year payback from its installation date.[53]

Fig 7.14 Pipes to the heat pump under the Menai

The heat pump (Fig 7.14) installation has already raised visitor numbers and has attracted media attention, from children's TV to BBC Radio 4. Of the 100,000 visitors per year to date, including cruise ships from America, New Zealand and Germany, the manager notes that the majority are tourists rather local visitors; 75% are members and 25% non-members.[54] Reciprocal relationships with Australia and New Zealand's National Trust organisations draw organised tours. The key issue at Plas Newydd and in the context of the National Trust Estate is one of demonstrable improvement and global outreach. The theatricality of the site and the National Trust's core remit to enhance access will assist in the amplification of results, yet its relative remoteness highlights the intangible nature of the gain. Beyond its setting, the life of the house as opposed to its architecture forms the focus of its interest, and the fact that its refurbishment is fundamentally addressing use as opposed to the alteration of its fabric is significant.

GLOBAL TRADITIONS: EARTH WALLS

Together with timber-framed buildings, traditional earth-walled buildings are among the least CO_2 intensive constructions as they use local materials from local sources and little embodied energy to translate them into enclosures. The range of earth-walled buildings in the UK runs from chalk (clunch) in the east to cob in the south-west. Clough Williams Ellis popularised interest in the method of building in the UK in 1919,[55] although Henry Holland had first presented FM Cointereaux's 1791 article on the subject to the Board of Agriculture in 1797.[56] The unique environmental properties of earth-walled buildings have been heralded in modern times, including their benefits to health. Pearson has noted their superior thermal properties.[57] The requirement for such buildings to 'breathe' is perhaps greater than any other. If immovable objects are left in close proximity to internal walls, dampness may form behind them. If concrete or impermeable floors are installed, they will force water to collect. The walls are particularly vulnerable to the ingress of concentrated water, and there are many examples of earth- and cob-walled buildings collapsing through dissolving. When clad with impregnable cementitious or plasticised skins, they are equally, if not more, vulnerable to the impact of moisture ingress.

Again, window-to-wall ratio may be considerably less than in modern buildings with pre-stressed concrete or steel lintels and plate glass. The R-value of the material may vary considerably, but Pearson has calculated it to be significantly better than that of cementitious constructions.[58] There are particular challenges associated with earth-walled buildings, and they do present a case where neither internal nor external wall insulation is an option. In addition, the risk of increasing concentration of dampness will preclude the use of conventional floor insulation and the use of associated damp-proof membranes. In the following case study, the most significant design component of the proposal is shown to be the adaption of the inhabitants in their use of the building, rather than the adaption of the building to its use by the inhabitants.

Fig 7.15 Manor Cottage
(1999)

Manor Cottage (Fig 7.15), although only four miles from Cambridge, was occupied by my client's aunt until 1998 without connections to mains water, electricity, gas or drainage. The site provided food from its garden and water from a well; paraffin lamps, a woodburning stove and a number of privies enabled inhabitation. Listed Grade II, the cottage is built partly of clunch (chalk block) with timber-framed extensions, and dates from between 1600 and 1850. It is located on land that originally belonged to Haslingfield Manor, which burned down in the 1920s. Clunch pits remain at a neighbouring village and its use as a building material is widespread in the area. A house or barn is shown on an 1814 Relham print of the manor.

In this project, the lean-tos were rebuilt to incorporate serviced areas and circulation, minimising alteration to the rooms. The clunch rooms at the east end of the house had brick on earth floors, and the timber-framed sections had either partial concrete or cardboard/linoleum and earth floors. It was agreed that the clunch-walled rooms be left as such, impervious coverings removed and the floor left as brick on earth, with open fires to provide heat, which would encourage the evaporation of moisture and the movement of air through the rooms.

Fig 7.16 Mason's signature
and key marks in clunch
block

Fig 7.17 Manor Cottage interior (1999)

The clunch was left to breathe for some weeks during the summer to help reduce the internal moisture levels and finally rendered in lime, as set out in the specification. The house was extended and rethatched, and without going into detail, the conservation of the clunch and the willingness of the client to use those rooms seasonally was the key achievement.

Fig 7.18 Exterior complete

Fig 7.19 Interior complete

CONCLUSION

Legal judgements are established through reference to both case law and statute. The one informs the other, and a principle of progress is in theory maintained by a marriage between principled theory and experience. Conventions and legislation elicit protocols of stage-by-stage progress in design, yet these are often extremely unhelpful in the context of historic buildings. Setting budgets, targets and timescales in advance is often counterproductive. The idea of the grand-scale operation afforded by an organisation such as the National Trust may appear to be ideal, but is it at all helpful to other modes of ownership? A key observation is that in all cases, presumptions of behaviour can be very misleading.

The four case studies presented here have aimed to illustrate various aspects of refurbishment practice. All historic buildings, their construction, their contexts, their past alterations, their past and future owners and operators present different economic opportunities and risks. By using several different case studies, I have tried to demonstrate a range of strategic responses that are all closely related to the specific opportunities and risks available in each case. The variety of considerations, even within this small sample, indicate that we should protect the need to approach energy renovations to historic buildings with extreme care, but also that they should still be considered a design solution.

Although the results are not eye-catching – in fact, design in this context often spends most effort to avoid interventions being seen – significant effort is expended to achieve such measures. Architectural design is commonly delivered as exceptional because it delivers visible innovation. Even conservation triumph in this context is dramatised by the contrast between 'before and after' images. But do architects show disdain for 'invisible mending' at their peril? The seats of judgement for building performance and heritage significance have been adopted by building physicists and archaeologists respectively, united in an apparently unambiguous scientific discourse, yet their assertions risk leaving the architectural profession behind. Although ICOMOS was established predominantly by architects, it is no longer closely related to the profession. Most architects today would not hesitate to claim an ambition for sustainability, but few do the same for the conservation of historic buildings.

The means to balance significance and gains in performance and the potential to correlate offsets require strategic design skill. Target-based guidance filtered from governmental directives undoubtedly presents risks of oversimplification. The appropriateness of elemental methods for assessing historic building fabric should be questioned in every case. Clients and architects should recognise the need to retain flexible interrelationships between new and old performance standards, expectations of thermal comfort, contextual constraints and peculiar opportunities as they arise. Fundamentally, the uncomfortable question of balancing values recurs, and as requirements to adapt to the impacts of climate change increase, we have a duty to address these more rigorously. Nevertheless, unlike conventional unilateral methods to procure improvements to building standards, the specific localised concerns of vernacular building traditions as well as variations in current economic contexts have huge impacts on what is reasonable or feasible to achieve, making most attempts at benchmarking for the purposes of implementing policies extremely difficult.

NOTES

1   Meredith Walker and Peter Marquis-Kyle, *The Illustrated Burra Charter: Good Practice for Heritage Places* (Burwood: Australia International Council on Monuments and Sites (ICOMOS), 2004).

2   It should be noted that the requirement to provide SAP ratings on listed buildings for sale or rent is currently suspended (Garston, Watford, WD25 9XX: BRE on behalf of DECC, 2014).

3   The Historic Houses Association defines a historic house as one whose nature is such that it affects the way its occupants live.

4   Carl Elefante, 'The greenest building is ... one that is already built', *Forum Journal*, 21:4 (2007), 26–38.

5   The quantity of pre-1919 housing stock in various European countries is estimated at around 20%. Frits Meijer et al, 'Comparing European residential building stocks: performance, renovation and policy opportunities', *Building Research & Information*, 37/5–6 (2009), 533–51.

6   Didier Bosseboeuf, *Energy Efficiency Trends in Buildings in the EU: Lessons from the ODYSSEE MURE Project* (ADEME, 2012).

7   Carl Elefante, 'Historic preservation and sustainable development: lots to learn, lots to teach', *APT Bulletin*, 36:4 (2005), 53.

8   Department for Communities and Local Government (DCLGC), *English Housing Survey: Energy Efficiency of English Housing* (London: DCLG, 2012).

9   Department for Communities and Local Government (DCLG), *English Housing Survey: Table Da7101 (Sst7.1): Energy Performance1 – Dwellings, 2012* (UK GOV, 2014).

10 Kathryn B Janda, 'Buildings don't use energy: people do', *Architectural Science Review*, 54:1 (2011), 15–22.

11 Elizabeth Shove, *How People Use and 'Misuse' Buildings*, ESRC Seminar Series: Mapping the Public Policy Landscape (ESRC, Technology Stategy Board, 2009), 18.

12 English Heritage, *Energy Efficiency and Historic Buildings: Application of Part L of the Building Regulations to Historic and Traditionally Constructed Buildings*, English Heritage, 2011). [Supersedes Building Regulations and Historic Buildings, 2nd ed (English Heritage, 2004).]

13 Elefante, 'The greenest building'.

14 Caroline Rye and Neil May, *A Short Paper on the Conventions and Standards That Govern the Understanding of Moisture Risk in Traditional Buildings*, http://stbauk.org/resources/index [accessed 30 June 2015]; Caroline Rye and Cameron Scott, *The Spab Research Report 1. U-Value Report*, http://www.spab.org.uk/downloads/SPABU-valueReport.Nov2012.v2.pdf [accessed 30 June 2015]; English Heritage, *Research into the Thermal Performance of Traditional Brick Walls* (English Heritage, 2013); English Heritage, *Research into the Thermal Performance of Traditional Windows: Timber Sash Windows* (English Heritage, 2009).

15 Historic England, *Practical Building Conservation: Timber Research into the Thermal Performance of Traditional Windows* (Farnham: Ashgate, 2012); Brian Ridout, *Timber Decay in Buildings: The Conservation Approach to Treatment* (London: E & FN Spon, 2000).

16 Rye and Scott, *The SPAB Research Report 1.*

17 N May et al, *Responsible Retrofit of Traditional Buildings* (London: Sustainable Traditional Buildings Alliance, 2012); English Heritage, *Research into the Thermal Performance of Traditional Windows.*

18 Jan Kunnas et al, 'Counting carbon: historic emissions from fossil fuels, long-run measures of sustainable development and carbon debt', *Scandinavian Economic History Review* (2014), 1–23.

19 David Greasley et al, 'Testing genuine savings as a forward-looking indicator of future well-being over the (very) long-run', *Journal of Environmental Economics and Management*, Vol 67 issue 2 (2014), 171–88.

20 'Cloudy2Clear UK was founded to fill a void that existed in the market for a company that focused exclusively on the replacement of failed double glazed windows. From this idea was born Cloudy2Clear , a concept that proved so successful, the head office management team decided to offer the opportunity to Franchisees all over the UK' http://www.cloudy2clearwindows.co.uk/about-us/ [accessed 30 June 2015].

21 Caroline Rye and Neil May, *A Short Paper on the Conventions and Standards that Govern the Understanding of Moisture Risk In Traditional Buildings; Davis Langdon LLP, Cost Impact Analysis for Low Carbon and Ecohomes Standard Housing Using Lifecycle Costing Methodology* (Edinburgh: Scottish Government Social Research, 2008).

22 Elefante, 'The greenest building'.

23 Eir Grytli et al, 'The impact of energy improvement measures on heritage buildings', *Journal of Architectural Conservation*, 18:3 (2012), 89–106.

24 May, *Responsible Retrofit of Traditional Buildings.*

25 John H Cluver and Brad Randall, 'Saving energy in historic buildings: balancing efficiency and value', *APT Bulletin*, 41:1 (2010), 5–12.

26 T Ramesh, Ravi Prakash and KK Shukla, 'Life cycle energy analysis of buildings: an overview', *Energy and Buildings*, 42:10 (2010), 1592–600.

27 Phil Oxley (Oxley Conservation), 'Insulating Timber-Framed Walls', in Ian Brocklebank and Chris Wood David Pickles (ed), *Energy Efficiency and Historic Buildings* (2012).

28 Ibid.

29 Deutsches Fachwerkzentrum Quedlinburg eV, *Ökologisches Pilotprojekt Unter Wissenschaftlicher Begleitung – Lange Gasse 7 Quedlinburg* (2014).

30 Hans Valkhoff, 'An environmental assessment of insulation materials and techniques for exterior period timber frame walls', in *PLEA Conference Proceedings 2011* (Louvain-la-Neuve: Google Books, 2011).

31 TE Faber and Laura Napran, *An Intimate History of the Parish of St Clement in Cambridge, 1250–1950* (Cambridge: privately published, 2006), xxiv.

32 [Unknown], 'Houses on E side of Thompsons Lane near junction Bridge St.', B.Tho.K2 20487 *Cambridgeshire Collection* (Cambridge Central Library).

33 Society, Cambridge Antiquarian (1938), 'Back of St Clements old vicarage, Thompson Lane.', in IX Thompsons Lane (ed.), *Cambridgeshire collection* (Cambridge Central Library).

34 HS Johnson, 'The Old Vicarage Thompson's Lane', B.Tho.K3 25953 Copy Negative: and 94/20/21, *Cambridgeshire Collection* (Cambridge Central Library, 1930 (circa)).

35 Nathaniel Lloyd, *A History of English Brickwork: With Examples and Notes of the Architectural Use and Manipulation of Brick from Mediaeval Times to the End of the Georgian Period* (London: Montgomery, 1925).

36 Aykut Erkal et al, 'Assessment of wind-driven rain impact, related surface erosion and surface strength reduction of historic building materials', *Building and Environment*, 57 (2012), 336–48.

37 English Heritage, *Research into the Thermal Performance of Traditional Brick Walls* (English Heritage, 2013).

38 Rye and Scott, *The SPAB Research Report 1*.

39 Paul Baker, *Historic Scotland Technical Paper 10: U-Values and Traditional Buildings* (Edinburgh: Historic Scotland, 2011).

40 Ibid.

41 Grytli et al, 'The impact of energy improvement measures on heritage buildings'.

42 Tim Forman and Chris Tweed, 'Solid wall insulation retrofit in UK dwellings: critical factors affecting management and quality', in A Raiden and E Aboagye-Nimo (eds), *Proceedings 30th Annual ARCOM Conference, 1–3 September 2014, Portsmouth, UK* (Portsmouth: Association of Researchers in Construction Management, 2014), 1367–76.

43 Debbie Crockford, 'Sustaining our heritage: the way forward for energy-efficient historic housing stock', *The Historic Environment: Policy & Practice*, 5:2 (2014), 196–209.

44 Pennant et al, *A Tour in Wales*, 236.

45 Thomas Pennant et al, *A Tour in Wales* (London: Printed for Benjamin White, 1784).

46 National Trust, *Annual Report 2012/13* (Swindon: National Trust, 2013).

47 Ibid, Richard Haslam et al, *Gwynedd: Anglesey, Caernarvonshire and Merioneth*, Pevsner Architectural Guides (New Haven; London: Yale University Press, 2009), xviii.

48 Haslam et al, *Gwynedd*.

49 Roy Milnes, 'Draft Assessment of Energy Saving Opportunities for Plas Newydd Anglesey', in Carbon Trust (ed), (Prepared for Jane Richardson National Trust Wales, 2008).

50 Paula Lester, 'Lean, green country-house machines', *Country Life* (Aug 2010).

51 Roy Milnes, 'Draft Assessment of Energy Saving Opportunities for Plas Newydd Anglesey', in Carbon Trust (ed), (Prepared for Jane Richardson National Trust Wales, 2008).

52 Ibid.

53 Ibid.

54 National Trust, *Annual Report 2012/13.*

55 Clough Williams-Ellis and John St Loe Strachey, *Cottage Building in Cob, Pisé, Chalk & Clay* (London; New York: Office of Country Life; C Scribner's Sons, 1919).

56 Henry Holland and Samuel John Neele, *Pisé, or, the Art of Building Strong and Durable Walls, to the Height of Several Stories, with Nothing but Earth or the Most Common Materials* (England: sn, 1797).

57 Gordon T Pearson, *Conservation of Clay and Chalk Buildings* (London: Donhead, 1992).

58 Ibid.

EIGHT

Sustaining heating in places of worship:
Physical, social, organisational and commercial factors as determinants of strategic decision-making and practical outcomes

··

Bruce Induni

INTRODUCTION

This chapter is based on field research undertaken as part of an Society for the Protection of Ancient Buildings (SPAB)-sponsored initiative to promote church maintenance cooperatives. The area covered included both rural and urban parishes in the West Midlands, Stoke-on-Trent, south Shropshire, Worcestershire and parts of Herefordshire. The areas chosen may or may not be representative of the United Kingdom as a whole.

Informal conversations were conducted with:

- churchwardens
- place of worship support officers
- vicars and archdeacons
- architects
- Diocesan Advisory Committee members
- Amenity Society staff.

This field research has been supported by extensive discussions with SPAB staff and review of casework notes.

During the informal conversations every effort was made to tease out the personal opinions of interviewees rather than to get them to repeat what they thought were the right answers. The success of this interview approach cannot easily be tested, and the reader needs to bear in mind that the conclusions reached in this chapter are not based on academically rigorous research methods. It should also be remembered that the interviewees were a self-selecting sample: they were the people who were prepared to be interviewed.

Research often generates more questions than it answers, and this chapter is no exception. The social and personal motivation that underlies decisions on church heating is complex, subtle and often illogical. It needs much more research. The commercial motivations behind the advice given by heating engineers can be assumed but rarely proven. This chapter should be seen as the beginning of a discussion and not as a final definition of the issues involved.

The nature of the problem

Britain's parish churches are the embodiment of our civilisation and are the physical evidence of our heritage of Christian faith, hope and charity. They are also an astonishingly rich resource of history and art. Churches currently face many challenges, one of which is heating them without diminishing their beauty or historical importance. There are few immediately obvious ways of answering this challenge. None of the currently available heating systems is wholly satisfactory, but that is not a reason for despair: the difficulties presented by church heating should be a spur to developing fresh solutions. Churchgoers do not deserve to be cold; being cold is more than being uncomfortable. If you are old and frail, being cold is the first step on the pathway to hypothermia and death. It therefore follows that churchgoers should be allowed to effectively heat their place of worship.

In practice, heating churches is more complicated than simply providing comfort to the elderly and frail. Churches themselves are elderly and delicate, and provide us with a tangible link to our past – they are culturally significant. Modifying their equilibrium state by heating them can and does have profoundly damaging physical side-effects.[1] Removing and modifying church fabric to permit the installation of heating systems risks destroying the historical authenticity that is the basis of the building's cultural significance. This potential conflict between creature comfort and cultural significance is greatly complicated by the need to protect our environment by using energy in a less profligate and more sustainable manner.

The definition of a church is not always straightforward, and estimates vary on the total number of places of worship in England, but it is commonly said to be around 16,000.[2] The size of these places of worship is hugely varied, from great cathedrals down to single-cell corrugated iron tabernacles. Despite this great variety, one factor is common to most of our churches: very few were originally designed to be heated. Adapting them to provide any form of heating is difficult enough, and provision of sustainable heating is one of the great challenges of our age. Technical difficulties abound. High ceilings steal useful heat from where it is needed. Beautiful but draughty windows leak heat to the outside environment. Damp solid walls remove heat effectively from the interior. These technical problems are only part of the story. There is also a cocktail of religious, social, organisational and commercial issues that add multiple layers of complication.

This chapter examines the history of attempts to heat places of worship, discusses the impact of strategic and practical decision-making on the installation of new heating systems, and places these discussions within the context of the dynamic development of the modern church. Although this discussion is based on the governance and buildings of the Church of England, much of it is relevant to most nonconformist chapels, the Catholic Church and to the Churches of Wales and Scotland. The physics of building heating are not denomination dependent, unless hell fire from the pulpit forms an integral part of the system.

HISTORY

Traditional heating of buildings has undergone several revolutions. In the 15th century the central hearths and open halls of early mediaeval architecture gave way to chimneys, ceilings and division into relatively small rooms. As the Industrial Revolution gained momentum, coal became cheap enough to allow the heating of previously unheatable buildings. Churches are the most spectacular example of this change.

Stoves
The simplest form of coal-based heating is the open grate, and this became common for heating small spaces within churches, such as vestries. The large open space of the nave demanded more efficient and more contained heating apparatus. Cast iron stoves were developed and installed in churches and all types of buildings to address this need. These ranged from simple potbellied stoves to the massive Gurney stoves placed in cathedral interiors (Fig 8.01). The introduction of coal-fired stoves immediately presented many of the problems that are still with us:

- Stoves provide efficient but the localised sources of heat. If you are close to the stove you are roasted, but on the other side of the nave you are frozen.
- Feeding solid-fuel stoves involves transporting dirty fuel and ashes through the space that you are heating.
- Problems with the efficient working of flues are common. Blocked flues and back draughts may not ever have been common, but they are unpleasant and dangerous when they occur.

Coal-fired boilers
By the late 19th century almost all churches that could afford to do so had abandoned interior stove heating, and constructed external boiler rooms. These used coal- or coke-fired furnaces to heat water, which was circulated inside the church through cast iron pipework

Fig 8.01 Gurney stoves like this one in Tewkesbury Abbey are beautiful objects in their own right. They were originally coke fuelled, but can be converted to gas. From an efficiency point of view they are poor performers. Although much of the fuel is converted to useful heat, most of this is convected to the higher parts of the building without having any useful warming effect for the parishioners seated at low level

and radiators. These heating pipes were frequently installed in trenches dug into the floor of the church and covered with elaborate cast iron gratings. The systems effectively distributed heat more evenly and removed the dirt and dust problems created by internal stoves. However, they were grossly inefficient and only sustainable in an era of cheap fuel. Boilers themselves were inefficient, and the heat distribution system contained large volumes of water that took a long time to heat. In other words, much heat was wasted in warming up the system before any heat could be transferred to the interior of the building. Where buildings are in constant use, this is not a significant problem; but if a church is only used on Sundays, system heating needs to be initiated well in advance of actual need, and the system will inevitably remain hot for a considerable time after need has passed. Providing sustainable heating where there is intermittent use remains an intractable problem.

Installation of these indirect coal-fired heating systems always required massive changes to the fabric of the church, and was only possible because the all-conquering Victorian fashion for church restoration had marginalised those opposed to the loss of historic fabric. The Victorian installation of floor-ducted indirect heating systems was often accompanied by the

Fig 8.02 Bottled gas cabinet heaters should never be used in churches. They are inherently dangerous and even if there were no fire risk from the storage of bottled gas, they invariably make the insides of churches much damper. Organs and other delicate fittings will be at particular risk from this increased dampness

installation of fixed pews. It is more than a little ironic that current conservation opposition to the installation of underfloor heating should focus on the retention of Victorian pews that were introduced as an integral part of a new heating system.

Oil, gas and electricity

Technical innovation, together with economic and social change after the Second World War, triggered the slow death of the coal industry. From a sustainability point of view this was no bad thing. Burning coal and its derivatives in inefficient heating systems cannot be defended on environmental grounds. Sadly, the abandonment of coal-fired church heating systems did not trigger a rational rethinking of church heating.

From the 1960s, oil- and gas-fired heating equipment was installed as a substitute for Victorian coal-fired boilers. More efficient and lower-volume piping and radiators were substituted for massive cast iron Victorian systems. Underfloor ducting was largely abandoned and a generally more domestic approach was taken. Where modified and updated wet central heating systems were not installed, the 1960s and 70s saw wide-scale application of directly gas- and oil-fired convector heaters (Fig 8.02). Electric storage heaters were also adopted on a fairly wide scale. By the end of the 1970s few parish churches were without a fixed heating system.

Into the modern age

Until the first oil price shock in the early 1970s, the efficiency of post-war heating systems was not a significant issue for most parishes. Oil and gas were cheap enough, and coke was still available at a reasonable price. Post oil price shock, this changed dramatically. The efficiency, and hence the cost, of church heating systems became a major issue. There was no organised national and effective response to this economic change. The Church of England had other crises to attend to. In particular, declining and ageing congregations became a

Fig 8.03 Under-pew heating is cheap to install, cheap to run and has little impact on historic church fabric. Oil filled electric heaters provide low level conducted and convected heat. Radiant heat is limited and under-pew heaters give warm bottoms and backs but can leave feet very cold. There have been instances where the apparently simple installation has led to amateur work and serious fire damage. Under-pew heaters find little favour with churches that want to remove their pews to allow flexible use of space

major issue. Dwindling congregations and increasing fuel prices caused the abandonment of many heating systems. They remained in place but were only partially used, or not used at all. Lack of a strategic response did not mean lack of experiment. In particular, gas-fired direct hot-air heating was developed. Under the trade name Crolla, this system was introduced into a significant number of the larger churches including Malmesbury Abbey.

A commonly used alternative to gas-fired space heating has been under-pew electric heating (Fig 8.03). Another widely adopted modern approach has been electrically powered quartz-ray overhead radiant heaters. In very recent times underfloor heating has been promoted as the most sensible way of heating churches. Whether its adoption is a rational, desirable or sustainable vision for the future is a matter of fierce argument. All of these new approaches offered some benefits, but none was without problems or unintended consequences.

STRATEGIC DECISION-MAKING

The basic unit of the Church of England, since its earliest days, has been the parish. Parish churches are not legally owned by anyone, but are in the practical, day-to-day care of churchwardens. Churchwardens are unpaid and largely untrained local volunteers. They may be supported or hindered in their work by a Parochial Church Council (PCC) and have an ill-defined and highly variable working relationship with their local priest. The voluntary nature of local church management does little to promote consistent or rational decision-making when it comes to church heating.

The task of imposing good order and discipline on church building and maintenance decisions falls first to area Deans and then to the Archdeacon. The Archdeacon is advised and assisted by the Diocesan Advisory Committee (DAC) and in some dioceses by a Place of Worship Support Officer (POWSO) or Church Buildings Officer (CBO). Some DACs have members with specialist knowledge of heating issues. Some POWSOs have significant expertise in church heating. Some dioceses (for example, Lichfield) have trained clergy to offer proactive heating advice. More general strategic advice is provided by Church Care (formerly the Council for the Care of Churches) and the Cathedrals Fabric Commission.

It cannot be overstressed that the way in which the Church of England supports and constrains the heating decisions of churchwardens is highly variable and complex. Individual personalities can play a major role in outcomes.

THE PHYSICS OF CHURCH HEATING

Church buildings obey rigid physical laws, and these underpin the way heating systems behave. All of us have some basic understanding of keeping warm. We know that heat will move from a hot thing such as a fire or central heating radiator. However, the physical laws governing the behaviour of heating systems are not well understood by many churchwardens.

Key issues that are not always fully grasped include the following.

Heating versus ventilation
By keeping buildings drier, effective ventilation prevents fungal decay and reduces insect infestation, but ventilation wastes heat. Conflicts between heating the inside of a church and ventilating that same space are inescapable. We need to ventilate churches so that we can breathe, and so that moisture from our breath does not cause condensation. If we introduce kitchens and toilets into churches, the risk of condensation becomes much more severe and the need for effective ventilation much more pressing. Good ventilation is an integral part of preserving building fabric.

Mechanical systems that drive effective ventilation and at the same time recover heat are widely available, but they are complex and expensive, and require ongoing maintenance. When badly installed and maintained, they can be noisy and ineffective. To be effective, heat recovery systems need to be combined with carefully designed insulation. In other words, a heat recovery system will only work within a designed environment and cannot simply be added to an existing building without major modifications to that building. This is a huge task and has so far ruled out the installation of heat recovery systems into historic churches.

Convection, radiation and conduction
The design of modern domestic heating systems concentrates on heating space. So-called radiators heat the air in a room, which circulates (convects) and transfers the heat from the radiators to ourselves. This has advantages: heating all the air in a room gives an even heat without hotspots or cold areas. However, in churches, or any building with high ceilings, it

is a wasteful system. The process of convection moves hot air to the top of the empty space and does not effectively push that heated air down to the lower levels where it is needed. This process is known as stratification. The problem of stratification can be reduced by mechanically moving air around inside the space being heated. A fan near the ceiling will help to do this. But mechanical air movement is always expensive, often noisy and rarely wholly satisfactory.

We do not have to heat the air space around us and rely on convection to move heat from its source to where it is needed. Heat can also be directly radiated. Picture the scene in a 17th-century inn where bewigged gentleman are sitting on high backed settles in front of a blazing fire. They are not being warmed by convection: all the convected heat is going up the chimney, and they are being warmed by heat energy directly radiated from the burning fuel. Roaring log fires may not be appropriate in churches, but there are more subtle ways of utilising radiated heat. Electric radiant heaters can be mounted at high level in churches to radiate heat directly at users of the building. When properly located, radiant heaters are highly efficient, with most of the heat they produce being focused where it is needed. Direct radiant heating is an effective way of dealing with the problem of intermittent use. The heating system itself does not absorb significant amounts of energy, and large volumes of water do not need to be heated in advance of the church being used. There is no significant residual heat in the system to linger on, heating the church after the congregation is gone; but direct radiant heating systems are highly visually intrusive, and can produce uneven levels of heat. It is difficult to avoid giving people hot heads and cold feet, and such uneven heating is never comfortable.

The third way of providing heat to the congregation is by conduction. The most common way of doing this is by means of under-pew heaters. For many years this has been typically arranged by installing an electric element in an oil-filled tube under each pew, a system that provides a modest level of heat, which is transferred directly through the pew to the parishioner by conduction and by a limited amount of convection. Opinions vary on the effectiveness of under-pew heating, but the low cost of operation and the lack of visual intrusion are widely popular. However, this popularity is tempered because under-pew heaters do little to ease the misery of cold feet.

In recent years there has been a great awakening of interest in underfloor heating. This type of heating is not new; the Romans used underfloor hypocaust heating, and modern variants have been installed domestically since the 1950s. Underfloor heating works by a combination of conduction and convection. Direct contact between the congregation's feet and the floor provides a route for conduction, while the heated surface of the floor also transfers energy to the air inside the church, which convects and distributes the heat. As with other forms of convection, much of the useful heat will be lost to stratification. Underfloor heating claims significant sustainability credentials, and these are examined in more detail below. However, it is also becoming something of a conservation battleground.

Fig 8.04 Domestic central heating systems have no place in churches. Radiators are mis-named: they radiate little heat and do most of their work by convection. This heats space and not people and is an extravagant luxury in an energy-conscious world. There is rarely anywhere sensible to put the radiators. Here a delicate and valuable medieval tomb has been damaged by drilling in fixings for the radiator and pipes. The localised heat from the radiator will draw dampness and soluble mineral salts into the fabric of the building and cause substantial long-term damage

All methods of transferring heat from its source to where it is needed present practical problems. From the sustainability point of view, there is little excuse for heating large volumes of air when stratification means that the heat is largely wasted. Yet space heating by convection remains popular because of the evenness of heat that it provides (Fig 8.04). It is luxury at a cost. Radiation and conduction have much more convincing sustainability credentials than space heating by convection. Heat goes directly to where it is required, and so lower heat inputs are necessary. The disadvantage to both approaches is that they provide uneven heat.

Draughts, insulation and heat loss

Heat inputs into a church interior are only one side of the story of personal comfort, because as heat is being put into the building it is also being lost. Heat delivered by convection is lost through air change, stratification and air leakage. Air change is another way of saying ventilation, and is both necessary and wasteful. As noted above, we need to breathe and we need to remove the moisture in our exhaled breath. If ventilation is carefully managed, its beneficial effects outweigh any problems of energy wastage; but if it is unmanaged, it can completely negate all efforts to heat a church. Unmanaged air change is popularly known as draughtiness. Badly fitting doors, open windows and poorly designed 19th-century air vents can all contribute to the problem. The intuitive response from many churchwardens is to block any aperture that might admit a draught. Such indiscriminate draughtproofing usually leads to significant condensation problems even if it succeeds in conserving some heat.

Insulation

Stratification leads to significant heat loss through air leakage. Few traditional church roofs have any effective insulation, and most have cracks and imperfections that allow significant leakage of heated and stratified air into the outside environment. It is true that boarded roofs and plaster ceilings do prevent heat loss, but neither is insulation in the modern sense. Solid walls, particularly when they are damp,[3] provide effective routes for heat loss by conduction. Leaded light windows are poor at retaining heat. In short, lack of design in insulation, together with the relatively poor heat retention performance of traditional church fabric, means that traditional churches cannot be sustainably heated without significant structural alterations to control heat loss.

Humidity, dampness and salt damage

Breathing, washing and cooking all introduce moisture into building interiors. Churches that restrict air change to conserve heat, and also install toilets and kitchens – but do not install effective alternative ventilation systems – will suffer condensation problems. Any given volume of air is capable of holding water vapour. How much water vapour this air can hold depends crucially on how hot it is. If the interior of a church is heated, the interior air can hold a considerable quantity of water vapour. This is not easy to explain to non-technical churchwardens, because we can neither see nor taste water vapour and have no easy way of detecting its presence.

When heating is switched off and the air inside the church cools, it can no longer hold all the water vapour that it has absorbed, and the excess water will condense on the coldest available surface (Fig 8.05). Churchwardens and clergy often fail to see the link between dampness, mould growth and intermittent heating. This is particularly unfortunate because condensation is one of the main drivers of timber, cloth and paper decay. Delicate decorative materials such

Fig 8.05 Detail of damp damage being caused by the radiator installation in Fig 8.04

as paint or the ivory on the keys of an organ are at particular risk when heating systems cause fluctuations in relative humidity levels.

Altering the relative humidity inside a church can also have profoundly damaging effects on interior masonry. Soluble salt damage is one of the most serious and widespread decay mechanisms affecting historic stonework. Soluble mineral salts become dissolved in groundwater and are drawn up into porous and permeable masonry by capillary attraction. As the salt-laden water reaches the surface of masonry inside the building it evaporates, leaving the salt behind. The growing salt crystals destroy the stone around them. Heating the interior of the church lowers the relative humidity of the air inside the church and allows it to hold more water vapour. This reduced relative humidity powerfully amplifies the evaporation of groundwater from interior masonry. In other words, the warmer and drier the inside of the church, the more salt will be drawn up into low-level masonry, and the worse salt crystallisation damage will become. The link between salt crystallisation damage and heating is often overlooked because there is no intuitive connection between providing a pleasantly warm interior environment and seeing low-level masonry crumble to dust.

Thermal shock

One last aspect of building physics deserves a mention. When a convection-based heating system inevitably causes stratification, surprisingly high temperatures may be reached in the higher parts of the church: 20°C at floor level might easily mean 40°C at the apex of the ceiling.[4] Such raised temperatures are not intrinsically damaging to timber and plaster – much higher temperatures may well be reached on summer evenings – but if the raised temperatures are attained very quickly there is a problem. This is known as thermal shock. Rapid changes in temperature stress fixing details such as wooden pegs or the key that holds plaster to lath. Repeated rapid changes in temperature will almost certainly cause premature failure.

Most church heating systems carry little risk of thermal shock. Indeed, in practice many may struggle to produce any increase change in temperature in roofing materials. For one particular system this is not the case. Direct gas-fired heating systems are capable of producing very rapid increases in temperature at high levels in churches. The risk of structural damage through thermal shock attributable to direct gas-fired heating systems is unproven. Tangible evidence of actual damage done does not exist, but that may well be because it has not been looked for.

Summary

Building physics has been intensively studied for many years. The effects of changes in relative humidity, the decay caused by condensation and salt crystallisation, and the risks of thermal shock are well known within architecture and surveying. However, research suggests that this knowledge is not be effectively passed on to those who have responsibility for the day-to-day management of heating in churches.

PERCEPTION

At first glance it seems obvious that church congregations feel cold because they simply
are cold. Mrs Jones thinks her feet are freezing because the temperature of the church floor
is almost at 0°C. However, the reality of feeling cold is much more complicated and is at
least partly driven by subjective personal perception. Our bodies are not thermometers. The
temperature of our lower limbs is real and physical, but our perception of that temperature is
constructed within our minds.

Colour

That colour affects our perception of the physical world is beyond doubt. We buy *red* apples
and *brown* eggs, and we associate *white* with cleanliness and sterility. *Black* and *yellow*
stripes are a universal indicator of dangerous insects. Colour and temperature have similarly
powerful associations. *White* and *blue* suggest cold; *reds, yellows, pinks* and *browns* suggest
warmth. This matters when it comes to the perception of warmth in a church. Interiors that
are lime-washed in brilliant white never look warm. If the actual temperature is adequate for
comfort, the wrong colour of interior decoration will make us feel colder.

Light

Just as the paint colour used on the walls will affect the congregation's perception of
temperature, so will the colour of the glass in the windows and the type of lighting used
throughout the church. Putting red and gold tinted glass into plain windows in place of
green or blue will make no real difference to the temperature inside the church, but the
congregation's perception of the temperature will be changed. Perhaps most powerfully of all,
harsh white or blue lighting or glazing chills the soul if not the fingers. Unheated medieval
churches were lit with candles, and these gave off not only a real heat but also a warm light.

Heads, bottoms and feet

Different methods of delivering heat focus warmth on the different parts of the body. This
matters, because different people derive comfort from heat differently. Heat delivered to the
wrong parts of cold people's bodies is heat wasted. Under-pew heating may be economical
and visually unintrusive, but does it give warmth where it is perceived to be necessary?

Toilets and kitchens

Church facilities also play an important role in the perception of heating-related wellbeing.
The promise of tea and cake served from the kitchen within the church makes the endurance
of cold much more bearable. Churches without other creature comforts need to be
disproportionately warm to make them attractive in winter.

Boredom

Our perception of discomfort and even outright pain does not just depend on the immediate
environment; it also depends on our state of mind. If we are bored and without distraction,

physical discomfort is greatly amplified. The relative popularity of house churches is probably due in part to the relative comfort offered by non-traditional buildings, but it is also often due to charismatic Ministry and the complete involvement of the congregation in the conduct of worship.

Other discomforts

Seating within churches plays a significant part in determining the comfort and well-being of the congregation. The agony offered by many pews multiplies the distress of white walls, boredom and poor heating, and makes one discomfort hard to separate from another.

RETREAT

Rather than looking for clever ways to heat church interiors, it is possible to radically alter the way the space is used: to admit that the whole space of the church is unheatable and to retreat into a manageable part of the whole.

Pods

Pods are perhaps the most imaginative and challenging way of creating heatable environments within an existing church building. Visually radical, and often requiring significant structural alterations as well as the removal of pews, pods have yet to find great favour within conservation. This may well be changing. For example, the Churches Conservation Trust has installed community-use pods in the redundant church of All Souls in Bolton. This represents a major departure for an institutional church carer, and has been grant aided by the heritage lottery fund. The popularity of pods among cold congregations has yet to be adequately researched.

Chancels and vestries

Informal retreat from unheatable naves has been going on for many years. As congregations have dwindled, it has become increasingly common for large churches to be subdivided by screens with only the chancel retained for regular worship. A fascinating example is Christ's Church at Melplash in Dorset, where the nave has been separated from the chancel and converted into a badminton court. Churches with suitable vestries formally use these to cater for reduced congregations. An example is St John the Evangelist at Goldenhill in Stoke-on-Trent.

Retreat into smaller and more heatable parts of a large church may be a rational solution to short-term heating problems, but it does nothing to secure future beneficial use and maintenance for the parts that have been abandoned.

Church halls

Conservation focus on ancient and consecrated church buildings inevitably diminishes attention to the role of subsidiary church buildings such as church halls. From the parishioners' point of view, such conservation focus is often irrelevant to their regular worship habits. It is not uncommon for small congregations and their priest to unofficially adjourn to the more heatable space offered by nearby parish rooms and church halls.

Such physical retreat from cold and damp churches may solve the problems of the congregation but exacerbate the problems of the church building. In effect, retreat to adjacent buildings is an unrecognised form of church redundancy.

House churches
Perhaps the ultimate expression of congregations retreating from unheatable traditional church space is the emergence and success of house churches. Though house churches are undoubtedly a complex and subtle social/religious phenomenon, comfortable accommodation is undoubtedly a factor in their success. Limited research suggests that satisfactory heating is a major factor in attracting families with young children.

SOCIAL FACTORS

Church heating problems obviously depend on the physics of the building and the heating system used, but they also depend on the way in which people use the building. Building use depends in turn on a complex and interlocking range of social factors. One facet of the connection between cold churches and social use is obvious. Victorian and 20th-century heating systems have fallen into disrepair and disuse because they were inefficient and expensive to run. Declining congregations have lacked the resource to turn them on, let alone maintain them. The scale of the decline in church attendance has been remarkable, with usual attendance at Sunday worship falling from over 1.6 million in 1968 to under 0.8 million in 2012.[5]

Intermittent use and connection with the community
We have become accustomed to the intermittent use of churches. Even well-attended churches often have only two services a week plus irregular use for 'rites of passage'. This was not always so. Although the evidence is not strong, it is likely that medieval use of nave space was not limited to religious services,[6] but the Reformation changed the whole nature of church use. The enforced removal of screens separating nave from chancel and Archbishop Laud's introduction of movable altar tables meant that the nave became as sacred a space as the chancel. This introduced new levels of formality into use of the nave. The whole church was now reserved for worship, whereas pre-Reformation nave use appears to have been much more flexible.[7] The accidental result of this change has been to separate church from community.

One way of approaching the problem of church heating is not to fiddle with different types of heating system, but to reinvigorate the use of the building. Bringing the community back into the church would be an excellent way of reducing heating costs and problems, but it requires a positive will on the part of the church to do so. Even where this will exists there are churches that have lost their community due to demographic change: there are insufficient people living within the parish to form a viable community. Where both the will and the possibility of reinvigorated community involvement exist, lack of flexible space may be a problem. Overcoming this may not be easy, but it is possible. A good example is St Michael's Church, Discoed near Presteigne. This church serves an isolated small community, but has been able to develop wider community involvement by converting its nave into a flexible space for concerts and art exhibitions.

Reinvigorating the use of church buildings by reconnecting with local communities may address heating problems, but it brings manifold difficulties of its own.

Public perception, pews and proper churches

Most churchgoers have a clear mental image of what a proper English church should be like. This image usually includes bells, high ceilings, stained glass and fixed pews. Up to the end of the Second World War new churches were almost always built along quasi-traditional lines, perhaps the most spectacular example being Scott's Anglican Cathedral in Liverpool. In the 1960s non-traditional designs did appear, for example Upper Basildon in Berkshire. However, this new spirit of architectural adventure has never caught the imagination of wedding planners. The public perception is that rites of passage should take place in a traditional church ... a 'proper church'.

An integral part of this vision of a 'proper church' is fixed pew seating. From a heritage point of view, some pews are both historic and beautiful. Most, however, are 19th-century mass-produced catalogue furnishings that offer little art and less comfort. That pews may lack age or rarity does not prevent heritage organisations from protesting forcefully against their removal. The influence of such heritage protest on church governance via the Diocesan Advisory Committees is formidable, and severe tension within the faculty system is commonplace. The common complaint from parishioners is that those concerned with preserving 19th-century heritage do not personally endure the discomfort that comes with historic seating.

Removal of fixed pews is intimately bound up with the installation of underfloor heating. If there are no pews, the effectiveness, unintrusiveness and simplicity of under-pew heating is irrelevant and the arguments for underfloor heating become much more persuasive.

PRACTICAL OUTCOMES AND AVAILABLE ALTERNATIVES

The perfect church heating system would cost nothing to run, require no alterations to the building, need no maintenance and would not create new environmental issues such as condensation. Such a system remains an impossible daydream; practical reality is constrained in many ways.

Refurbished existing wet systems

Victorian central heating systems almost always used external boilers to heat water which was then circulated through high-volume cast iron pipes and radiators. This pipework, and the radiators associated with it, was sometimes highly decorative. The system in Lady St Mary's church in Wareham is a good example. It is always tempting, from the heritage point of view, to retain the visible parts of decorative Victorian systems, but retention is never likely to provide efficient heating. Even with the most efficient modern gas boiler, the high thermal mass of the system means that a large proportion of the fuel used will go to heating the system rather than heating the congregation.

Dangers of abandoned boiler rooms

Victorian wet central heating systems rarely used pumps to circulate the heating water. Circulation was achieved by thermal siphoning. In other words, the boiler – the heat input into

Fig 8.06 The underground boiler houses of Victorian heating systems allow hot water to circulate through the system without the need for pumps: because the source of heat was at the lowest part of the system, natural convection moved the hot water into the church. Today such boiler houses are often converted to house oil-fired boilers driving more modern central heating systems. Be very cautious in entering: these boiler houses may well contain lethal concentrations of carbon monoxide

the system – was situated at the lowest point of the water flow and the decreased density of the heated water forced the whole loop to circulate.

Underground boiler houses present serious safety problems. The build-up of methane and/ or carbon monoxide is always a potential danger. Victorian attitudes to safety were not as developed as our own and they accepted the dangers inherent in subterranean boiler houses, but we probably should not (Fig 8.06). Thus conversion of Victorian systems not only presents efficiency challenges but also requires relocation of boilers and the careful design of conversion from thermal siphoning to pumped systems.

Conversion of pot-bellied and Gurney stoves

Once commonplace in both poorer churches and grand churches such as Tewkesbury Abbey, coke stoves were the Victorian alternative to wet central heating systems. It is unlikely that many simple cast iron pot-bellied stove heating systems still survive. Coke was the essential fuel for such stoves and was once a cheap by-product of town gas production, but it is now expensive and hard to find. Even if fuel were available, the unevenness of the heat provided by cast iron potbellied stoves makes them unattractive.

Some Gurney stoves used in cathedrals and major churches have attracted conservation conversion, principally because of their ornate magnificence. By converting them from coke to gas, the ornate cast iron exteriors of the stoves have been retained. Gurney stoves, in large spaces, do not behave in the same way as smaller potbellied stoves in smaller spaces. Rather than providing radiant heat to the immediate vicinity, Gurney stoves are convectors that heat the air within the building. While this does give a measure of evenness to the heating effect, it is inefficient due to stratification.

Conversion of historic heating systems is possible and, where they are particularly ornate, may be desirable on heritage grounds. However, it is never likely to be a cheap alternative. Conversion itself will not be simple, and overall efficiency (as opposed to boiler efficiency) is always likely to be poor compared with modern systems.

NEW INSTALLATIONS OF MODERN SYSTEMS

Modern heating systems are designed to meet the demands of specific markets and have markedly different characteristics.

Domestic systems

Most modern domestic central heating systems use pumped water circulation to transfer heat from the condensing boiler to the air space in a building via small-bore copper pipes and panel radiators. There is no doubt that it is a good system in the right circumstances. However, it does not adapt well to church heating:

- Heating the air inside buildings with high ceilings is inefficient due to stratification.
- Small-bore copper piping is ugly and intrusive and requires multiple fixings into potentially historic surfaces. Soldered joints are effective but are an avoidable fire hazard during installation. Alternative compression and plastic pipe fittings do not have an unblemished record for being leak free.
- Domestic panel radiators are ugly and intrusive, difficult to fix without causing damage to historic surfaces and susceptible to rapid corrosion damage.
- Domestic radiator valves are notorious for leaking due to gland seal failure. Such leaks tend to be minor but persistent and are potentially a major source of fungal timber decay.

In short, domestic wet central heating systems are precisely designed to meet the needs of domestic heating. Where stratification is a serious issue and leaks and fixings may cause irreparable damage to historic fabric, domestic central heating systems are not appropriate.

Wet or electric underfloor systems
All underfloor heating systems can be based on buried hot water pipes or on buried electric heating elements. There is likely to be little difference in principle between systems designed for domestic use and those for church or industrial use. It is unclear whether the reliability and running costs of domestic underfloor heating are relevant to church installation. Since church installation invariably involves retrofitting into damper environments than those found in domestic situations, reliability may turn out to be a key issue.

Industrial systems
Highly efficient heating systems are commonly installed in factories and retail warehouses. However, these are rarely relevant to church heating needs. They are generally noisy and involve the relatively violent movement of large volumes of air. Neither of these attributes is acceptable in the church environment.

Air handling and air conditioning systems
The large auditoria in concert halls and theatres, and the large open spaces in offices, civic buildings and educational buildings, often use heated and conditioned air delivered through elaborate ducting systems. These have little relevance to church heating since the cost of retrofitting would be prohibitive and the visual intrusion enormous. All air handling and air conditioning systems require regular high-level maintenance that would be hard to resource from church funds.

RADICAL SOLUTIONS

All the possible heating approaches discussed above might be called traditional. Creating your own individual source of heat by burning fossil fuels such as oil or gas is an approach essentially unchanged from Victorian times. Heating designers have responded to climate change and rising fuel prices by developing radical new solutions. One of these – ground source heat pumping (GSHP) – could be particularly relevant to church heating.

GSHP recovers solar energy from soil and subsoil. Over the summer the sun warms the surface of the Earth, and although dramatically high temperatures are not reached, the mass of the warmed material is enormous so the amount of heat is considerable. GSHP harvests the store of low-grade heat and converts it into the high-grade heat needed to warm the interior of the church. The principle is simple enough, but the equipment needed is relatively complex and expensive and is currently uneconomic for smaller buildings. Applicability is also limited by building density. The amount of heat that can be recovered is not infinite, and if too much is taken, by too many buildings, from too small an area, the ground can become seriously chilled. Rural churches usually have significant graveyards, and these spaces could offer a significant heat recovery resource, making GSHP an attractive alternative to conventional systems.

Other innovatory heating systems, such as district heating, co-generation and biofuels, may have much less obvious application to church heating, but still deserve serious consideration. We should not be content with continuing to adapt existing proprietary systems intended for domestic use.

One area of innovative energy harvesting needs special mention. Generation of electricity via photovoltaics (solar panels) is uneconomic and not in the slightest environmentally friendly. The current energy cost of producing photovoltaics significantly exceeds the amount of energy that they will produce in their lifetime. The reason for their current popularity is an ill-advised and probably temporary government subsidy. Do not put photovoltaics on the roof of your church.

CHURCH-SPECIFIC SYSTEMS

The above brief overview of commercially available heating systems suggests that most are not specifically designed for church use, and indeed this is the case. Eighteen thousand or so parish churches is far too small a market to attract specific design and development. All commercially available church heating systems are thus adaptations and compromises. The advantages and disadvantages that come with these compromises are analysed here.

Direct radiation systems: gas-fired or electric 'quartz ray'
Quartz ray heaters are usually electric radiant elements mounted to wall surfaces at high level. Their radiant heat is directed downwards onto the congregation. Gas-fired high-level radiant heaters are available, but they are not known to have been deployed in churches.

Advantages
- Low cost: quartz ray heaters are cheap to buy and relatively cheap to install.
- High reliability: simplicity and absence of moving parts make for high levels of reliability.

- Low maintenance: electric systems require little or no maintenance during their service life.
- High efficiency: because they deliver heat by radiation, losses to stratification and space heating are low.
- Instant controllability/very low warm-up time: negligible time lag between initial switch-on and the delivery of useful heat combined with near instant switch-off mean that heat is only provided when it is needed.
- Excellent focus: heat is delivered to a narrowly focused area so that unintended and pointless heating of the surrounding fabric is largely avoided.

Disadvantages
- Overly focused: the focus of quartz ray heaters is both an advantage and a disadvantage. Little heat is wasted, but the concentration of heat to head and shoulders may not produce high levels of comfort. Many complain that high-level focused radiant heat does nothing to alleviate the misery of cold feet.
- Visual impact: the visual impact of quartz ray heaters is severe. Even when switched off, their shiny concoctions of metal contrast dramatically with historic wall surfaces.
- Moderate wiring damage: power supply to these heaters always involves fixing cabling across potentially delicate wall surfaces. Research suggests that ancient plaster, often with wall paintings, is surprisingly common, and poorly mapped or catalogued. Cutting chases or driving in cable clips poses a severe risk to any such historic fabric. Electricians have a poor track record for inadvertently damaging the surfaces to which they fix equipment.

Direct gas-fired
Direct gas-fired heating for churches passes external air directly over an exposed gas burner and blows this heated air into the interior of the church. In other words, the church is directly heated by the combustion products of the gas burner. Fairly widely installed in the 1970s and 1980s, direct gas-fired church heating is no longer a popular alternative.

Advantages
- Low installation costs: the equipment is simple and generally installed externally, the simple, if large, entry point required.
- High output: the system is capable of delivering large quantities of heated air in a short space of time.
- Controllability: the system is easy to turn on and off and requires relatively short preheating periods before use.

Disadvantages
- Dampness and potential toxicity: direct use of gas combustion products to deliver heat also delivers large quantities of water vapour. The product of perfect combustion is 50% carbon dioxide and 50% water. No amount of planning can accurately predict how much condensation will be produced by blowing large quantities of hot water vapour into a cold

church. In fairness, most direct gas-fired heating systems are designed to suck out moist heated air when the heating system is switched off. How successful this retrieval system is at reducing condensation is debatable. The heated air is not only damp, but also potentially toxic. Little is known about the long-term health effects of breathing the elevated levels of nitrogen oxides that direct gas-fired heating is likely to produce.

- Thermal shock: an undoubted advantage of direct gas-fired heating is its ability to heat large volumes of air quickly. However, this is also a disadvantage. The rapidly heating air will also rapidly heat delicate items such as church organs. In the absence of reliable research-based evidence, it must be assumed that direct gas-fired heating will deliver significant thermal shock to vulnerable fabric.
- Cost: although low running costs have always been claimed an advantage of direct gas-fired heating systems, research suggests that parishes are rarely happy with the actual gas bills. This is less the fault of the system than the fundamental problem of space heating: if you have a large space you will get stratification, and you will waste heat to areas where it is not needed.

Under-pew heating

Under-pew heating has proved moderately popular in the sense that it has been widely deployed. Whether the scale of deployment has more to do with the promptings of heritage advisers than the overt satisfaction of users is hard to say. More research would not go amiss.

Advantages

- Low cost: under-pew heating is cheap to install and cheap to run.
- High efficiency: heating by conduction, and to a limited extent by radiation, dramatically reduces the inefficiency of heating unoccupied space.
- Low visual impact: however, because under-pew heaters are sited under the pews, they are largely hidden. Skilful installation wiring, at or near floor level, can also mean low levels of visual intrusion.
- Moderate controllability/reasonable warm-up time: under-pew heating is not instantaneous in the way that quartz ray heaters are. Significant warm-up times unnecessary before the congregation arrives, and there is significant residual heat after people have left.
- Good focus: heat is extremely well focused, with direct conduction of all the bottoms and backs.

Disadvantages

- Over-focused: because heat is delivered primarily by direct conduction, with very little space heating, some parishioners complain that warm bottoms and backs do not compensate for cold noses and feet.
- Moderate wiring damage: skilfully installed wiring may do little damage, but as with quartz ray heaters, sensitivity to delicate and historic surfaces is not a common attribute among electricians.

- Fixing damage to historic woodwork: where pews are ancient, applying localised heating may be detrimental. Joints may be damaged and shakes opened, and unpredictable warping may be triggered. These are all theoretical risks that have proved real enough in other situations, but there does not appear to be a significant body of evidence that historic pews have been damaged in this way
- Safety issues: though intrinsically safe, under-pew heaters have proved attractive to amateur installers. A serious fire at Ugborough in Devon is thought to have been caused by defective amateur installation of under-pew heaters. Though amateur installation is a hazard for any form of heating, the apparent simplicity of wiring in under pew heaters poses a potentially dangerous temptation.
- Retention of fixed pews: under-pew heating requires pews! In the wider context of providing flexible space to encourage greater community use, under-pew heaters are potentially restrictive.

Underfloor heating

Installation of underfloor heating in churches (Fig 8.07) has become the primary focus of a battle between those determined to maintain the existing character of churches, and those determined to provide a flexible space, comfort and community use. Both cases have weaknesses. The heritage lobby frequently dignifies Victorian pews with historic status that they hardly deserve, while flexible space advocates probably overstate the comfort and usability advantages of pew removal. Quite aside from these theoretical advantages and disadvantages, underfloor heating has straightforward practical plusses and minuses.

Advantages
- Negligible visual intrusion: when complete, underfloor heating is capable of near invisibility.
- Compatible with movable seating and flexible space: the evenness with which underfloor heating delivers warmth allows maximum flexibility in the use of space.
- Possibly low running costs: advocates of underfloor heating, and in particular the commercial suppliers of systems, claim that it offers low running costs. There is, as yet, insufficient evidence for this to be claimed as a real practical advantage. The main problem is the comparison of like with like. Churches that install underfloor heating almost always do so as part of a determined attempt to encourage greater use. If that greater use does materialise, heating costs will also rise, making comparison with a low-use, low-cost scenario difficult.
- Efficiency: advocates of underfloor heating suggest that congregations are primarily heated by conduction and radiation, and that space heating is minimal. If this is true, underfloor heating will produce true efficiency gains, but the potential transfer of heat from the floor to the air space above it is complex and unpredictable. Considerably more practical field research is needed before the inefficiency of underfloor heating in high-ceiling buildings can be assessed.

Fig 8.07 The iron grilles in the floors of many churches restored by the Victorians used to contain large diameter hot water pipes fed from an external boiler. Such systems were always grossly inefficient and depended on very cheap coal. The sub-floor space can be adapted to accommodate modern central heating systems, but such adaptions are always likely to conduct much of the delivered heat into the ground under the church. At best, such systems heat space rather than people, which is inherently wasteful as it is people who mind being cold whilst space remains largely indifferent

Disadvantages
- Poor controllability: underfloor heating is a high thermal mass system. Low levels of heat input are applied over extended periods to warm the floor slab. Any system that slowly heats large masses needs extended warm-up times and will remain hot for a long time after it is needed. When use is intermittent, these extended warming and cooling times make accurate control difficult and are likely to lead to considerable heat wastage. Where use is continuous, such inefficiencies will not arise. If a church is installing underfloor heating as part of a campaign to increase usage of the building, accurate prediction of increased use is needed to determine whether the new heating will be efficient or wasteful.
- Potentially poor focus: well-designed underfloor heating systems can be zoned to allow partial heating that is focused on areas actually being used. Whether such zoning will yield real operational efficiencies in a large open church is a matter of debate. If heated areas of the floor do not lose excessive quantities of heat to the air above them, zoning will work. If, however, there is significant transfer of heat from the floor to the air above it, circulation and stratification may negate any theoretical advantages of zoning.
- Very high installation costs: underfloor heating is without doubt the most initially expensive of any available heating option. The new floor slab that contains the heating elements must be isolated from sources of dampness and insulated to prevent heat loss into the ground. In a historic church these needs will always demand extensive and complex building work.

- Potentially severe disruption/loss of historic fabric: installation of a new floor will inevitably lead to the loss of and damage to historic flooring materials. Church floors often contain mediaeval altar slabs and tomb covers. Medieval floor tiles are not uncommon, and much fine 18th-century flooring survives. All this material is highly vulnerable when non-specialists lift and attempt to relay it.
- Changed patterns of water movement and salt crystallisation: inserting a waterproof floor in place of one that previously allowed evaporation of groundwater will divert extra flows of salt-laden ground water into column bases and the lower parts of walls. Increased masonry damage in these areas is inevitable.
- Potentially high maintenance costs: when underfloor heating systems go wrong, they are difficult and expensive to maintain. A current example of the problem is the partial failure of the system in Wakefield Cathedral.[8]
- Visual intrusion: this is perhaps the most surprising of the disadvantages of underfloor heating. Floors in churches frequently fail to get the attention that their design deserves. Many Victorian architects placed great emphasis on restoring visually and liturgically significant floor levels. Underfloor heating almost always raises floor levels and poses a significant temptation to take out steps and changes in the level. Major changes to the appearance and atmosphere of a church can be introduced by default when floors are altered.

CONCLUSION

Church heating in the Victorian era was a simple business. Churches were full. The newly rich were mindful of their place in heaven. Coal and coke were cheap. Cast iron was proof of God's blessing for new technology. The environment was a rich fruit, ripe for picking. Loss of historic fabric was a concern for only a tiny minority: Ruskin, Morris and the SPAB were marginal, if vocal, eccentrics. Victorian parishioners, clergy, architects and heating engineers were sure they were right.

Our current angst is, as much as anything else, a direct reaction to that Victorian certainty. We are no longer so sure that historic material or the world environment are toys for our amusement. This uncertainty means that practical heating outcomes are now likely to be the result of a complex blend.

Philosophy
The input of the Amenity Societies (SPAB, the Victorian Society, the Georgian Group, the Twentieth Century Society, the Ancient Monuments Society and the Council for British Archaeology) have had a powerful input into DAC decision-making. This has tended to emphasise the need to retain historic fabric more than the desirability of providing comfortable places of worship.

Emotion

The popular public view of a 'proper church' for rites of passage makes the adaptation of churches to make them more heatable difficult and sensitive. Pods have yet to achieve popularity as a setting for white weddings.

Ambition

Individual parishes remain responsible for the maintenance and management of their churches. Churchwardens, PCCs and clergy have hugely varied ambitions for the buildings in their care. For some, heatable and comfortable space is a priority. For others, increased community use is vital. For both these groups, the flexible use of space offered by underfloor heating is the obvious solution.

For others, whose main ambition is the conservation of historic fabric, any heating system threatens potential fabric loss, and underfloor heating will lead to the worst losses. Current practical heating outcomes largely depend on the local winners of this debate over beneficial use versus fabric retention.

Commercial pressure

This can be a significant factor. Heating installers are part of the same building industry that is home to the double-glazing salesman. Limited research suggests that many heating installations have been adopted because local parishes accepted an overoptimistic estimate of their running costs that was provided by a commercial installer.

Locally available skills

Where the installation of heating systems is not grant aided, initial cost is the overriding factor in choice of system. Only a small minority of parishes are rich enough to choose anything but the cheapest. If a local volunteer claims the necessary skill to install a system, such as under-pew heating, poverty will make such an offer hard to resist. Evidence of amateur wiring and plumbing is neither rare nor historic. As you read this, a parish volunteer somewhere will be adapting a church wiring system.

Process

The process of church decision-making has a profound effect on practical heating outcomes. From the parish point of view, the Church of England has a complex and sometimes impenetrable system of advice-giving on technical building matters. Despite the efforts of many highly skilled and approachable church employees, the process of church governance is problematic. Research strongly suggests that many parishes see their DACs as hostile and remote, and their quinquennial architects as disinterested and expensive. The interventions of the Amenity Societies are rarely seen as sympathetic or helpful. For their part, quinquennial architects, archdeacons and DACs often see themselves as defenders of rational behaviour adrift in a sea of ignorance.

Ignorance

A wealth of excellent advice and guidance is available to local parishes, but this is rarely pro-active: it has to sought out and understood. Seeking and understanding are high-level skills that are not always gifted to churchwardens. The current state of church heating is driven as much by ignorance as by any other factor. Trailing leads, multi-plugs and electric fan heaters are currently overloading church wiring. Worst of all, bottled gas cabinet heaters still lurk in vestries and under bell towers. Such risk-taking is not deliberate delinquency; it is well-meant ignorance.

Ignorance of heating physics means local parish decision-making is often heavily influenced by the experience of neighbouring parishes. If heating in one parish is perceived to be effective and economical, it is highly likely that neighbouring parishes will adopt the same approach. This does not necessarily produce good results. The success of the heating system depends on the system itself and how it is used. Neighbouring parishes may see the success of a system and assume that it will work for them, when in practice their own pattern of use may demand a completely different installation.

Church heating and the future of the church

Ambition on the part of local parishioners and their clergy is an essential part of any plan to improve church heating. Without local ambition to make the local church a better place, for whatever purpose, the whole future of the building is thrown into doubt.

None of our medieval churches were designed to be heated. Installing heating is not a response to the needs of the building, but a response to the needs of the occupants. There is no reason why these two sets of needs should ever be compatible.

The organisation of the Church of England around semi-autonomous local parishes is a key part of its institutional character. It is also a key factor in the survival of local church building and decoration. The survival of details such as rood screens, monuments and wall paintings probably owes more to local autonomy than any other reason. For example, the carvings at Kilpeck have survived because local parishioners were deaf to the national commands. On the other hand, this same local autonomy makes the current resourcing and organising of church heating much more difficult.

From a heritage point of view, all church heating decisions are part of a dangerous game. Installation of heating systems always risks damage to historic fabric. The scale of that damage risk varies between different heating systems, but it is always there. However, unheated churches defy attempts to create beneficial use, and without beneficial use buildings do not survive.

From a religious worship point of view, church heating is no less complicated. Cold and damp churches diminish congregations. Expensive and uneven heating systems, especially those that demand fixed pews, effectively prohibit flexible use of space. This makes increased community use of the building all but impossible.

Heating is only one part of the wider problem of church redundancy. Cold and damp churches are certainly more likely to become redundant, but heating does not guarantee reinvigorated congregations or beneficial use. Unless the Church regains its centrality to community life, our rural parish churches do not have an obviously rosy future, regardless of how they are heated.

NOTES

1   The equilibrium state is achieved when the heat being put into the church is balanced by the heat being lost, so that the temperature inside the church is stable.

2   https://www.churchofengland.org/about-us/our-buildings.aspx [accessed 30 June 2015].

3   Caroline Rye and Neil May, *A Short Paper on the Conventions and Standards That Govern the Understanding of Moisture Risk in Traditional Buildings*, http://stbauk.org/resources/index [accessed 30 June 2015].

4   Based on temperatures recorded during repair work at Duxford church in Cambridgeshire.

5   https://www.churchofengland.org/media/2112070/2013statisticsformission.pdf [accessed 30 June 2015].

6   JH Betty, *Church and Parish* (London: Batsford, 1987).

7   Ibid.

8   Personal communication, SPAB Churches Casework Officer, January 2015.

Conclusions

....

Oriel Prizeman

It is feasible to imagine that the political and ideological values of sustainability and conservation are interchangeable. However, the philosophical starting points can be very disparate. Arguments are often won by the reassociation of prejudices and can span the political spectrum. In the 21st century, Libertarian fears over protecting energy security and a reassertion of responsibility towards future generations can take the place of the CND campaigners of the 1970s. Regulating the lever that swings between control and risk in this context aims to use theory developed in a scientific manner to drive policy and practice, which somehow is expected to take heed of the protected species of traditional knowledge at the last minute.

The ICOMOS Venice Charter 1964 (Article 9)[1] extended the William Morris/SPAB principle that restoration 'must stop at the point where conjecture begins' to a global audience. Today, UNESCO acknowledges a gulf in policy regarding conservation and sustainable development, and a working group is addressing the issue in 2015.[2] Fukuyama, in his recent study of political order and the globalisation of democracy, notes: 'The economic, social, and political dimensions of development proceed on different tracks and schedules, and there is no reason to think that they will necessarily work in tandem.'[3] This is relevant to the globalisation of policy regarding heritage and sustainable development. In the context of UNESCO, it is relevant to question whether policy is still entirely dominated by European colonial and patriarchal models. China's growth, not America's, is always referred to as the evil force of environmental risk to future generations.

The critical importance of economic and environmental contexts is reflected by differing perspectives presented in these few western texts. Equally, historic reflections on heritage, and pride or shame associated with the past, influence the prospects of physical artefacts. The key point in the field is that all responses, judgements and approaches are specific to a place and time. Principles are useful where regulations are not. It is not insignificant to note that ICOMOS has struggled to revise its simple guidelines to accommodate concerns of sustainability. The enormous quantity of detail required for assimilation in the first steps of thinking about a sustainable response in the historic environment can serve to crush strategic thinking. It is the architect's role to bring that thinking to fruition, and the role of academics and software developers to continue to make the tools available to make the best evidence accessible for evaluation.

The various contributors here add evidence through practice and research to the assertion that while the concerns are becoming more widely realised, responses are becoming more varied. Douglas Kent asserts how the anti-restoration attitude relates to adaptation and sustainable building conservation. He relates how anxiety over retaining fabric breathability in the context of the Green Deal led to research initiatives moving away from the initial anti-academic stance of the Society for the Protection of Ancient Buildings (SPAB). The movement is towards greater measurement and monitoring to substantiate the defence of existing building performance.

Dean Hawkes illustrates the changing attitudes to the environmental performance of buildings in Britain across a 500-year period. He introduces the unmeasured perception of comfort and highlights its understanding as a relative concept historically. The adjustment of people's behaviour to the seasonal condition of the building is noted. In characterising Christopher Wren as an environmentalist, he essentially provokes a reaction to 20th-century architecture and a return to design philosophy that works with, as opposed to against, its climate.

Lannon et al review the modelling potential for the mass retrofit of the UK building stock. Working from a national power-generation scale through to housing upgrades, they demonstrate the range of variables in play. The nationwide dependence on fossil fuels and the definition of fuel poverty are asserted. The work highlights the quantity of fuel-poor occupants living in traditional buildings in the UK today. By taking a more generalised view of pre-1919 buildings, they defend the usefulness of the reduced standard assessment procedure (RdSAP) for drawing conclusions regarding the energy use of traditional buildings. This work appears to be in almost direct opposition to the element-specific approach taken by the SPAB research. It challenges the protection of listed buildings from adaptation and advocates the development of more user-friendly tools and making decisions on retrofit at a local level.

Peter Cox's chapter outlines the position in legislative terms within the European context and highlights the key challenges that face the ICOMOS International Scientific Committee (ISC) on Energy and Sustainability (ISCES). Cox notes the key concerns of controlling the quality and knowledge of 'actors' working in the retrofit industry. The requirement for reversibility and practices of risk assessment are outlined among a phased scenario for essentially taking sensible steps. He concludes with a pointed demand for national governments to give urgent attention to the risks of not considering the implication of hastily floated incentives to meet carbon reduction targets.

The contrasts in theoretical approach reflect differences that can be seen in the practice chapters. Buildings that are the responsibility of one organisation may have the benefit of longer-term perspectives on investment. Smaller projects illustrate the benefits of working iteratively and without compliance to layered client policies. To a great extent the question of standardisation, of codes and policies, emerges as the front line of the problem. Where buildings are sufficiently protected by conservation legislation, these concerns are not an item on the mandatory agenda. However, instances where they are and where they are becoming so by contrast with other buildings are occurring at an increasingly agitated pace.

Tom Hotaling's American examples are all for private non-profit academic institutions. They offer a finer definition of heritage but also show the added impetus of a client organisation's sustainability policy. In outlining the National Park Service's distinction of preservation into four categories, he introduces an approach that, if not seen as so vigorously policed, is at least clear to the practitioner. So why is UK legislation the envy of the US preservation practitioner? Hotaling highlights the variance in depth and complexity of control between projects. To some extent the same is true of the UK because of interest groups and other bodies, but institutional missions may in fact be quite specific. The issue of changing demands for building performance is brought to the fore in examples of changing use acoustically at Pennsylvania and at MIT, working with the growing pains of a 100-year-old development plan.

Interestingly, at MIT it was a sustainability code that ensured that all the sash windows remained openable, 'to allow interior occupants to temper the amount of fresh air'. This contrasts with EU legislation, which through its preference for airtightness veers towards the reverse point of view. This may be a reflection of a different and much broader experience of the operation of 20th-century buildings in the United States.

Hotaling's examples reveal the context of dealing with the legacy of buildings which remain in the possession of their founders. The University of Chicago building was cited as 'the best investment I ever made' by John D Rockefeller. Hotaling mentions the implied English architectural heritage being applied to more modern educational aspirations. It is perhaps now worth noting the care with which such bequests are being tended. For example, in all Ann Beha Architects' projects there is a sensitivity shown to the finish and also the colour of the original intention of building – something that would rarely be observed for buildings of a similar era in the UK. At Louis Khan's Exeter library, there is an intention to work with the principles of the original design, to unearth an unexecuted landscape plan. Nevertheless, the scheme also adjusts the interior fixtures to allow the changing teaching and studying methods. Hotaling coins the term that the building is in the process of being 'grandfathered' in terms of code compliance – for disability access and fire. The work demonstrates that heritage status is an active process. Although at both MIT and Chicago Hotaling notes that no installation was added to the walls and LEED checklists are cited to demonstrate compliance with sustainable agendas, the emphasis of health as a part of the sustainable agenda harks back to earliest aspirations for environmental standards.

By contrast, Oliver Smith's example at Trinity shows how under what are arguably tighter and more well-established planning objectives in the UK, the architect's role becomes one of pointing out contradictions. Beyond the demands of the design brief, that of enabling each side of the established policy arguments to be addressed becomes a design in itself, one of creating a convincing argument that can be applied to the site concerned. His note about the arbitrariness of standards of acceptability for levels of humidity is valuable also – it illustrates the risks of over-simplification in the decision-making process. Most importantly, the project illustrates how a redefinition of significance, in this case that of the building's continuous occupation, can be used to enable management for change.

Bruce Induni raises the issue of uncertainty and clearly extrapolates the driving forces and historic distinctions behind our approaches to adaption in the case of church occupation. His chapter highlights the importance of the changing perception of the balance to be struck between human comfort and heritage protection – the rights of future generations to access their own heritage set against the current need to encourage their parents and grandparents to use it. Induni also notes the ironies of our current situation – where people arguing against new heating installations seek to protect pews that were part of far more insensitive Victorian heating interventions in medieval churches.

When William Morris wrote the SPAB manifesto in 1877, he railed against a tide of building development that bears no relation to our current situation. We, in the UK, are now predominantly engaged in adapting our existing building stock. Architects as agents for the implementation of necessary change find themselves in a thicket of guidance, incentives and legislation that, as the various sources for this book reveal, come from international, European, national and local sources. Often, with the two imperatives of conservation and sustainability, the messages are contradictory and our job is to negotiate between them to make them relevant to our context. In addition, our clients may be driven more by shorter-term economical than longer-term ecological motives. Although certain key considerations and principles such as reversibility of intervention and the breathability of traditional materials may be universal, the whole issue with historic buildings is that they were not built under conditions of global standards. They respond independently and subtly to the climate in which they were constructed, as Dean Hawkes makes very clear. The one factor that is sometimes more adaptable is that of use. Through the chapters, three broad typologies in practice are collated here – churches, educational estates and domestic buildings – and they all offer certain interests, constraints and opportunities. A key conclusion remains that were the people to adapt as well as the buildings, there would be significantly more scope for progress in the reduction of energy use within these buildings.

The concerns illustrated here collectively demonstrate the extent to which legislative direction and generalised standards are at risk of inhibiting innovation, or at least of dominating the design agenda, whereby more thought may end up being devoted to the negotiation of compliance than of developing sensitive and optimal interventions that respond to very specific contextual conditions. While it might be desirable to assert scientific principles, quantities translated from the micro scale to the macro are not relevant here. Case studies provide a traditional form of reference tool but they do not establish ground rules. Vernacular, native or indigenous architecture is of interest because it specifically responds to a local context, climatically, socially and seasonally. By definition, the impact and relevance of its technical innovation is localised, not globalised. While it is stimulating to observe alternative responses, we must not generalise from the particular. The climatic location of a building can totally alter its chances of survival – it is readily observed that a building technique in one part of a country may be completely absent in an area only a few miles away because the regional climate is different. To a great extent the path forward appears to be one of anti-standardisation, one that is wary of benchmarks. As Oliver Smith points out, it is ludicrous to set dividing lines: 80% relative humidity should not be the deciding factor over 79% when reaching significant conclusions aiming to progress with the remodelling of a huge historic building and its huge energy consumption. There is a gulf between legislation and traditional knowledge – a gulf between dictat and practice, where the architect can and must recognise her or his requirement to act.

The aim of collating a group of impassioned but diverse voices on the subject here has been to stimulate further debate, not provide prescriptions. The authors' respective approaches vary to reflect their respective roles, which range from academic researchers to consultants, practitioners and members of NGOs. All are charged with the goal to consider conflicting issues that concern the adaptation of heritage assets to climate change from perspectives of formulating the rationale for policy directives to implementing contradictory directives. None has the upper hand, as practice continually informs theory and vice versa. The greatest threat in this context would appear to be the imposition of any form of benchmarked datum for performance, which is by definition ill suited to fit the contours of our built identity in relation to its climate. To develop the means to adapt, each of these arguments will need to be developed further, understood better and negotiated with more care than ever previously, by all concerned.

NOTES

1 International Council on Monuments and Sites, *International Charter for the Conservation and Restoration of Monuments and Sites (The Venice Charter): IInd International Congress of Architects and Technicians of Historic Monuments, Venice, 1964* (ICOMOS, 1964).

2 'Decision 36 COM 5C – Developing a proposal for the integration of a sustainable development perspective within the processes of the World Heritage Convention' http://whc.unesco.org/en/sustainabledevelopment/ [accessed 30 June 2015]. World Heritage Committee, 'Decision 36 Com 5c – Developing a Proposal for the Integration of a Sustainable Development Perspective within the Processes of the World Heritage Convention', in Scientific and Cultural Organization United Nations Educational (ed), Convention Concerning the Protection of the World Cultural and Natural Heritage (St Petersburg, Russian Federation, 2012, Thirty-sixth session).

3 Francis Fukuyama, *Political Order and Political Decay: From the Industrial Revolution to the Globalization of Democracy* (London: Profile Books, 2014).

Glossary

....

absolute humidity	a measure of moisture in the air, regardless of temperature
ATTMA	Air Tightness Testing and Measurement Association
BER	building energy rating
BREEAM	Building Research Establishment Environmental Assessment Methodology
breathable	the capacity and the requirement for traditional built fabric to 'breathe' allowing the permeation of vapour between external and internal environments
CBO	Church Buildings Officer
CEN	Comité Européen de Normalisation
CHP	combined heat and power
cortile	(Italian) an internal court
DAC	Diocesan Advisory Committee
DECC	Department of Energy and Climate Change
dew point	the temperature to which the air would have to cool (at constant pressure and constant water vapor content) in order to reach saturation
EH	English Heritage
EPC	Energy Performance Certificate
gasolier	a gas-fired light fitting
GHG	greenhouse gas
GIS	geographical information system
grandfathered building	a building which is subject to an exemption clause in US law, meaning it only needs to meet the laws, codes and regulations in effect at the time it was constructed or altered
GSHP	ground source heat pumping

Gurney stove	a stove, designed by Sir Goldsworth Gurney and patented in 1856, that used external ribs to increase the surface area available for heat transfer
heritage building	an historic building
HHSRS	Housing Health and Safety Rating System
IBP	Institute for Building Physics
ICOMOS	International Council of Monuments and Sites
IHGM	Interstitial hygrothermal gradient monitoring
ISC	International Scientific Committee
ISCES	International Student Conference on Environment and Sustainability
LED	light-emitting diode
LEED	Leadership in Energy and Environmental Design
LIM	limiting isopleths for mould
LPG	liquefied petroleum gas
millwork	woodmill-produced building materials
muntin	a glazing bar in a window
MVHR	mechanical ventilation heat recovery
NPPF	National Planning Policy Framework
OSCAR	Online Sustainable Conservation Resource
Passivhaus	an international standard developed in Germany in the early 1990s by Professors Bo Adamson of Sweden and Wolfgang Feist for a building which delivers internal thermal comfort through air movement without additional heating or cooling
PCC	Parochial Church Council
POWSO	Place of Worship Support Officer
PPS	Planning Policy Statements
pugging	the infill between the joists of a separating floor for either acoustic or fire insulation
PV	photovoltaics
SAP	Standard Assessment Procedure
SHPO	State Historic Preservation Officer
sistered wood joists	joists repaired with additional timbers side by side
sole plate	the bottom horizontal member of a timber frame to which vertical studs are fixed
SPAB	Society for the Protection of Ancient Buildings
spandrel	a triangular panel between the shoulders of two neighbouring arches
STBA	Sustainable Traditional Buildings Alliance
sun burner	a ventilating gas lamp used for public buildings – patented by William Sugg and Co. circa 1830
SWI	solid wall insulation

travertine   limestone formed in geothermic springs widely used as a building
                          material by the Romans
U-value   measure of heat loss expressed in W/m^2k. Shows the amount of heat
                          lost in watts (W) per square metre of material when the temperature
                          (k) outside is at least one degree lower
USGBC   United States Green Building Council
VAV system   variably air volume system
VCL   vapour control layers
WUFI®   Frauenhofer's WUFI® is a software tool used for modelling the
                          hydrothermal performance of layered constructions

Bibliography

Air Tightness Testing and Measurement Association (2010) *Measuring Air Permeability of Building Envelopes (Dwellings), Technical Standard L1* (Northampton: ATTMA). Retrieved 31st October 2014 from http://www.attma.org/wp-content/uploads/2013/10/ATTMA-TSL1-Issue-1.pdf

Anderson, Brian, *Conventions for U-Value Calculations* (Watford: BRE Scotland, 2006).

Baeli, Marion, *Residential Retrofit: 20 Case Studies* (London: RIBA Publications, 2013).

Baillie Scott, MH, *Houses and Gardens* (London: George Newnes, 1906).

Baker, Paul, *Historic Scotland Technical Paper 10: U-Values and Traditional Buildings* (Edinburgh: Historic Scotland, 2011).

Banham, Reyner, *The Architecture of the Well-tempered Environment*, 2nd rev ed (London: The Architectural Press, 1969).

Bassett, T, et al, 'Calculating the solar potential of the urban fabric with SketchUp and HTB2', presented at *Solar Building Skins* (Bressanone, Italy: 6–7 December 2012).

Betty, JH, *Church and Parish* (London: Batsford, 1987).

Bordass, William and Colin Bemrose, *Heating Your Church* (London: Church House, 1996).

Bosseboeuf, Didier, *Energy Efficiency Trends in Buildings in the EU: Lessons from the ODYSSEE MURE Project* (ADEME, 2012).

Boynton, Lindsay, *The Hardwick Inventory of 1601* (London: The Furniture History Society, 1971).

Brimblecombe, Peter, *The Big Smoke: A History of Air Pollution in London since Mediaeval Times* (London: Methuen, 1987).

British Standards Institution, *Hygrothermal Performance of Building Components and Building Elements – Internal Surface Temperature to Avoid Critical Surface Humidity and Interstitial Condensation – Calculation Methods*, BS EN ISO 13788: 2002, (London: BSI, 2002).

—— , *Hygrothermal Performance of Building Components and Building Elements – Assessment of Moisture Transfer by Numerical Simulation*, BS EN 15026: 2007 (London: BSI, 2007)

Brooks, Chris and Andrew Saint, *The Victorian Church: Architecture and Society* (Manchester: Manchester University Press, 1995).

Bruegman, Robert, 'Central heating and forced ventilation: origins and effects on architectural design', *Journal of the Society of Architectural Historians*, 37 (1978), 141–60.

Brunskill, RW, *Traditional Buildings of Britain: An Introduction to Vernacular Architecture* (London: Gollancz in association with Peter Crawley, 1981).

Burke, Edmund, James Dodsley, and Isabella Metford (1790), *Reflections on the revolution in France: and on the proceedings in certain societies in London relative to that event. In a letter intended to have been sent to a gentleman in Paris*, The fourth edition (London: Printed for J Dodsley, in Pall-Mall, 1790).

Cambridge Antiquarian Society, 'Back of St Clements old vicarage, Thompson Lane', in *IX Thompsons Lane, Cambridgeshire Collection* (Cambridge: Cambridge Central Library, 1938).

Campbell, Colen, *Vitruvius Britannicus, or The British Architect* (1715, 1717 and 1725; unabridged facsimilie ed New York: Dover, 2006).

Carbon Trust, *Building the Future Today* http://www.carbontrust.com/resources/reports/technology/building-the-future [accessed 30 June 2015].

Chambers Dictionary of Etymology (Edinburgh & New York: Chambers, 1988).

Chambers, William, *A Treatise on the Decorative Part of Civil Architecture* (London, 1759).

Chartered Institution of Building Services Engineers (CIBSE), *Guide to Building Services for Historic Buildings: Sustainable Services for Traditional Buildings* (London: CIBSE, 2002).

Clarke, R (2009) 'The Crazy Energy Police Want to Cover My Historic House in Cladding' in *The Mail on Sunday*, 19th July

Cluver, John H and Brad Randall, 'Saving energy in historic buildings: balancing efficiency and value', *APT Bulletin*, 41:1 (2010), 5–12.

Crobu, E, et al, 'Simple simulation sensitivity tool', presented at *Building Simulation 2013 (BS2013): 13th International Conference of the International Building Performance Simulation Association* (Chambéry, France: 25–28 August 2013).

Crockford, Debbie, 'Sustaining our heritage: the way forward for energy-efficient historic housing stock', *The Historic Environment: Policy & Practice*, 5:2 (2014), 196–209.

Davies, MG, *International Journal of Energy Research*, 11:1 (1987).

Davis Langdon LLP, *Cost Impact Analysis for Low Carbon and Ecohomes Standard Housing Using Lifecycle Costing Methodology* (Edinburgh: Scottish Government Social Research, 2008).

Department for Communities and Local Government (DCLG), *Planning Policy Statement: Planning and Climate Change Supplement to Planning Policy Statement 1* (London: TSO, 2007).

—— , *Planning Policy Statement 5: Planning for the Historic Environment* (London: TSO, 2010).

—— , *Energy Performance Certificates for the Marketing, Sale and Let of Dwellings* (London: DCLG, 2012).

—— , *English Housing Survey: Energy Efficiency of English Housing 2012* (London: DCLG, 2012).

—— , *Improving the Energy Efficiency of Our Buildings* (London: DCLG, 2012).

—— , *National Planning Policy Framework* (London: DCLG, 2012).

——, *English Housing Survey: Headline Report 2012-13*, (London: DCLG, 2013)

Department of Energy and Climate Change (DECC), *DECC 2050 Pathways Calculator* (2011).

—— , *Fuel Poverty Methodology Handbook* (London: DECC, 2013).

—— , *An Investigation of the Effect of EPC Ratings on House Prices* (London: DECC, 2013).

—— , *United Kingdom Housing Energy Fact File: 2013* (London: DECC, 2013).

—— , *Annual Fuel Poverty Statistics Report* (London: DECC, 2014).

—— , *English Housing Survey: Table DA7101 (SST7.1): Energy Performance1 – Dwellings, 2012* (London: DECC, 2014).

—— , *Fuel Mix Disclosure Data Tables* (London: DECC, 2014).

—— , *The Government's Standard Assessment Procedure for Energy Rating of Dwellings*, rev February 2014 to include TER calculation for Wales, rev June 2014 to include RdSAP, 2012 (Watford: BRE on behalf of DECC, 2014).

Derham, William, 'The history of the great frost in the last winter 1703 and 1708/9', *Philosophical Transactions of the Royal Society*, 26 (1708–09), 454–78.

——, 'Concerning frost in January 1730/1', *Philosophical Transactions of the Royal Society*, 37 (1731–32), 16–18.

Deutsches Fachwerkzentrum Quedlinburg eV, *Ökologisches Pilotprojekt unter wissenschaftlicher Begleitung – Lange Gasse 7 Quedlinburg* (2014)

Durrant, David N, *Bess of Hardwick: Portrait of an Elizabethan Dynast*, rev ed (London: Peter Owen, 1999).

Elefante, Carl, 'Historic preservation and sustainable development: lots to learn, lots to teach', *APT Bulletin*, 36:4 (2005), 53.

——, 'The greenest building is ... one that is already built', *Forum Journal*, 21:4 (2007), 26–38.

EnergyPlus, *EnergyPlus Energy Simulation Software*, http://apps1.eere.energy.gov/buildings/energyplus/ [accessed 30 June 2015].

English Heritage, *Climate Change and the Historic Environment* (English Heritage, 2008).

—— , *Conservation Principles, Policies and Guidance for the Sustainable Management of the Historic Environment* (London: English Heritage, 2008).

——, *Research into the Thermal Performance of Traditional Windows: Timber Sash Windows* (English Heritage, 2009).

—— , *Energy Efficiency and Historic Buildings: Application of Part L of the Building Regulations to Historic and Traditionally Constructed Buildings* (English Heritage, 2011). [Supersedes *Building Regulations and Historic Buildings*, 2nd ed, English Heritage, 2004].

—— , *Energy Efficiency and Historic Buildings: Insulating Timber-Framed Walls* (English Heritage, 2012).

—— , *Energy Efficiency and Historic Buildings: Advice for Domestic Energy Assessors and Green Deal Advisors* (English Heritage, 2015).

—— , *Research into the Thermal Performance of Traditional Brick Walls* (English Heritage, 2013). Erkal, Aykut, Dina D'Ayala and Lourenço Sequeira, 'Assessment of wind-driven rain impact, related surface erosion and surface strength reduction of historic building materials', *Building and Environment*, 57 (2012), 336–48.

European Parliament and the Council of the European Union, *Directive 2002/91/EC of the European Parliament and of the Council of 16 December 2002 on the Energy Performance of Buildings* (EC, 2003).

Evelyn, John, *Fumifugium, or The Inconveniencie of the Aer and Smoak of London Dissipated Together With Some Remedies Humbly Proposed* (London, 1661).

Faber, TE and Laura Napran, *An Intimate History of the Parish of St Clement in Cambridge, 1250–1950* (Cambridge: privately published, 2006).

Fagan, Bryan, *The Little Ice Age: How Climate Made History 1300–1830* (New York: Basic Books, 2000).

Farnum, Jonathan E, Acting Preservation Director City of Philadelphia Historical Commission (27 July 2007), in University of Pennsylvania Richard Russell (ed) (Philadelphia).

Fawcett, Tina, 'Exploring the time dimension of low carbon retrofit: owner-occupied housing', *Building Research & Information*, 42:4 (2013), 477–88.

Forman, Tim and Chris Tweed, 'Solid wall insulation retrofit in UK dwellings: critical factors affecting management and quality', in A Raiden and E Aboagye-Nimo (eds), *Proceedings 30th Annual ARCOM Conference, 1-3 September 2014, Portsmouth, UK* (Portsmouth: Association of Researchers in Construction Management, 2014), 1367-76.

Friedman, Steven Morgan, *A Brief History of the University of Pennsylvania* (Philadelphia: University of Pennsylvania Archives & Records Center, 1998).

Fukuyama, Francis, *Political Order and Political Decay: From the Industrial Revolution to the Globalization of Democracy* (London: Profile Books, 2014).

Greasley, David, et al, 'Testing genuine savings as a forward-looking indicator of future well-being over the (very) long-run', *Journal of Environmental Economics and Management*, 67:2 (2014), 171-88.

Grytli, Eir, et al, 'The impact of energy improvement measures on heritage buildings', *Journal of Architectural Conservation*, 18:3 (2012), 89-106.

Hens, H, et al, 'Brick cavity walls: a performance analysis based on measurements and simulations', *Journal of Building Physics*, 31:2 (2007), 95-124.

Harris, John, 'The architecture of the house', in Andrew Morris (ed), *Houghton Hall: The Prime Minister, the Empress and the Heritage* (London: Philip Wilson, 1996).

Harrison, William, *The Description of England, 1587* (New York: Dover, 1994).

Haslam, Richard, et al, *Gwynedd: Anglesey, Caernarvonshire and Merioneth*, Pevsner Architectural Guides (New Haven; London: Yale University Press, 2009).

Hassan, Thomas E, Principal, Phillips Exeter Academy (4 Feb 2013), 're. U.S. Department of Education's Green Ribbon Schools Program', in Division Director Dr Judith D Fillion, New Hampshire Dept of Education (ed) (MS NH).

Hawkes, Dean, *The Environmental Tradition: Studies in the Architecture of Environment* (London & New York: E & FN Spon, 1996).

——, *The Environmental Imagination* (London & New York: Routledge, 2008).

——, *Architecture and Climate* (London & New York: Routledge, 2012).

Higgins, Mary Clerkin, 'Stained glass report: Chicago Theological Seminary', *Stained Glass Report* (Brooklyn, 2010).

Historic England, *Practical Building Conservation: Timber* (Farnham: Ashgate, 2012).

Holland, Henry, and Samuel John Neele, *Pisé, or, The Art of Building Strong and Durable Walls, to the Height of Several Stories, with Nothing but Earth or the Most Common Materials* (England: sn, 1797).

Hopkinson, RG, *Architectural Physics: Lighting* (HMSO, 1964).

'Houses on E side of Thompsons Lane near junction Bridge St', *Cambridgeshire Collection* (Cambridge: Cambridge Central Library).

Howard, Luke, *The Climate of London*, 2nd ed (London, 1833).

Hulme, Mike, 'Climate', in Bruce Smith (ed), *The Cambridge Shakespeare Encyclopedia: Volume I, Mapping Shakespeare's World* (Cambridge: Cambridge University Press, 2015 p. 35, n. 3 states 2015.).

International Council on Monuments and Sites, *International Charter for the Conservation and Restoration of Monuments and Sites (The Venice Charter 1964): IInd International Congress of Architects and Technicians of Historic Monuments, Venice, 1964* (ICOMOS, 1964).

International Organization for Standardization (1994) *Thermal Insulation - Building Elements - In-Situ Measurements of Thermal Resistance and Thermal Transmittance* (ISO 9869: 1994, Geneva: ISO).

Iorwerth, Heledd Mair, et al, 'A SAP sensitivity tool and GIS-based urban scale domestic energy use model',
    presented at: *Building Simulation 2013 (BS2013): 13th International Conference of the International
    Building Performance Simulation Association*, Chambéry, France: 25–28 August 2013.

Janda, Kathryn B, 'Buildings don't use energy: people do', *Architectural Science Review*, 54:1 (2011), 15–22.

Jankovic, Vladimir, *Reading the Skies: A Cultural History of English Weather, 1650–1820* (Chicago: University of
    Chicago Press, 2000).

Jarzonbek, Mark M, *Designing MIT: Bosworth's New Tech* (Boston: Northeastern University Press, 2004).

Jeffrey, Paul, *The City Churches of Sir Christopher Wren* (London: Hambledon Continuum, 1996).

Johnson, HS, 'The old vicarage Thompson's Lane', *Cambridgeshire Collection* (Cambridge: Cambridge Central
    Library).

Kelly, Scott , Crawford-Brown, Douglas and Pollitt Michael G, *Building Performance Evaluation and Certification
    in the UK: is SAP Fit for Purpose?*, Tyndall Working Paper 155 (Tyndall Centre for Climate Change Research,
    2012).

Kunnas, Jan, et al, 'Counting carbon: historic emissions from fossil fuels, long-run measures of sustainable
    development and carbon debt', *Scandinavian Economic History Review*, 62:3 (2014), 243–65.

Lawrence Berkeley National Laboratory (LBNL), *Therm Two-Dimensional Building Heat-Transfer Modeling*,
    http://windows.lbl.gov/software/therm/therm.html [accessed 30 June 2015].

Le Corbusier, *Precision on the Present State of Architecture and City Planning* (Cambridge: MIT Press, 1991).

Lea, FM, *Science and Building: A History of the Building Research Station* (London: HMSO, 1971).

Lester, Paula, 'Lean, green country-house machines', *Country Life* (Aug 2010).

Liscombe, RW, *William Wilkins 1778–1839* (Cambridge: Cambridge University Press, 1980).

Lloyd, Nathaniel, *A History of English Brickwork: With Examples and Notes of the Architectural Use and
    Manipulation of Brick from Mediaeval Times to the End of the Georgian Period* (London: Montgomery, 1925).

Lowell, Mary S, *Bess of Hardwick: First Lady of Chatsworth* (London: Abacus Books, 2007).

Manley, G, 'Central England temperatures record: monthly means 1659 to 1973', *Quarterly Journal of the Royal
    Meteorological Society*, 100 (1974), 389–405.

Marks, Brian and Ian G Hanna, *Heat and Light: A Practical Guide to Energy Conservation in Church Buildings*
    (Edinburgh: St Andrew Press, 1994).

May, N et al, *Responsible Retrofit of Traditional Buildings* (London: Sustainable Traditional Buildings Alliance,
    2012).

Meijer, Frits, et al, 'Comparing European residential building stocks: performance, renovation and policy
    opportunities', *Building Research & Information*, 37:5–6 (2009), 533–51.

Middleton, WE Knowles, *The Invention of the Meteorological Instruments* (Baltimore: Johns Hopkins University
    Press, 1972).

Milnes, Roy (2008), 'RESTRICTED – COMMERCIAL Draft Assessment of Energy Saving Opportunities for Plas
    Newydd Anglesey', in Carbon Trust (ed), (Prepared for Jane Richardson National Trust Wales).

Morris, Robert, *Lectures on Architecture: Consisting of Rules Founded upon Harmonic Architectural Proportions
    in Building* (London, 1734).

Morris, William, *The Manifesto of the Society for the Protection of Ancient Buildings*, http://www.spab.org.uk/
    downloads/The SPAB Manifesto.pdf [accessed 30 June 2015].

Murphy, GB, et al, 'A comparison of the UK Standard Assessment Procedure and detailed simulation of solar
    energy systems for dwellings', *Journal of Building Performance Simulation*, 4 (2011), 75–90.

Muthesius, Herman, *Das Englische Haus*, Denis Sharp (ed), Janet Seligman (trans) (London: Frances Lincoln, 2007).

National Meteorological Library and Archive, *Climate of the British Isles Fact Sheet* 4 (Exeter: Met Office, 2013).

National Trust, *Annual Report 2012/13* (Swindon: National Trust, 2013).

Ochsendorf, John, *Guastavino Vaulting: The Art of Structural Tile* (New York: Princeton Architectural Press, 2010).

Olley, John, 'The Reform Club', in Dan Cruickshank (ed), *Timeless Architecture* (London: The Architectural Press, 1985).

Oxford Dictionary of National Biography (Oxford: Oxford University Press, 2004–09).

Lewis, PT and DK Alexander, 'HTB2: A flexible model for dynamic building simulation', *Build Environment*, 25:1 (1990), 7–16.

Partners for Sacred Places, 'Free articles & tutorials', www.sacredplaces.org [accessed 30 June 2015].

Pearson, Gordon T, *Conservation of Clay and Chalk Buildings* (London: Donhead, 1992).

Pennant, Thomas, et al, *A Tour in Wales* (London: Printed for Benjamin White, 1784).

Prizeman, Oriel, *Philanthropy and Light: Carnegie Libraries and the Advent of Transatlantic Standards for Public Space* (Farnham: Ashgate, 2012).

Prowler, Donald and Robert Bruceman, 'Nineteenth century mechanical system designs', *Journal of Architectural Education*, 30:3 (1977), 11–15.

Ramesh, T, Ravi Prakash, and KK Shukla, 'Life cycle energy analysis of buildings: An overview', *Energy and Buildings*, 42:10 (2010), 1592–600.

RIBA Joint Committee on the Orientation of Buildings, *The Orientation of Buildings* (London: RIBA, 1933).

Richardson, Charles James, *A Popular Treatise on the Warming and Ventilation of Buildings Showing the Advantage of the Improved System of Heated Water Circulation* (London: John Weale Architectural Library, 1837).

Ridout, Brian, *Timber Decay in Buildings: The Conservation Approach to Treatment* (London: E & FN Spon, 2000).

Rosoman, TS, 'The Chiswick House inventory of 1770', *Furniture History*, 22 (1986), 81–105.

Rye, Caroline, and Neil May, *A Short Paper on the Conventions and Standards that Govern the Understanding of Moisture Risk in Traditional Buildings* (Sustainable Traditional Buildings Alliance, 2014), available at http://stbauk.org/resources/index [accessed 30 June 2015].

Rye, Caroline and Cameron Scott, *The SPAB Research Report 1. U-Value Report* (Society for the Protection Ancient Buildings, 2012), available at http://www.spab.org.uk/downloads/SPABU-valueReport.Nov2012. v2.pdf [accessed 30 June 2015].

Saint, Andrew, *Towards a Social Architecture: The Role of School Building in Post-War Britain* (New Haven & London: Yale University Press, 1987).

Shove, Elizabeth, *How People Use and 'Misuse' Buildings*, ESRC Seminar Series: Mapping the Public Policy Landscape (ESRC, Technology Strategy Board, 2009).

Smith, Denis, 'The building services', in MH Port (ed), *The Houses of Parliament* (New Haven: Paul Mellon Center for British Art/Yale University Press, 1976).

Society for the Protection of Ancient Buildings (1877) *Manifesto*, available at http://www.spab.org.uk/what-is-spab-/the-manifesto [accessed 30 June 2015].

— — , *William Morris' SPAB: 'A School of Rational Builders'* (London: SPAB, 1982).

— — , (2011–14), Research Reports 1-3, available at http://www.spab.org.uk/advice/energy-efficiency [accessed 30 June 2015].

Spellman, Catherine and Karl Unglaub, (eds), *Peter Smithson, Conversations with Students: A Space for our Generation* (New York: Princeton Architectural Press, 2005).

Summerson, John, *Architecture in Britain: 1530–1830*, 9th rev ed (Yale University Press, New Haven, 1993).

Thomas, George E and David B Brownlee, *Building America's First University: An Historical and Architectural Guide to the University of Pennsylvania* (Philadelphia: University of Pennsylvania Press, 2000).

UNESCO, *Hangzhou Declaration: Placing Culture at the Heart of Sustainable Development Policies* (Hangzhou, China: UNESCO, 2013).

University of Chicago, *Architecture: University of Chicago*, http://architecture.uchicago.edu [accessed 30 June 2015].

–– , *History: The University of Chicago*, http://www.uchicago.edu/about/history [accessed 30 June 2015].

Ürge-Vorsatz, Diana, Sonja Koeppel, and Sebastian Mirasgedis, 'Appraisal of policy instruments for reducing buildings' CO_2 emissions', *Building Research & Information*, 35:4 (2007), 458–77.

USGBC, *United States Green Building Council*, http://www.usgbc.org [accessed 30 June 2015].

Valkhoff, Hans, 'An environmental assessment of insulation materials and techniques for exterior period timber frame walls', in *PLEA Conference Proceedings 2011* (Louvain-la-Neuve: Google Books, 2011).

Viitanen, H, AC Ritschkoff, T Ojanen and M Salonvaara (2003) 'Moisture Conditions and Biodeterioration Risk of Building Materials and Structure', in *Proceedings of the Second International Symposium Integrated Lifetime Engineering of Buildings and Civil Infrastructures*, Kuopio, 1–3 December, 151–66.

Voysey, CFA, 'Ideas in Things II', in T Raffles Davidson (ed), *The Arts Connected with Building* (London: Batsford, 1909).

Walker, Meredith and Peter Marquis-Kyle, *The Illustrated Burra Charter: Good Practice for Heritage Places* (Burwood, Australia: International Council on Monuments and Sites, 2004).

Warm, P and R Oxley, (2002) *CIBSE Guide to Building Services for Historic Buildings* (London: CIBSE 2002).

Watkin, David, *Sir John Soane: Enlightenment Thought and the Royal Academy Lectures* (Cambridge: Cambridge University Press, 1996).

Weeks, Kay D, and Anne E Grimmer, *The Secretary of Interior's Standards for the Treatment of Historic Properties, with Guidelines for Preserving, Rehabilitating, Restoring, and Reconstructing Historic Buildings* (Washington, DC: National Park Service, 1992).

Weiss, Edith Brown, In *Fairness to Future Generations: International Law, Common Patrimony, and Intergenerational Equity* (Tokyo, Japan; Dobbs Ferry, NY: United Nations University Transnational Publishers, 1998).

Welsh Assembly Government, *The Welsh Housing Quality Standard – Revised Guidance for Social Landlords on Interpretation and Achievement of the Welsh Housing Quality Standard* (Cardiff: Welsh Assembly Government, 2008).

Welsh School of Architecture, *SAP Sensitivity Tool* http://www.lowcarboncymru.org.uk/tools [accessed 30 June 2015].

White, Gilbert, *The Journals of Gilbert White* (London: Futura, 1982).

–– , *The Natural History of Selborne 1788–1789* (Harmondsworth: Penguin Classics edition, 1987).

Williams, CW, 'Mr Oldham's system of warming and ventilating', *Civil Engineer and Architects' Journal*, 2 (1839), 96–7.

Williams-Ellis, Clough and John St Loe Strachey, *Cottage Building in Cob, Pisé, Chalk & Clay* (London; New York: Office of Country Life; C Scribner's Sons, 1919).

Willis, Robert and John Willis Clark, *The Architectural History of the University of Cambridge, and of the Colleges of Cambridge and Eton ... Edited with Large Additions, and Brought up to the Present Time, by J. W. Clark [With plans, etc.]* (Cambridge: Cambridge University Press, 1886).

Wilmert, Todd, 'Heating methods and their impact on Soane's work: Lincoln's Inn Fields and Dulwich Picture Gallery', *Journal of the Society of Architectural Historians* 1:2 (1993), 26–58.

Wiseman, Carter, *Louis I Kahn: Beyond Time and Style: A Life in Architecture* (New York; London: WW Norton, 2007).

World Commission on Environment and Development, *Our Common Future* (Oxford: Oxford University Press, 1987).

World Heritage Committee, 'Decision 36 COM 5C – Developing a proposal for the integration of a sustainable development perspective within the processes of the World Heritage Convention', in United Nations Educational Scientific and Cultural Organization (ed), *Convention Concerning The Protection of the World Cultural And Natural Heritage, Thirty-sixth session* (St Petersburg, Russian Federation: UNESCO, 2012).

Wren, Christopher, *Parentalia: Or, Memoirs of the Family of Wren ...* (London: T Osborn and R Dodsley, 1750).

Image credits

· ·

5th Studio	160, 162, 165, 166, 173, 178 (top), 181, 184–186
5th Studio, after Willis and Clark	163
Ann Beha Architects	119, 121, 122, 128, 129 (top), 130, 132, 133, 137, 147, 148, 151, 152 (bottom), 153
Archimetrics	178 (bottom), 179
Architects and Building Branch[1]	33
Richard Bentley[2]	9
Cambridgeshire Collection[3]	198, 199 (top)
Cambridge UL	13, 22
Bernard Cox / RIBA Collections	18
Peter Cox	70 (bottom), 71, 73, 82, 84
DBOX / OTTO	142 (bottom)
David Lamb Photography (2010)	123, 124
Devonshire Collection	19
Charlotte Ellis	31
Ian Ford	146
Fraunhofer Institute for Building Physics	176
Christopher Harting – DP	127
Dean Hawkes	4, 6–8, 11, 14, 23–25, 29 (bottom), 34
Historic Scotland	66, 70 (top), 74, 75
Bruce Induni	222–224, 227, 228, 234, 241

---

[1] Architects and Building Branch, Ministry of Education, 'Building Bulletin 6, Primary School Plans, HMSO London, 1951
[2] 'Bentley's Miscellany', Volume 9, Richard Bentley, 1841, p. 133
[3] Courtesy of Cambridgeshire Collection, Cambridge Central Library

Heledd Iorwerth	44–45, 47, 56–58
Douglas D Kent	89, 91, 92
Simon Lannon	40, 52, 59
Xiaojun Li	60, 61
Max Fordham LLP	175, 177
Raymond McGrath[4]	32 (top)
Motco Enterprises	12
National Gallery Picture Library	180
Thomas Pennant et al.[5]	208
Oriel Prizeman	Front Cover, 199 (middle, bottom), 201–204, 206, 207, 209, 210, 212–214
RIBA Drawings Collection	27
RIBA Photograph Collection	17 (top), 32 (bottom)
Tom Rossiter	140, 141, 142 (top)
SPAB	94, 96, 101, 106, 109
Royal Society	10
Timothy Soar	188
The Master and Fellows of Trinity College Cambridge	164
University of Chicago Library[6]	136
Courtesy of the University of Pennsylvania Archives	118
Peter Vanderwarker	129 (bottom), 152 (top)
Vitruvius Britannicus – Dover Publications	17 (bottom)
Charlotte Wood	29 (top)

---

[4] Raymond McGrath, 'Twentieth Century Houses', Faber and Faber, 1934, p. 38
[5] Thomas Pennant et al, 'A Tour in Wales', 1784
[6] University of Chicago Photographic Archive, [apf2-01615], Special Collections Research Center, University of Chicago Library

Index

···

Page numbers in **bold** refer to tables and in *italic* refer to figures.

5th Studio 161–2
12–14 Lincoln's Inn Fields, London 22, *22*
48 Storey's Way, Cambridge 28–9, *29*

absolute humidity 104, **104**
academic buildings
    Building 2, Massachusetts Institute of
        Technology 126–35, *127, 128, 129, 130, 132,*
        133
    Class of 1945 Library, Phillips Exeter Academy
        145–54, *146, 147, 148, 151, 152, 153*
    Lerner Center, University of Pennsylvania 117–26,
        118, 121, 122, 123, 124
    Saieh Hall, University of Chicago 135–45, *136, 137,*
        140, 141, 142
    see also New Court, Trinity College, Cambridge
accessibility 123
acoustic treatments 121, 124–5, 149
Adam, Robert 22
aesthetics, traditional buildings 68, 77, 81, 90
air conditioning 30, 236
    see also mechanical ventilation heat recovery
        (MVHR) systems
air pollution, London 10, 12, 21
air quality, indoor 107–8, **107**
Air Tightness Testing and Measurement Association
    (ATTMA) 99, 100
airtightness 59, 99–100, **99**, 162
All Souls Church, Bolton 231
alternative energy sources *see* renewable energies
American Baptist Education Society 135–6
Americans with Disabilities Act 123
Anglesey, 5th Marquess of 207, 208
Anglesey, 6th Marquess of 208
Anglesey, 7th Marquess of 208–9, *210*
Anglican Cathedral, Liverpool 233
Ann Beha Architects (ABA), Boston, Massachusetts 115,
    118, 138
Antonello de Messina *180*

ArchiMetrics Ltd 97, 181
Architecture of the Welltempered Environment, The
    (Banham) 20
artificial lighting 13, 25, 30
    see also low energy lighting
Arts and Crafts 20, 26–9, *27, 29*
Association for Preservation Technologists
    International 196–7
asthma 90
authenticity, traditional buildings 77, 90, 169–70,
    174

Baillie Scott, M.H. 26, 28–9, *29*
Baker, Paul 176
Banham, Reyner 20, 35
Bank of England 22, 25
Bank of Ireland 25
Barry, Sir Charles 21, 23–5, *23, 24, 25*
battery storage systems 59
Bayly, Sir Nicholas 208
Beacon Planning 167
BER *see* Building Energy Rating (BER)
Bess of Hardwick 5
biofuels 237
Bordass, Bill 196
boredom 230–1
Bosworth, William Welles 127
box pews 13
BR 443 *Conventions for U-Value Calculations* 95
breathable materials 71, 78, 80, 89, 211
BS EN ISO 13788 105
BS EN ISO 15026 105
BuildDesk software 95–7, *96*
Building Energy Rating (BER) 67, 69
building envelope 74–5, *74, 75*
building fabric
    risks to 81, 90, 108–9, *109*
    see also solid wall construction; timber-framed
        buildings; U-values; walls

building materials, traditional building retrofitting
      70–1, 78, 80
building performance modelling see energy modelling
      techniques
Building Regulations 43–4, 66, 95, 100, 162, 166, 182
Building Research Station 31, 33
building services, traditional buildings 75–6
      see also heating systems; ventilation systems
Building the Future Today report 41, **41**
building use see occupant behaviour
Burlington, Lord 18–19, *18, 19*

Cambridge
      48 Storey's Way 28–9, *29*
      Manor Cottage 212–13, *212, 213, 214*
      Old Vicarage, Thompson's Lane 197–205, *198, 199,
          201, 202, 203, 204*
      Thurso House 31, *31, 32*
      see also New Court, Trinity College, Cambridge
Cambridge City Council 167–8, 171–2, 186–7, 189
*Cambridge Local Plan Policy 4/10 – Listed
          Buildings* 167–8
Campbell, Colen 14
carbon dioxide emissions 40, 41–2, **41**, 65–6, 183, *184*,
      194
carbon dioxide, internal levels 107–8, **107**
carbon monoxide 235
Carbon Trust 41, **41**, 209
carpets 18
case studies
      Castleland renewal area, Wales 54–6, **54**, **55**, *56*,
          57, 58
      dynamic simulation of terrace house 56–61, *59*, **60**,
          60, 61
      earth-walled building 211–13, *212, 213, 214*
      house with solid walls 205–7, *206, 207*
      Plas Newydd, Anglesey 207–11, *208, 209, 210*
      timber-framed building 197–205, *198, 199, 201, 202,
          203, 204*
      see also United States historic buildings
cast iron stoves, in churches 221, *222*, 235
Castleland renewal area, Wales 54–6, **54**, **55**, *56, 57, 58*
cathedrals
      Gothic Revival restoration 88
      see also church heating
Cathedrals Fabric Commission 225
cavity wall insulation recommendations **50**
cavity walls 89, 94, 207
CBOs see Church Buildings Officers (CBOs)
cement-based render 81, 203
Central European Standards Committee, EU 69
Chambers, William 14, 16, 18, 19, 20
chancels 231
Checkley, George 31, *31, 32*
Chicago Theological Center (CTS) 136
chimneys 16, 19, 100
Chiswick House, London 18–19, *18, 19*
CHP (combined heat and power) 82
Christ's Church, Melplash, Dorset 231
Christ's College Cambridge *180*
Church Buildings Officers (CBOs) 224–5
Church Care 225
church halls 231–2

church heating 219–45
      converting existing systems 233–5, *234*
      direct gas-fired heating systems 224, 229, 238–9
      electric radiant heaters 224, *224*, 226, 237–8
      history of 221–4, *222, 223, 224*
      installing modern systems 235–6
      perception of cold 230–1
      under-pew heating 224, *224*, 226, 233, 239–40
      physics of 225–9
      renewable energies 236–7
      retreating into smaller spaces 231–2
      social factors 232–3
      stoves 221, *222*, 235
      strategic decision-making 224–5, 242–5
      underfloor heating 223, 224, 226, 233, 236, 240–2,
          241
church maintenance cooperatives 219
Church of England organisation 224–5, 244
churches
      Gothic Revival restoration 88
      Wren's London 11–14, *11, 12, 13, 14*
      see also church heating
Churches Conservation Trust 231
churchwardens 224, 225, 243
Cité de Rèfuge, Paris 30
Class of 1945 Library, Phillips Exeter Academy 145–54,
          146, 147, 148, 151, 152, 153
Classical Revival 127
classicism 8
climate 76–7
      see also English climate
climate change 49, 65
Climate Change and the Historic Environment (EH)
      171
Climate of London, The (Howard) 21
clunch wall construction 212–13, *212, 213*
cluster analysis technique 51–2, 54
Cluver, John 197
co-generation systems 237
coal 10, 12, 41, **41**
coal-fired heating systems, in churches 221–3
Coates, Wells 30
cob wall construction 93
      see also earth-walled buildings
Cobb, Henry Ives 136
Cointereaux, F.M. 211
coke stoves, in churches 221, *222*, 235
cold, perception of 230–1
Colefax, Sibyl 207
combined heat and power (CHP) 82
comfort
      16th century 5–6
      17th century 13
      18th century 18
      19th century 20, 21–2, 26, 28
      and traditional building retrofitting 108–9, *109*
Comité Européen de Normalisation (CEN), EU 69
condensation 90, 228–9
condensation risk analysis 105–7, 205
condition, traditional buildings 75
conduction 226, 227
conservation areas 43
conservation issues 77–8

Conservation Principles, Policies and Guidance for the Sustainable Management of the Historic Environment (EH) 169–71
conservative repair 88
convection 225–6, 227
Cooper, John 208
Cope and Stewardson, Philadelphia 118
copper piping, small-bore 235–6
Cram, Ralph Adams 146
Crolla heating system 224
crown glass 196
curtains 79, 195, 196, 205

DACs *see* Diocesan Advisory Committees (DACs)
damp-proof membranes 211
dampness 75, 164–5, 211, 228
  see also interstitial hygrothermal conditions
Dartmoor National Park Authority 97
Darwin, Charles 180, *180*
daylighting 12–13, 15–16, 18, 19, 28, 33
decarbonisation 41–2
demonstrator software 51
Department of Energy and Climate Change, UK 47, *47*, 90
Derham, William 15
Description of England, The (Harrison) 4
dew point margins 105, *106*
Dickens, Charles 21
Diocesan Advisory Committees (DACs) 224–5, 233, 242, 243
direct gas-fired church heating systems 224, 229, 238–9
district heating systems 82, 237
documentation, traditional building retrofitting 80, 82
domestic central heating systems, in churches *227*, 235–6
domestic traditional building retrofitting 39–40, 42–4, 193–215
  Castleland renewal area case study 54–6, **54**, **55**, *56*, *57*, *58*
  dynamic simulation of terrace house 56–61, *59*, **60**, *60*, *61*
  earth-walled building case study 211–13, *212*, *213*, *214*
  energy efficiency at local authority scale 52–3
  Plas Newydd, Anglesey 207–11, *208*, *209*, *210*
  risks to building fabric 90, 108–9, *109*
  solid wall retrofitting case study 205–7, *206*, *207*
  stock profile 43–4, *44–5*
  timber-framed building case study 197–205, *198*, *199*, *201*, *202*, *203*, *204*
  see also SPAB building performance survey
doors 75, 195
double glazing **50**, **55**, *57*, *58*, 59
draughtproofing 99, 100
  churches 227
  costs **55**, *57*, *58*
  effects on traditional buildings 90
  recommendations **50**
Drewsteignton, Devon *see* SPAB building performance survey
dry rot 107, 164–5
dynamic simulation models 48–9, 56–61, *59*, **60**, *60*, *61*

earth-walled buildings 93, 211–13, *212*, *213*, *214*
Edinburgh Register Office 22
Edison, Thomas 30
EH *see* English Heritage
electric radiant heaters, in churches 224, *224*, 226, 237–8
electric storage heaters 223
electricity generation 40–2, **41**
electricity supply 30
Elefante, Carl 194, 195, 196
elemental methods of evaluation 195
Elizabeth, Countess of Shrewsbury 5
embodied energy 49, 79–80, 211
Energy Company Obligation 50–1
energy efficiency
  government policy 40–3
  at local authority scale 52–3
  see also retrofitting
energy modelling techniques 44–5, 196–7
  dynamic simulation models 48–9, 56–61, *59*, **60**, *60*, *61*
  Standard Assessment Procedure (SAP) 45–8, *47*, 52, 55, *56*, *57*, *58*, 95
Energy Performance Certificates (EPCs) 46, 54, 55, 90, 95
  exemptions 43, 44, 67, 69
  retrofit recommendations 49, **50**
Energy Performance of Buildings Directive, EU 66
English climate 3
  16th century 4, 5
  17th century 9–11, 12
  18th century 15
  19th century 21, 26
  Little Ice Age 4, 9, 12, 26
English Gothic 136
English Heritage 46, 182, 195, 196, 205
  guidance 161, 169–71, 197
  New Court, Trinity College, Cambridge 171–2, 186–7
English Housing Survey 194
environmental design
  16th century 3–8, *4*, *6*, *7*, *8*
  17th century 8–14, *11*, *12*, *13*, *14*
  18th century 14–20, *17*, *18*, *19*
  19th century Arts and Crafts 20, 26–9, *27*, *29*
  19th century London 20–5, *22*, *23*, *24*, *25*
  20th century 30–3, *31*, *32*, *33*, *34*
  modes of environmental control 35
environmental design optimisation 49
environmental sustainability policies 115–16, 144, 154
EPCs *see* Energy Performance Certificates (EPCs)
European Standard for Energy Efficiency of Culturally, Historically and Architecturally Important Buildings 69
European Union 66, 67, 69, 194
Evelyn, John 9–10
exclusive mode of environmental control 35
external wall insulation 44, 59, *84*, 97, 102, 201, 205–7

fabric first retrofitting 54, **54**, 55, *57*
fabric heat loss *see* U-values
fire detection measures 139
fireplaces 7, 16, 18, 19, 28, 29
floor insulation **50**, **55**, *57*, *58*, 195, 211

floors 75
fog 21
Foulke and Long Institute, University of
    Pennsylvania 118, *118*
Franklin, Benjamin 117–18
Fraunhofer Institute for Building Physics (IBP),
    Germany 83, 107
Freeman, Ripley 127
Frost Fairs on Thames 9, *9*, 15
Fry, Maxwell 30, 31–2, *32*
fuel poverty 39, 42–3
Fukuyama, Francis 247

gas-fired heating systems, in churches 223
gas lighting 25
geothermal energy 79, 209–10
    see also ground source heat pumps (GSHP)
Glaser method 105
Glasgow Caledonian University 91, 93, 176
Goodhart-Rendel, H.S. 208
Gormley, Antony 131
Gothic Revival 88, 208
Gothic style 164, *164*
grandfathered buildings 151
grape harvest 15
Great Storm (1703) 15
green building certification 85, 117
    see also Leadership in Energy and Environment
        Design (LEED)
Green Deal 43, 90
Green Footsteps of Cumbria 99
greenhouse gas emissions see carbon dioxide emissions
grid decarbonisation 41–2
ground source heat pumps (GSHP) 183, *184*, 210, 211,
    237
Gurney stoves 221, *222*, 235
gutters 75

hand-blown glass 196
handmade bricks 195
Hardwick Hall, Derbyshire 3–5, *4*, 6–8, *6*, *7*, *8*, 18
Harkness table 150
Harper, William Rainey 136
Harris, John 16
Harrison, William 4
health problems, traditional building retrofitting 90
heat pumps 183, *184*, 210, 211, 237
heating
    16th century 7–8
    17th century 13
    18th century 18, 19
heating systems 76, 164–5, 209
    19th century 20, 21–2, 24–5, 28
    20th century 30
    design temperatures 59
    district 82, 237
    upgrade costs **55**, *57*, *58*
    upgrade recommendations **50**
    see also church heating
heavyweight walls 93–5, *94*
hemp/lime plaster 81, 97, 98, 101, 197
hempcrete construction 95
Herbert H. Riddle, Chicago 136

heritage buildings 67–8, 193–4
    see also domestic traditional building retrofitting;
        New Court, Trinity College, Cambridge;
        traditional building retrofitting; United States
        historic buildings
heritage value
    vs public benefit 167, 169, 170–1, 188–9
    traditional buildings 77, 81, 159, 169–71
Hertfordshire County Council 33
heterogeneous walls 93, 95
HHSRS see Housing Health and Safety Rating System
    (HHSRS), UK
high-performance buildings 85
Histoglass 186
historic buildings 193–4
    see also domestic traditional building retrofitting;
        New Court, Trinity College, Cambridge;
        traditional building retrofitting; United States
        historic buildings
Historic England 93, 97
Historic Scotland 93, 182, 186, 196, 205
Holland, Henry 211
homogeneous walls 93–5, *94*
hot box methods 196
Houghton Hall, Norfolk 16–18, *17*
house churches 231, 232
house prices, and energy efficiency 42
Houses and Gardens (Baillie Scott) 28
Housing Health and Safety Rating System (HHSRS),
    UK 54, 55
housing in multiple occupation regulations 162, 166
Howard, Luke 21
HTB2 dynamic simulation tool 49, 56
humidity
    absolute 104, **104**
    relative 102–3, **103**, **107**, 228–9
Hyde Park-Kenwood Historic District, Chicago 138
hygrothermal modelling 105–7, 195, 205
    New Court, Trinity College, Cambridge 174–80, *175*,
        176, *177*, *178*, *179*
hygrothermal sections 105, *106*

ICOMOS see International Council on Monuments and
    Sites (ICOMOS)
IHGM see interstitial hygrothermal gradient monitoring
    (IHGM)
immersion heaters, photovoltaic 59
impermeable wall insulation 90, 104, 107
in situ U-value monitoring 92, 173, 205
incandescent light bulb 30
indoor air quality 107–8, **107**
industrial buildings, conversion to residential 79–80
industrial heating systems 236
Industrial Revolution 20, 196
insulation
    churches 228
    floor **50**, **55**, *57*, *58*, 195, 211
    recommendations **50**
    sheep's wool 203–4
    see also roof insulation; solid wall insulation (SWI)
integrity, traditional buildings 77
internal panelling 205
internal temperatures, residential buildings 47–8, *47*

internal wall insulation 97, 101–2, 103, 104, 107, 201, 205
International Council on Monuments and Sites (ICOMOS) 66, 68, 215, 247
International Scientific Committee on Energy and Sustainability (ISCES) 67, 68, 69
interstitial hygrothermal conditions 102–7, **103**, **104**, *106*
interstitial hygrothermal gradient monitoring (IHGM) 102, 176, 178–80, *178, 179*
ISCES *see* International Scientific Committee on Energy and Sustainability (ISCES)
ISO 9869 92
isopleths for mould growth 108–9, *109*, 174, *176*

Janda, Kathryn 194
Jerome, St 180, *180*
Jones, Keith 210
Jones, Nerys 207–8, 209

Kahn, Louis 146, 148
Kelly, Scott 46
Kindergarten, Kensal Rise, London 31–2, *32*
Kyoto Protocol 65, 66

Lady St Mary's Church, Wareham 234
Law Courts, Westminster 22
Le Corbusier 30
leaded light windows 228
Leadership in Energy and Environment Design (LEED) 85, 117, 125, 134
LED lighting 59
Lerner Center, University of Pennsylvania 117–26, *118, 121, 122, 123, 124*
Lethaby Scholarship 89
life cycle costs 49, 195
lighting
    artificial 13, 25, 30
    gas 25
    LED 59
    low energy **50**, **55**, *57, 58*
    natural 12–13, 15–16, 18, 19, 28, 33
lightweight walls 95
LIM *see* limiting isopleths for mould (LIM)
lime-based mortars 195
lime-based render 81, 97, 203
    see also hemp/lime plaster
limiting isopleths for mould (LIM) 108–9, *109*
listed buildings 43, 67, 69, 159
Little Ice Age 4, 9, 12, 26
Little, Owen Carey 208
Liverpool Cathedral 233
local authorities 52–3, 83
    see also Cambridge City Council
local authority planning policies 161, 167–8, 171, 188–9
loft insulation *see* roof insulation
London
    19th century environmental design 20–5, *22, 23, 24, 25*
    air pollution 10, 12, 21
    Chiswick House 18–19, *18, 19*
    Kindergarten, Kensal Rise 31–2, *32*

SPAB headquarters building 91–3, *91, 92*
    Wren's churches 11–14, *11, 12, 13, 14*
longevity of buildings 90
low-E double glazing 59
low energy lighting **50**, **55**, *57, 58*
Lubetkin, Berthold 30

Malmesbury Abbey 224
Manor Cottage, Cambridge 212–13, *212, 213, 214*
Marrakesh Accords 65
Massachusetts Institute of Technology, Building 2 126–35, *127, 128, 129, 130, 132, 133*
Max Fordham LLP 174, 181
mechanical ventilation heat recovery (MVHR) systems 59, 162, *164*, 182–3, *184*, 225
meteorological instruments 15
meteorology 9, 10–11, *10*, 15, 21
methane 235
mini CHP (combined heat and power) units 82
Modern House 30–1, *31, 32*
modernism 30–3, *31, 32, 33, 34*
moisture 100–2, *101*, 211
    see also dampness; interstitial hygrothermal conditions
Monet, Claude 21
Moorcrag, Windermere, Cumbria 27–8, *27*
Morgan, Emslie 33, *34*
Morgan's Road School, Hertford 33, *33*
Morris, Robert 14, 15–16, 20
Morris, William 20, 26, 87, 88, 242, 250
mould growth 90, 108–9, *109*, 164–5, 174, *176*, 228
Muthesius, Hermann 26
MVHR *see* mechanical ventilation heat recovery (MVHR) systems

National Historic Districts, US 120, 138
National Park Service, US 116
National Planning Policy Framework (NPPF), UK 161, 167, 168–9, 171, 188–9
National Register of Historic Places, US 116, 120
National Trust 208, 209–11
natural gas 41, **41**
Natural History of Selborne, The (White) 15
natural lighting 12–13, 15–16, 18, 19, 28, 33
naves, church 221, 231, 232–3
New Court, Trinity College, Cambridge 159–89, *160, 162, 163, 164*
    design approaches 180–2, *180, 181*
    hygrothermal modelling 174–80, *175, 176, 177, 178, 179*
    policy context 167–72
    previous refurbishments 164–5, *165, 166*
    proposals 182–8, *183, 184, 185, 186, 188*
    understanding existing building 173–4, *173*
Newton, Isaac 15
non-breathable materials 71, 78
non-statutory guidance 169–70
NPPF *see* National Planning Policy Framework (NPPF), UK
nuclear power 41, **41**

occupant behaviour 48, 52, 76, 211, 213
oil-fired heating systems 76, 209, 223

Old Vicarage, Thompson's Lane, Cambridge 197–205,
    198, 199, 201, 202, 203, 204
Oldham, John 24–5
open fires 28
orientation 196, 205
    16th century 7–8
    18th century 15–16, 18–19
    19th century 24, 27–8
    20th century 31–2, *32*, 33
Orientation of Buildings, The (RIBA) 31
OSCAR (Online Sustainable Conservation
    Resource) 196–7

Palace of Westminster 23, *23*, 24
Palazzo Farnese, Rome 23–4
Palladianism, English 14–20, *17, 18, 19, 164*
Palladio, Andrea 14, 16, 18
Parnassus project, UCL 205
Parochial Church Councils (PCCs) 224, 243
passive solar warming 6–8, 18, 27–8, 29, 33, *34*
Passivhaus 85
PCCs *see* Parochial Church Councils (PCCs)
Pearson, Gordon T. 211
perceived energy performance 79
Percent-for-Art Program, MIT 131
perception of cold 230–1
performance gap 45
Perkins systems 22
pews 13, 233
    see also under-pew church heating
Philadelphia Historical Commission 120
Phillips Exeter Academy, Class of 1945 Library 145–54,
    146, 147, 148, 151, 152, 153
photovoltaic immersion heaters 59
photovoltaics 59, 183, *184*, 210, 237
    costs **55**, *57, 58*
    recommendations **50**
    on traditional buildings 79, 81
PIR *see* polyisocyanurate (PIR)
Place of Worship Support Officers (POWSOs) 224–5
planning authorities 83
Plas Newydd, Anglesey 207–11, *208, 209, 210*
pods, within churches 231
pointing 75
polyisocyanurate (PIR) 95, 97, 101–2
*Popular Treatise on the Warming and Ventilation of
    Buildings, A* (Richardson) 22, *22*
pot-bellied stoves, in churches 221, 235
Potter, James 208, 210
POWSOs *see* Place of Worship Support Officers
    (POWSOs)
preservation 116
professional competence, traditional building
    retrofitting 78–9
protected structures 67, 69
public benefit vs heritage value 167, 169, 170–1, 188–9

qualifications, professional 71–2, 83
quartz ray heaters 226, 237–8, 239

radiant heaters, in churches 224, *224*, 226, 237–8
radiation 226, 227
radiators 76, 210, 225, *227*, 235–6

rainwater goods 75
reconstruction 116
Reduced SAP (RdSAP) 46, 95
Reform Club, Pall Mall 23–5, *25*
rehabilitation 116
Reid, David Boswell 23
relative humidity 102–3, **103**, **107**, 228–9
renders
    cement-based 81, 203
    hemp/lime plaster 81, 97, 98, 101, 197
    lime-based 81, 97, 203
renewable energies 41, **41**, 79, 81–2
    church heating 236–7
    geothermal energy 79, 209–10
    ground source heat pumps 183, *184*, 210, 211, 237
    New Court, Trinity College, Cambridge 183
    Plas Newydd, Anglesey 209–11
    solar thermal **50**, **55**, *57, 58*
    wind turbines 81, 210
    see also photovoltaics
residential traditional buildings *see* domestic traditional
    building retrofitting
restoration 88, 116
retrofitting 49
    costs **55**
    fabric first vs systems first 54, **54**, 55, *57, 58*
    recommendations 49, **50**
    reversibility 78, 80, 170
    stepwise retrofit 50–1
    whole house retrofit 49–50
    see also domestic traditional building retrofitting;
        New Court, Trinity College, Cambridge; SPAB
        building performance survey; traditional
        building retrofitting; United States historic
        buildings
reuse of existing buildings 79–80
reversibility, of retrofitting projects 78, 80, 170
Richardson, Charles James 22, *22*
Riddlecombe, Devon *see* SPAB building performance
    survey
risk assessment 78
Rockefeller, John D. 136
roof insulation 59, 195, 210
    churches 228
    costs **55**, *57, 58*
    recommendations **50**
roofs 75
Royal Institute of British Architects (RIBA) 31
Ruskin, John 88, 242
Rye, Caroline 93

Saieh Hall, University of Chicago 135–45, *136, 137,
    140, 141, 142*
St George's School, Wallasey 33, *34*
St James's, Piccadilly, London 11–13, *11, 12, 13, 14*
St John the Evangelist, Goldenhill, Stoke.on.Trent 231
St Mary's Church, East Knoyle, Wiltshire *89*
St Michael's Church, Discoed, Presteigne 233
salt damage 229
Sanders, Chris 176
SAP *see* Standard Assessment Procedure (SAP)
sash windows 196
school buildings 31–3, *32, 33, 34*

Scott, Cameron 93
secondary glazing 100, 210
selective mode of environmental control 35
Shakespeare, William 5
sheep's wool insulation 203–4
Shrewsbury, Shropshire see SPAB building performance
    survey
shutters 79, 182, 195, 196, 205
significance assessment 174
simulation see dynamic simulation models
single-glazed windows 196
SketchUp software 49
Skipton, North Yorkshire see SPAB building performance
    survey
Smirke, Robert 21, 22
Smithson, Peter 6–7
Smythson, Robert 3–5, *4*, 6–8, *6, 7, 8*
Soane, John 21–2, *22*
Society for the Protection of Ancient Buildings
    (SPAB) 87–90, 109–10, 193, 205, 219, 242, 250
  headquarters building U-values 91–3, *91, 92*
  survey of solid wall U-values 93–7, *94, 96*
  see also SPAB building performance survey
solar panels see photovoltaics
solar thermal **50, 55**, *57, 58*
solar walls 33, *34*
solid floor insulation 195
solid wall construction 43, 68, 89
  breathable materials 71, 78, 89, 211
  churches 228
  costs **55**, *57, 58*
  dew point margins 105, *106*
  earth-walled buildings 93, 211–13, *212, 213, 214*
  heavyweight walls 93–5, *94*
  heterogeneous walls 93, 95
  homogeneous walls 93–5, *94*
  interstitial hygrothermal conditions 102–7, **103**,
      104, *106*
  lightweight walls 95
  retrofitting case study 205–7, *206, 207*
  surface and sub-surface moisture 100–2, *101*
  U-values 91–8, *94, 96*, **98**, 205
  see also timber-framed buildings
solid wall insulation (SWI) 90, 110
  external 44, 59, *84*, 97, 102, 201, 205–7
  internal 97, 101–2, *103*, 104, 107, 201, 205
  New Court, Trinity College, Cambridge 177, *178*
  problems with 44, 90, 104, 107
  recommendations **50**
  SPAB building performance survey 97–8, **98**, 101–2,
      103, 104, 107
  timber-framed buildings 201
soluble salt damage 229
Southall, Paul 210
SPAB see Society for the Protection of Ancient Buildings
    (SPAB)
SPAB building performance survey
  airtightness 99–100, **99**
  comfort and fabric risk 108–9, *109*
  fabric U-values 97–8, **98**
  indoor air quality 107–8, **107**
  interstitial hygrothermal conditions 102–7, **103**,
      104, *106*

surface and sub-surface moisture 100–2, *101*
spatio-temporal visualisation tools 51
sprinklers 123, 139, 151
stained glass windows 139
Standard Assessment Procedure (SAP) 45–8, *47*, 52, 55,
    56, 57, 58, 95
State Historic Preservation Officers (SHPOs), US 116,
    120
STBA see Sustainable Traditional Buildings Alliance
    (STBA)
steam engines 23, 25
stepwise retrofit 50–1
stoves, in churches 221, *222*, 235
straw/clay construction 95
streetscape 68, 78
sub-surface moisture 100–2, *101*
sun burners 25
surface moisture 100–2, *101*
suspended timber floors 195
sustainability, use of term 117
Sustainable Traditional Buildings Alliance (STBA) 90,
    196
Swan, Joseph 30
SWI see solid wall insulation (SWI)
systems first retrofitting 54, **54**, 55, *58*

temperature gradient across walls 105, *106*
temperatures, internal 47–8, *47*
Tewkesbury Abbey *222*, 235
Thames, river 9, *9*, 15
thermal mass 7, 46, 79, 97, 178, 206
thermal shock 229
thermal siphoning 234–5
Thurso House, Cambridge 31, *31, 32*
timber decay 90
timber-framed buildings 68, 93
  retrofitting case study 197–205, *198, 199, 201, 202,
      203, 204*
Tower of London 186
traditional building retrofitting
  concerns 69–71
  conservation issues 77–8
  green building certification 85, 117
  health problems 90
  key components 72
  planned interventions 80–2
  professional competence 78–9
  professional qualifications 71–2, 83
  research 83
  reversibility 78, 80, 170
  risks to building fabric 81, 90, 108–9, *109*
  understanding the building 73–80
  see also domestic traditional building retrofitting;
      New Court, Trinity College, Cambridge; SPAB
      building performance survey; United States
      historic buildings
traditional buildings
  aesthetics 68, 77, 81, 90
  authenticity 77, 90, 169–70, 174
  condition 75
  heritage value 77, 81, 159, 169–71
  public benefit vs heritage value 167, 169, 170–1,
      188–9

traditional wall construction *see* solid wall construction
TSB Retrofit for the Future project 49–50
Turner, J.M.W. 21

U-values 81, 91
    measuring 73–4, *73*, 92, 173, 205
    in situ versus calculated results 95–7, *96*
    solid walls 91–8, *94*, *96*, **98**, 205
    standard values 196
UK Energy Research Centre (UKERC) 41
under-pew church heating 224, *224*, 226, 233, 239–40
underfloor church heating 223, 224, 226, 233, 236,
    240–2, *241*
underground church boiler houses 234–5, *234*
UNESCO 68, 247
United Nations Framework Convention on Climate
    Change 65
United States Green Building Council (USGBC) 117
United States historic buildings 115–56, 194, 196–7
    Building 2, Massachusetts Institute of
        Technology 126–35, *127*, *128*, *129*, *130*, *132*,
        133
    Class of 1945 Library, Phillips Exeter Academy 145–
        54, *146*, *147*, *148*, *151*, *152*, *153*
    Lerner Center, University of Pennsylvania 117–26,
        118, *121*, *122*, *123*, *124*
    Saieh Hall, University of Chicago 135–45, *136*, *137*,
        140, *141*, *142*
University of Chicago, Saieh Hall 135–45, *136*, *137*,
    140, *141*, *142*
University of Pennsylvania Campus Historic District
    120
University of Pennsylvania, Lerner Center 117–26, *118*,
    121, *122*, *123*, *124*

Valkhoff, Hans 197
vapour-closed materials 89
vapour control layers (VCLs) 107, 195, 203–4
vapour-open materials 89
ventilation, churches 225, 227, 236
ventilation systems 20, 23, 24–5, *24*, 30
    see also mechanical ventilation heat recovery
        (MVHR) systems
vestries 221, 231
Villa Rotonda, Vicenza 18
Vitruvius Britannicus (Campbell) 14

Voysey, Charles Francis Annesley 26–8, *27*

Wakefield Cathedral 242
wall linings 18
wall-to-window ratio 74, 196, 205, 211
walls
    cavity 89, 94, 207
    solar 33, *34*
    see also solid wall construction; timber-framed
        buildings
Walpole, Sir Robert 16
Warm Wales 55
Washington University, St Louis, Missouri 118
water heating
    photovoltaic immersion heaters 59
    solar thermal **50**, **55**, *57*, *58*
Waterhouse, Alfred 21
weather clocks *10*, 11
weather diaries 15
Webb, Philip 88, *89*
Westminster *see* Palace of Westminster
wet rot 107
Whistler, Rex 207
White, Gilbert 15
whole house retrofit 49–50
Wilkins, William 163, 180
William Morris Craft Fellowship 89
Williams-Ellis, Clough 211
wind turbines 81, 210
window-to-wall ratio 74, 196, 205, 211
windows 74, 195, 196, 210
    17th century 12–13
    18th century 16, 18, 19, 20
    19th century 28, 29
    churches 228
    double glazing **50**, **55**, *57*, *58*, 59
    New Court, Trinity College, Cambridge 162, 164, 182,
        183–6, *185*, *186*
    secondary glazing 100, 210
Wolfson Building, Trinity College, Cambridge 162
woodfibre board insulation 97, 101–2, 103, 107
Wren, Christopher 9, 10–14, *10*, *11*, *12*, *13*, *14*
WUFI software 107, 174–7, *175*, *177*
Wyatt, James 208, 210

zero emission retrofit 40